Social Functions of Emotion and Talking About Emotion at Work

WITHDRAWN

Social Functions of Emotion and Talking About Emotion at Work

Edited by

Dirk Lindebaum

Professor in Management and Organisation, Cardiff Business School, Cardiff University, UK

Deanna Geddes

Professor in Human Resource Management, Fox School of Business, Temple University, USA

Peter J. Jordan

Professor of Organisational Behaviour, Griffith Business School, Griffith University, Australia

Edward Elgar
PUBLISHING

Cheltenham, UK • Northampton, MA, USA

Published by
Edward Elgar Publishing Limited
The Lypiatts
15 Lansdown Road
Cheltenham
Glos GL50 2JA
UK

Edward Elgar Publishing, Inc.
William Pratt House
9 Dewey Court
Northampton
Massachusetts 01060
USA

A catalogue record for this book
is available from the British Library

Library of Congress Control Number: 2018944734

This book is available electronically in the **Elgar**online
Business subject collection
DOI 10.4337/9781786434883

ISBN 978 1 78643 487 6 (cased)
ISBN 978 1 78643 488 3 (eBook)

Typeset by Columns Design XML Ltd, Reading
Printed and bound by CPI Group (UK) Ltd, Croydon, CR0 4YY

Contents

Figures

Tables

Contributors

Neal M. Ashkanasy is Professor of Management, UQ Business School, the University of Queensland, Australia. He obtained his PhD in Social and Organizational Psychology from the University of Queensland, Australia. He worked as a professional engineer before joining the University of Queensland. His research on emotion, leadership, culture, and ethical behaviour has been published in, among others, the *Academy of Management Review*, the *Academy of Management Journal*, the *Journal of Applied Psychology*, the *Journal of Management*, and the *Journal of Organizational Behavior*. ORCID: 0000-0001-6422-1425

Robert A. Baron is Regents Professor, Mike and Robbie Holder Chair in Entrepreneurship and William S. Spears Chair, Spears School of Business, Oklahoma State University, USA. He received his PhD in Social Psychology from the University of Iowa. He worked at Purdue University and the Rensselaer Polytechnic Institute before joining the Spears Business School. His research on social psychology and entrepreneurship has been published in, among others, the *Academy of Management Review*, the *Academy of Management Journal*, the *Journal of Applied Psychology*, the *Journal of Business Venturing*, and the *Journal of Management*. ORCID: 0000-0002-0779-8751

Shane Connelly is Professor of I/O Psychology at the University of Oklahoma and an Associate Director for the Center for Applied Social Research. Her research interests include emotions in the workplace, leadership, ethics, and ideological communication in online settings. ORCID: 0000-0002-2686-6836

Marie T. Dasborough is Associate Professor in Management at the University of Miami Business School. She has a PhD in Organizational Behavior from the University of Queensland Business School in Australia. Her research focuses on leadership, emotions, attributions, and teams. She co-edits the JOB Annual Review, plus serves on the editorial boards of *Journal of Organizational Behavior*, *Leadership Quarterly*, and *Group & Organization Management*. ORCID: 0000-0001-5323-5119

Cynthia D. Fisher (MS, PhD Purdue) is Professor of Management at Bond Business School, Bond University, Australia. She writes on moods and emotions at work and employee attitudes and work behavior. She is a Fellow of the Society for Industrial and Organizational Psychology. ORCID: 0000-0002-2274-1366

Deanna Geddes is Professor in Human Resource Management and Associate Dean of Graduate Studies for the Fox School of Business at Temple University. She received her doctorate degree from Purdue University in the fields of organizational communication and industrial psychology. Her conceptual work and empirical studies focus on emotion at work, especially workplace anger, and performance feedback practices. ORCID: 0000-0001-7272-4321

Paul Harvey is the James R. Carter Professor of Management at the University of New Hampshire's Peter T. Paul College of Business and Economics. He has a PhD in Organizational Behavior from Florida State University and studies perceptual workplace phenomena such as psychological entitlement and abuse perceptions. He is an associate editor for the *Journal of Organizational Behavior* and *Group and Organization Management*, also serving as co-editor of the Annual Review issue for the former. ORCID: 0000-0001-7310-0537

Mathew L. A. Hayward is Professor, Department of Management, Monash Business School, Monash University, Australia. He received his PhD from Columbia University in Strategy, and worked at the University of Colorado, Boulder before joining Monash University. His research on behavioral decision theory explanations of strategy and entrepreneurship decisions and outcomes has been published in, among others, the *Academy of Management Review*, the *Academy of Management Journal*, *Administrative Science Quarterly*, *Management Science*, and the *Strategic Management Journal*. ORCID: 0000-0003-1557-7622

Peter J. Jordan is Professor of Organizational Behavior and Deputy Director of the Work Organization and Wellbeing Research Centre at the Griffith Business School, Griffith University. He gained his PhD in Management at the University of Queensland. Peter's current research interests include emotional intelligence, emotions in organizations, team performance and entitlement in organizations. Peter has published extensively in this field in leading international journals and has been awarded funding from the Australian Research Council for research in the area of emotional intelligence. ORCID: 0000-0001-8228-5457

Sandra A. Kiffin-Petersen is a Senior Lecturer at the Business School of the University of Western Australia. Her main research interests are in emotions at work, individual differences and trust in organizations. She has published this research in journals such as *Human Relations, Personality and Individual Differences, Journal of Business Ethics* and the *International Journal of Human Resource Management.* ORCID: 0000-0002-9422-304X

Heather C. Lench is Professor and Department Head of Psychological & Brain Sciences at Texas A&M University. Her research examines the role of affective reactions and their impact on people's beliefs about their future, as well as their role in guiding judgments and decision-making. ORCID: 0000-0002-6555-5811

Dirk Lindebaum is Professor of Organisation and Management at Cardiff Business School. His main preoccupation rests with the ways workers can experience repression at work, be they emotional or technological in kind. He is one of the book review editors at *Organization Studies.* For background on media engagement and publications, please visit his website: www.dirklindebaum.eu. ORCID: 0000-0002-5155-4359

Kathryn E. Moura is a doctoral candidate at the Griffith Business School. Her main area of research is in emotions, more specifically, anger within the workplace. Kathryn has extensive cross-cultural and human resource management experience, having lived and worked on three continents. Kathryn's experience includes being one of the directors of an international company for 14 years, founding her own company and working in the areas of HRM consulting, training and business coaching. ORCID: 0000-0001-5127-3453

Kenneth A. Perez is a doctoral student in the Department of Psychological and Brain Sciences at Texas A&M University. His research interests involve the examination of emotions, particularly the experience of awe, and their impacts on individuals' attitudes and behaviors. ORCID: 0000-0002-5785-8505

Richard H. Smith is Professor of Psychology at the University of Kentucky (PhD, the University of North Carolina at Chapel Hill). His research focuses on social emotions. He has co-edited two volumes on envy, *Envy: Theory and Research*, 2008; *Envy at Work and in Organizations*, 2016, and has a book on Schadenfreude, *The Joy of Pain: Schadenfreude and the Dark Side of Human Nature.* ORCID: 0000-0002-4698-9251

Rosanna K. Smith is Assistant Professor of Marketing at the University of Georgia. Rosanna completed her PhD in Marketing at the Yale School of Management and her BA in Art at Yale University. Her main area of research explores how beliefs about the nature of the creative process influence perceptions of authenticity and value. Her second line of research examines how marketing messages about the nature of beauty and the body affect self-esteem and social comparison processes. ORCID: 0000-0001-5276-9733

Peter N. Stearns is University Professor of History at George Mason University. He has written widely on the history of emotions and has also studied work in comparative context. ORCID: 0000-0001-7596-2878

Ashlea C. Troth is Associate Professor at Griffith Business School and Deputy Head of the Department of Employment Relations and Human Resources. Her areas of research expertise are in emotional intelligence and regulation, communication and performance. Ashlea's work has been published in leading international journals and she is currently a member of a research team with funding from the Australian Research Council to examine emotional regulation in the workplace. ORCID: 0000-0001-8768-7594

Megan R. Turner is a doctoral student in the University of Oklahoma's doctoral program in industrial and organizational psychology. Her research interests include emotions, ethics, and organizational citizenship behavior. ORCID: 0000-0002-8836-5105

Kristi Lewis Tyran is Professor of Organizational Behavior at Western Washington University, located in Bellingham, Washington, USA. She does research in the areas of Leadership, Emotion, Teaching Leadership, and International Service Learning and has published her work in the *Journal of Organizational Behavior*, *International Journal of Management Education*, and *Group and Organization Management Journal*. Prior to her career as an academic, she was a Vice President at Bank of America.

Tanja S. H. Wingenbach is a post-doctoral Research Fellow in the Social and Cognitive Neuroscience Laboratory at Mackenzie Presbyterian University (Sao Paulo, Brazil). Tanja completed her PhD in Psychology at the University of Bath (UK), her MSc in Clinical Psychology at the University of Basel (Basel, Switzerland), and her BSc in Psychology at the University of Luxembourg (Luxembourg, Luxembourg). Her main area of research is emotion science with a particular focus on facial expressions of emotion. ORCID: 0000-0002-1727-2374

Preface

The intellectual genesis of this book is rooted in substantial collaborations the three of us have enjoyed over several years. Many prior, shared projects have direct bearings in formulating the aim and scope of this book (Lindebaum and Geddes, 2016; Lindebaum and Jordan, 2014). However, a decisive moment for the development of this book was in Rome in 2016. Paul Harvey, Marie Dasborough, Sandra Kiffin-Petersen, as well as Ashlea Troth, Neal Ashkanasy and Peter Jordan kindly agreed – with minimal arm-twisting – to support this book with projects presented in Rome. Better still, we were thrilled that Peter Jordan also accepted our invitation to join the editorial team.

While being wary not to overstate, we wanted to open a fresh line of inquiry. Through connecting hitherto unconnected literatures (e.g., emotionologies and social functions of emotion), we saw the potential to substantively advance understanding of how the social functions of emotion and talking about emotion at work can mutually affect each other. Collaborating over several years, we grew appreciably convinced that our ideas were worth being nurtured and developed further. Rather than opting for a special issue, we felt strongly that the edited book could prove a better conduit in the generation of fresh and perhaps more unorthodox thinking (for more details on this, see Lindebaum et al., 2018). Overall, we recognise that the ideas presented in this edited volume may appear at first abstract and elusive. It is for this reason that we have opted for a book cover that depicts human profiles, internal dialogues, and emotion in rather abstract ways.

Looking back, we are both grateful and excited that all participants in the aforementioned symposium supported this edited volume with their outstanding scholarship. That same gratitude and recognition applies, needless to say, to our other accomplished contributors as well. To state that explicitly at this juncture is not only an act of courtesy, but also one of appreciation. Our authors could have decided that writing book chapters may not yield the dividends for career progression that journal publication oftentimes yields in this day and age. However, from personal author feedback, we have learned that writing the chapters actually provided a source of intrinsic satisfaction and joy because of the liberty of *what to say* rather than *where to say* it.

We also are indebted to all contributors for their willingness to constructively comment on the work of fellow authors, their receptiveness to the suggestions received from editors and colleagues, and their generous punctuality in adhering to completion deadlines. Any reader will understand what pleasure it was to handle and edit this book project.

Now that all is said and done, we also express our sincere thanks to Francine O'Sullivan, Rachel Downey, and Marina Bowgen at Edward Elgar for their uncomplicated approach in the pre-contract stage, as well as their diligence in subsequent stages of the book project.

REFERENCES

Lindebaum, D., and Geddes, D. (2016). The place and role of (moral) anger in organizational behavior studies. *Journal of Organizational Behavior*, 37(5): 738–757.

Lindebaum, D., and Jordan, P. J. (2014). When it can be good to feel bad and bad to feel good: exploring asymmetries in workplace emotional outcomes. *Human Relations*, 67(9): 1037–1050.

Lindebaum, D., Pérezts, M., and Andersson, L. (2018). Why books? *Organization Studies*, 39(1): 135–141.

1. Theoretical advances around social functions of emotion and talking about emotion at work

Dirk Lindebaum, Deanna Geddes and Peter J. Jordan

INTRODUCTION

Our aim in this book is to consider workplace emotion from a social functional perspective (Keltner and Gross, 1999; Keltner and Haidt, 1999; van Kleef, 2017) in relation to societal "talk about emotion" (see Solomon, 2003). Social functional accounts differentiate discrete emotions and provide a theoretical understanding of their consequences for goal-directed action. They are intended to explain behavior important to social relationships and ongoing interactions (Keltner and Gross, 1999). This framework has the benefit of examining what emotions *do* in social interaction rather than what they *are* (van Kleef, 2017). In contrast, the "talk about emotion" focuses on varying language practices (e.g., word choice, narratives and metaphors) and subsequent interpretations regarding emotions across cultures,[1] and, in turn, how these perceptions influence the causes, expressions, and consequences of emotions (Solomon, 2003). Solomon elaborates on this juxtaposition between the functional emotion, and the talk about it, using anger as an example:

> "Both are interpretations, and the same concepts often enter into the structure of each. Being angry [i.e., the emotion] may be one thing, questioning the legitimacy of one's anger [i.e., the talk about it], something else. But crucial concepts (e.g., of legitimacy, blame or responsibility) are just as much part of the anger as they are part of the questioning." (p. 87)[2]

He argues further that, in the absence of "righteous" (or useful) anger, it would be vain to discuss anger's legitimacy and/or value in society.

Contrasting social functional accounts of emotion and how society talks about these emotions can advance theoretical conversations around how they can be at odds with, as well as reinforce each other in organizations. Given Solomon's perspective, anger provides an excellent illustration of the theoretical and practical ramifications for emotion research if the emotion *per se* and the talk about it are at odds. For example, since a key social function of anger is to redress injustice (Keltner and Gross, 1999; Lindebaum and Geddes, 2016b), promoting "negative" talk about it (e.g., calling it a "negative emotion" in scholarship or "unacceptable" at work) can undermine its beneficial role in promoting necessary social change (for background and examples, see Geddes et al., 2018; Geddes and Callister, 2007; Lindebaum and Geddes, 2016b). Needless to say, although anger is not useful all the time for all people in all situations, a world without moral anger (appropriately expressed), for instance, lacks the corrective energy to restore justice and fairness in all walks of life – including work (Lindebaum and Gabriel, 2016).

The emotion of anger, however, is not an isolated case where the emotion and the talk about it can be at odds, as the following chapters will demonstrate. Another example comes from Cynthia Fisher's (2018) erudite chapter on boredom included in this book. She posits that "the function of the emotion of boredom is to stimulate exploration and the pursuit of new and more rewarding opportunities". Nevertheless, in an era of relentless talk about self-optimization at work and beyond (Spicer and Cederström, 2017), when corporations consider casual remarks at work "time theft" (Anderson, 2017, p. 1), there are potentially real consequences for workers confiding in co-workers that they are "bored". As Fisher (2018) states, "dedicated professionals in enriched jobs would not normally give voice to their feelings of boredom, particularly if these feelings conflicted with organizational or professional discourses about the nature of the work and the passion that should be felt toward it".

This book also opens debate around how social functions of the emotion and our talk about it can be mutually reinforcing. A classic example of this pairing is found with the emotion of happiness. Stearns's (2018) insightful chapter outlines the complicated evolution of happiness at work, the current emphasis on employee wellbeing, and how happiness dominates efforts behind employee engagement and satisfaction. Perhaps less intuitive, and requiring more "boundary conditions", is talk reinforcing emotions traditionally viewed as unwanted. As lucidly exemplified in the chapter on shame by Kiffin-Petersen (2018), in order for the talk about emotion to be able to reinforce its social function, it is necessary to break the taboo of *not talking* about the emotion. She argues that the taboo of talking about shame is so distinct, that we sometimes behave as if this emotion did not exist. But whether we *ought* to talk about shame so that its social functions are more likely to be fulfilled depends heavily on the shame-eliciting event. For instance, if a moral transgression occurred at work (e.g., lying to colleagues who trusted the transgressor), then appeasing efforts may entail a sincere apology that could – if credible and accepted – restore trust in the relationships. In such cases, talking about experienced shame can heal one's own rumination about the transgression and repair valued work relationships.

Beyond these examples of the talk about emotion and its social functions in society being either at odds or mutually reinforcing, there are also circumstances when both processes can operate simultaneously. Such is the case with schadenfreude as illustrated in the thought-provoking chapter by Harvey and Dasborough (2018). Schadenfreude is commonly kept private, and "civil" society generally frowns upon anyone demonstrating pleasure from another's downfall. The reason for this is partly rooted in schadenfreude's association with the experience of shame and guilt, as well as perceptions that its expression is unkind and cruel. However, expressing the emotion among co-workers can indicate the existence of performance norms and consequences that are likely if the behavior in question violates shared views of acceptable behavior. Schadenfreude can also play an important role in socializing workers to be more ethical in their work behaviors. In an anticipatory sense, new employees learn to avoid becoming the target of schadenfreude by acting in an ethically appropriate manner and conforming to normative standards of behavior in that workplace. Thus, schadenfreude, as Harvey and Dasborough (2018) note, serves social functions such as bonding, socialization and self-image protection, despite "individuals [being] often reluctant to acknowledge [it] – sometimes even to themselves". Bearing in mind multiple caveats, the talk about schadenfreude can both be at odds with as well as reinforce valued social functions. Further to this, there may be cases when particular emotions (e.g., hubristic pride, see Hayward et al., 2018) are less "functional" and more "dysfunctional" and a manifestation of problematic individual dispositions. In such a case, it is not whether or not the function of an emotion can be at odds with or reinforces social functions of emotions. Instead, the talk about the emotion reinforces its social undesirability.

Taken together, our dual focus emphasized in the following chapters help "problematize" portions of current emotion research. While we reiterate the variety of interactions between social function of emotions and how we talk about them, it strikes us as central to ponder if our talk about emotion potentially weakens and overrides the emotion's social functions?[3] If this is the case, a fundamental re-orientation in current theorizing around social functions of discrete emotion may be required.

This re-orientation would acknowledge that the talk about emotion can potentially inhibit these functions, given that what they produce in ongoing social interactions at work are malleable, not fixed. Since functions can be affected by the talk about emotion (as we discuss later in the section "the talk about emotion"), it may shift the way we appraise emotion. In other words, since the talk about emotion can fluctuate across different periods of time and locales, if appraisals change, so do subsequent cognitive processes and related affective, physiological and behavioral responses (Scherer et al., 2001). Thus, the entire causal chain is altered, and a different course of action is enabled, or a different outcome might be observed, as studies on different elicitors for sadness (Gray et al., 2011) or anger (Lindebaum and Gabriel, 2016; Lindebaum and Geddes, 2016b) have shown.[4]

In addition, what if the social function of an emotion and the way we talk about it can be mutually reinforcing, or be present simultaneously? What finer theoretical nuances and contours might emerge as a result of these scenarios, especially in terms of how boundary conditions may sway theorizing among them? How might this impact an individual's emotional experience and collective emotion episodes at work? Might this affect how management engages in and views others' emotional expression at work? These are some guiding questions that inspired this collection of chapters. We believe that a paucity of detailed attention to this line of inquiry in psychological and management studies (and beyond) limits theoretical, empirical, and practical progress, especially in relation to better understanding social interactions in and around work. In the following section, we elaborate on our two intersecting constructs to help address some of these concerns and lay the groundwork for our featured chapters.

THE EMOTION AND ITS SOCIAL FUNCTIONS

Theoretically, we situate our work alongside a significant body of research interested in the social functions of emotion (Dasborough and Harvey, 2016; Keltner and Kring, 1998; van Kleef, 2017). Simply, social functional accounts help circumvent definitional ambiguities that arise vis-à-vis diverging ontological and epistemological assumptions about the question "what is an emotion?" (contrast e.g., Ashkanasy, 2003; Elfenbein, 2007; Frijda, 1986; James, 1884; Parrott and Harré, 1996; Solomon, 2003; Zeelenberg et al., 2008).[5] Broadly, functions are recognized in etiological accounts of the genesis and development of a behavior, trait or system (Wright, 1973). Seen in this way, functions "refer to the history of a behaviour, trait, or system, as well as its regular consequences that benefit the organism, or … the system in which the trait, behaviour, or system is contained" (Keltner and Gross, 1999, p. 469). More specifically, functional accounts differentiate discrete emotions in relation to consequences of goal-directed behavior, and assert that they can help solve problems important to social relationships and ongoing interactions (Keltner and Gross, 1999). The social functional perspective suggests that responses linked to "each discrete emotion is theorized to address the adaptive problem that gave rise to that emotion" (Lench et al., 2015, p. 91). Others elaborate on this point by arguing that evolutionary perspectives define emotions in terms of their genesis. As Nesse and Ellsworth (2009) note:

> "Emotions are modes of functioning, shaped by natural selection, that coordinate physiological, cognitive, motivational, behavioral, and subjective responses in patterns that increase the ability to meet the adaptive challenges of situations that have recurred over evolutionary time … they are adaptations that are useful only in certain situations." (p. 129)

In other words, a discrete emotion evolved to help us (either as individuals or collectives) respond adaptively to social opportunities and challenges in ways that often, though not always, benefit us (see also Connelly and Turner, 2018).

An important clarification on the detail of "goal-directed" behaviors is that these are far more than simply purporting to decide on a goal and then express an emotion to achieve it (such as generating enthusiasm to improve relationships among team members). Goals, crucially, are also involved in our reactions to external events. So while it may seem counter-intuitive to suggest that we experience, for instance, shame or guilt because it has been our goal to do so, a closer look at the socio-functional emotion literature helps resolve this conundrum. Solomon (1993) insists that "emotions are judgments" and constitute "ways of seeing and engaging with the world", our ways of "being tuned" into the world (pp. viii–ix). He also argues that every emotion is a strategy, "a purposive attempt to structure our world in such a way as to *maximize our sense of personal dignity and self-esteem*" (p. xviii, italics added). The emphasis in the quote indicates the presence of a goal. If we turn to social functional accounts of shame, for instance, we can see that the experience of shame is far more than a "reaction". Rather, felt shame is related to negative self-evaluations based upon actual or anticipated depreciation by valued others due to a violation of standards (Creed et al., 2014). We may have transgressed important moral principles held dear by co-workers. As a result, we can experience shame as self-accusation, and perhaps open up and confess to restore a damaged personal relationship with someone close to us (Solomon, 1993). From a social functional perspective, shame motivates behaviors that help preserve "positive" self-views (de Hooge et al., 2010), including approach or reparation behaviors like apologies. Thus, "an unpleasant emotion may be desirable if it promotes goal pursuit, despite the fact that it involves displeasure, which itself is undesirable" (Tamir et al., 2016, p. 68).

THE TALK ABOUT EMOTION

We build on previous work (Lindebaum, 2017; Lindebaum and Geddes, 2016a) emphasizing that language use (e.g., metaphors) and emotion-ologies influence how we talk about emotion. Solomon insists on the pervasive nature of metaphors across cultures, for example, with any vocabulary of physiological self-references. In this regard, Solomon invokes several common examples, such as being "struck by jealousy", "plagued by remorse", "paralyzed by fear" (2003, p. 3) and anger's "hydraulic" metaphor of "blowing one's top" (see Perez and Lench, 2018 for more examples). But why exactly do metaphors matter theoretically and practically in the context of talking about emotion? Lakoff and Johnson (2006, p. 112) offer some light and astutely point out:

> "Metaphors may create realities for us, especially social realities. A metaphor may thus be a guide for future action. Such actions will, of course, fit the metaphor. This will, in turn, reinforce the power of the metaphor to make experience coherent. In this sense metaphors can be self-fulfilling prophecy."

Metaphors are so pervasive in society they can dominate our thinking about these feelings even though, as cultural artifacts, they can be invalid representations and systematically mislead attempts to understand our own and others' emotions.

Inherently influential for societal metaphors and other forms of emotion "talk" are emotionologies, or what Stearns and Stearns (1985) refer to as "the attitudes or standards that a society ... maintains toward basic emotions and their appropriate expression; ways that institutions reflect and encourage these attitudes in human conduct" (p. 813). Fineman (2008) adds that they influence how we perceive the appropriateness of both experiencing and expressing emotions in the self and others. The Dual Threshold Model (DTM) of emotion (Geddes and Callister, 2007) further illustrates the varied and changeable cultural standards regarding emotional expression tendencies among organizational members. Favorable outcomes from emotion expression at work, they argue, are most likely with emotion displayed in a manner deemed appropriate for the social context and/or circumstances. Using DTM terminology, the emotion remains in the "space between" the "expression and impropriety thresholds" or what Fineman (1993) calls the "zone of expressive tolerance". Here displayed emotion may promote dialogue and reactions that can benefit organizations and their members.

Emotionologies as a phenomenon have received only embryonic attention in management and organization studies. Nevertheless, Fineman (1993) argues that emotionologies are generated and reproduced through a variety of discursive and organizational practices, with some enjoying greater resilience and visibility compared to others. Yet, their pervasive influence in shaping everyday emotion and behavior is tangible:

> "We inherit emotionologies that soon appear natural and typically go unchallenged. They will inform how we should feel, and express our feelings, about ourselves ('happy,' 'positive,' 'fine') as well as how to feel about others – such as a love of winners, disgust for muggers, cynicism about politicians, and ambivalence towards teenagers. They shape and underpin the deference patterns of particular social encounters – what to feel or reveal at weddings, funerals, dinner parties, places of worship, or before a judge." (Fineman, 2008, p. 2)[6]

Emotionologies develop both over time and locale to define emotional standards for various categories of people (see Stearns and Stearns, 1985), thus reflecting both a chronological and geographical dimension. In terms of the chronological dimension, Stearns and Stearns (1985) note that emotionologies are liable to change over time for several reasons, including the media, advertising, popular culture, religious organizations, political parties, social movements and activist groups (Fineman, 2008). In terms of the geographical dimension, recent studies (Tamir et al., 2016) examined samples from eight distinct regions[7] to test the hypothesis that, across cultures, individuals desire emotions that are consistent with their core values. Findings suggest that individuals endorsing values of self-transcendence (e.g., benevolence) sought to feel more compassion, whereas individuals who endorsed values of self-enhancement (e.g., power) wanted to feel more pride and anger. Further to this, individuals appreciating openness to change (e.g., self-direction) wanted to feel more excitement and interest, while individuals who endorsed values of conservation (e.g., tradition) wanted to feel more calmness and less fear (Tamir et al., 2016). Therefore, Tamir and her colleagues (2016) argue that different cultures influence and reflect different individual values regarding the desirability of experiencing particular emotions.

Emotionologies both tell us much about the forces of social change and contribute to (or inhibit) these over time and space. In the context of work, attitudes toward emotion provide the expectations of emotional expression in relation to specific issues, subjects, genders, or occupational groups and hierarchies. Crucially, they also provide varying standards of "appropriate" emotional expressions for various professions such as doctors, social workers or service workers (see e.g., Fineman, 2010; McMurray and Ward, 2014; van Maanen and Kunda, 1989), which is why this is so central in the context of this book. Emotionologies shape, maintain and challenge standards of emotional expressions within organizations and professions. Therefore, emotionologies represent a critical cultural variable (Stearns and Stearns, 1985) that has bearing upon the formation of individual attitudes and values (Tamir et al., 2016) and can help explain why social functions of emotions can be at odds with how we currently talk about them (Lindebaum, 2017).

An important caveat must be emphasized in summary. Although emotionologies along with metaphors and other language use have considerable explanatory power in shaping how individuals perceive the expression of emotion by others, they can also indicate a lack of sophistication from the point-of-view of established theoretical frameworks. That is, while narratives around emotions are real, personal, and meaningful to us, they can nevertheless be misleading. As noted earlier, to label anger as a "negative emotion" may lead scholars and practitioners to pursue efforts meant to eliminate this feeling (and, particularly, its expression) from work, preventing management from learning about upset employees and damaging workplace situations (Geddes et al., 2018). They also can prompt individuals to make inaccurate attributions about the causes and consequences of emotions experienced and expressed by others especially. More precisely, this "talk about emotion" (internal or interpersonal) can potentially introduce attribution errors such as attributing the display of emotion to an expresser's personality trait, rather than recognizing external, situational factors triggering that emotion. Having clarified this important caveat, we offer an overview of the chapters below.

OVERVIEW OF CHAPTERS

In this section, we offer a brief overview about the aims and content of each chapter. As we think all discrete emotions contribute to our understanding of how people behave, respond, and talk in organizations, we arranged chapters in alphabetical order by discrete emotion.

The prevalence of workplace *anger* has prompted significant exploration of this complex emotion which has both positive and negative outcomes at work. Authors Moura, Jordan, and Troth (2018) conducted interviews focusing on anger targets and witnesses to better understand how people make sense of a colleague's anger display (i.e., the "talk" about the perceived cause of another's anger) and how that influenced their own emotion regulation strategies in response (a social functional response). Moura and her colleagues note that the frequency of anger expression and various attributions, including locus of control (internal vs. external), stability and controllability behind another's anger expression helped explain varying responses of study interviewees. Key also was how these anger observers judged the appropriateness of the anger display in light of organizational norms of emotion expression – with findings that those in managerial positions were held to a higher standard of behavior regarding anger expressions. They also note that the emotion management strategies practiced by anger targets included both expressing and suppressing their own emotions (e.g., anger, fear, surprise) to better control the situation – especially if they felt threatened by these expressions. Based on these data, Moura and her colleagues show how the talk about emotion varies depending on who is being talked about, but this talk helps produce a functional outcome.

Perez and Lench (2018) examined an emotion that is not often discussed in the literature in the context of work, *awe*. They define awe as an emotion that occurs when people are in the presence of something extraordinary and beyond their typical experiences. Significantly, they differentiate awe from other "positive" emotions (such as joy) suggesting that awe introduces a "small self" which promotes unique benefits around connection with others. They note that something that does not happen with awe, frankly, is talk about it. Generally, they describe the experience of awe as a private experience that is not often shared. The central reason for this is, they propose, that talking about awe may limit the ability to experience the benefits of the experience. In essence, awe in the chapter is described as an existential activity that is diminished by overthinking the experience. Examining their chapter from a social functional perspective, however, it is clear that awe does have beneficial effects in terms of enabling individuals to shift focus to big picture perspectives and to consider others and, therefore, it is linked to prosocial behaviors, including more creativity.

Once a neglected topic, over the last five years *boredom* has emerged in scholarship with a significant number of articles, particularly in psychology. Fisher (2018) notes, however, that a lot of this research is not specific to the work context. She explains that boredom has been explored as a trait (boredom susceptibility) and a state (emotion). Interestingly, boredom can manifest with low arousal levels (resignation) to high levels (restlessness and agitation). She argues that as a state, boredom has all the attributes of a unique, discrete emotion. Further, she noted that there is often a lack of talk during the experience of boredom. Quite often it is a very personal experience; thus, the presence of others may indeed relieve boredom. From a social functional perspective, Fisher notes that boredom can become dangerous and isolating, with people who talk about boredom appearing childish or uncreative. As a result, she discusses different types of boredom, such as indifferent, calibrating, searching, reactant, and apathetic boredom, indicating how these may affect others' perceptions of boredom. Finally, Fisher provides excellent examples of how the social functional processes linked to some emotions, including boredom, often discourage talk.

In their chapter on *envy*, Smith, Wingenbach and Smith (2018) describe envy as "a painful recognition of inferiority in reaction to an unflattering social comparison". As a consequence, feelings of envy can serve as an adaptive response to perceived disadvantage and can inspire individuals to find ways to "close the gap" between themselves and the envied person. Unfortunately for some, this is done by "tearing down" the other in an effort to feel better about themselves. Classical views of envy often focus on this "malicious" form, associated with hostility toward the more successful individual. Although the envying person may be aware their feelings are not completely legitimate, he or she wants to be justified in feeling negatively toward another's success. In contrast, envy in its "benign" form, although still an unpleasant state, is without hostility toward the other and instead reflects a sense of admiration and longing. As a result, envy can be the impetuous for significant efforts toward self-improvement and performance enhancement as the means to close the social comparison gap. Using the tragic case of Harvard student Sinedu Tadesse, the authors frame their argument beyond university cultures to illustrate how organizational talk about personal deservingness and control of individual achievements can generate envy of either the benign or the malicious variety.

Fear is given insightful scrutiny in the chapter by Connelly and Turner (2018). Their basic argument suggests that while fear's adaptiveness from an evolutionary perspective is well-documented (i.e., escaping threats), individuals are often reluctant to talk about it at work to avoid being perceived as weak or vulnerable. The authors offer an overview on the causes and consequences of fear, noting that "the functional or adaptive nature of fear has not been examined with respect to the workplace ... [and] ... a need for a more nuanced and balanced narrative regarding fear at work, one that is informed by theory and data". A salient feature of their chapter is that it offers dual perspectives on fear at work, considering organizational research on functional and dysfunctional experiences and outcomes associated with this emotion across levels of analysis. Importantly, both functional and dysfunctional experiences and outcomes are examined vis-à-vis experiencing fear in oneself, observing fear in others, and having a climate of fear at work. The chapter closes by offering both fruitful implications for future research, as well as hands-on practical strategies across levels of analysis regarding how to manage fear at work so as to avoid undesirable consequences.

In his chapter on *happiness*, Stearns (2018) provides a fascinating historical insight into the way our talk about happiness has changed over time. Using the innovative method of Google Ngram, Stearns notes that the talk about happiness has changed significantly over time. By examining the mention of happiness in literature, Stearns argues that a discussion of happiness was missing from eighteenth- and nineteenth-century writings about work, where the focus was on work ethic and personal advancement. He argues that by the early twentieth century, the concept of happiness emerged in the literature, but was hidden by a focus on satisfaction. Finally, he reveals that the modern focus on well-being is another way in which the talk about happiness has changed over time. The conclusion one can draw from this is the way in which talk about emotion varies over time and the focus of that talk can change focus to meet social norms. This is in contrast to social function accounts of emotion, which generally see emotional goals as being relatively stable over history. Stearns provides useful insight into the differences between these two ways of considering emotion.

Pride is considered one of the most impactful, positive emotions at work. However, Hayward, Ashkanasy and Baron (2018) argue that the emotion emerges in two distinctive forms – authentic and hubristic, both reflecting a direct emotional response to success. Authentic pride is viewed as emerging from concrete performance achievements based on one's own efforts. Consequently, it functions to promote beneficial work behaviours and attitudes, including confidence and self-esteem, as individuals attribute their success to hard work and perseverance. In contrast, hubristic pride emerges when individuals over-attribute personal or organizational achievements to their own stable, internal characteristics such as their personality and charisma. In other words, success came because of "who they are" rather than "what they did". Such feelings tend to promote "arrogance, overconfidence, aggression, and hostility" and can also be "powerfully socially dysfunctional and self-destructive". In this view, the emotion of authentic pride and the talk about it mutually reinforce each other, with the emotion seen as a positive condition promoting favourable outcomes to individuals and their organizations. In contrast, hubristic pride appears at odds with what we consider beneficial social functions, which in turn generates talk that warns against that particular form of pride, given it may be unwarranted and, ultimately, destructive.

In her chapter on *sadness*, Tyran (2018) starts with a description of the Pixar film *Inside Out* which specifically exemplifies the difference between talk about emotions and the social functional nature of emotions. Tyran notes that sadness impacts individual and organizational outcomes and affects the social aspects of an organization. She notes that sadness is differentiated from other related emotions (e.g., melancholy, unhappiness, grief, depression and hopelessness) by the sense of irrevocable loss associated with sadness. In terms of how we talk about emotions, the chapter explores issues around others' responses to sadness at work, noting that the collective experience of sadness in the workplace may lead to more cohesion and solidarity after tragedy. Indeed, this chapter helps demonstrate that talk and social functions of emotion at work can often be linked symbiotically. She notes that in organizations, leaders have a responsibility to address the talk, and particularly with collective sadness, leaders have a responsibility to facilitate healing and renewal. She argues from a social functional perspective that caring is a key component of authentic leadership and being caring assists employees to cope with sadness. Tyran shows that sadness as an emotion has significant social functional elements that are often promoted by talking about it.

Discussing *schadenfreude*, Harvey and Dasborough (2018) identify bonding, socialization and self-image protection as social functions of schadenfreude. One argument recognizes that schadenfreude is commonly kept private. However, its expression can help socialize workers into particular directions by providing valuable information for observers, reinforcing organizational norms. That is, schadenfreude signals the presence of ethical norms for workers so that they grasp colleagues will take pleasure in their downfall if the behavior in question violates shared views of moral behavior or performance standards. Workers thus fear becoming the target of schadenfreude, rather than sympathy. However, the authors also argue that the experience and expression of schadenfreude can have other effects. They can reflect (and, thus, be thwarted by) observer perceptions of so-called "dark" personality traits in the expresser. If this occurs, observers are more likely to attribute a lack of empathy on the part of the expresser for those individuals who are the target of schadenfreude. Thus, the authors argue that schadenfreude is a particularly sinister threat to social relationships, "because the experience of this positive emotion requires the suffering of another". Overall, talking about schadenfreude can have upsides as well as downsides, depending on how it is perceived by others.

Shame is the focus of the chapter by Kiffin-Petersen (2018), which aims to better understand its function in interpersonal relationships at work. She argues that shame evolved to increase an individual's chances of acceptance in social groups by signaling to them when they have violated the group's moral standards or norms. Appeasement is thus both a function and outcome of shame. In discussing how shame is "talked about", she acknowledges that emotions have biological roots. Yet, we also internalize societal expectations about how shame should be expressed, which then shapes how we respond to that emotion. Thus, the talk about shame influences workers' appraisals of shame-inducing events and how they respond. She argues that the talk about shame can reinforce its social function as soon as we drop the taboo of not talking about shame and appreciate that it can be "adaptive if it ultimately increases inclusivity into a social grouping". By contrast, observers who respond with negative "talk" in the workplace can further stigmatize shame, and this can encourage maladaptive responses. Also, once moral imperatives are substituted by economic ones, the "talk about", or use of, shame by line managers to signal poor performance enables organizations to manipulate workers into exerting greater effort that benefits the organization economically, but at the expense of workers' health.

CONCLUDING THOUGHTS AND LOOKING AHEAD

The collective contribution of all chapters in this book resides in the hitherto under-explored argument that the talk about emotion – in the form of metaphors and emotionologies – can shape emotion-eliciting events across time and location. In shaping emotion-eliciting events, the talk about emotion can alter the entire emotion chain; from the experiential to physiological to behavioral of employees. This, in turn, can imply that the social function of emotion and the talk about emotion can sometimes mutually reinforce each other, while at other times, remain at odds. When the talk is at odds with the social function of emotions, the foundation for this contention is often organizational control (Connelly and Turner, 2018; Harvey and Dasborough, 2018; Lindebaum and

Courpasson, 2017; Scheff, 1988). In other circumstances, as the chapters
in this volume demonstrate, they can be present simultaneously. This in
itself raises intriguing questions about deeper causes as to if two
opposing (some would say paradoxical) tendencies can share a common
cause? Alternatively, are there multiple causalities at play? Exploring
answers to these questions will help us characterize, examine, and
perhaps resolve these different combinations, as well as influence future
emotion research and how we view and respond to emotion at work.

In terms of future research, we already suggested that emotionologies
are liable to change over time due to, for instance, the influence of the
media, advertising, popular culture, religious ideologies, political ideologies, social movements, as well as practices in the workplace. Given
these vested interest groups, it is likely that emotionologies are sometimes orchestrated or manipulated to serve political purposes. For
instance, Rogers (1977) argues that politics are the manipulation of
power and control which emerges as strategies and tactics designed to
control the thoughts, emotions and behavior of oneself or other people.
This definition clearly reflects a social functional view of emotions. As
the chapters in this edited volume show, several emotions (either explicitly or implicitly) can be used in the context of work to impose
emotional and behavioral control – often in the sense of anticipatory
emotion (Harvey and Dasborough, 2018).

To render the argument around the control and politics of emotionologies more visible for the purpose of our book, turning to studies on
organizational climate may prove insightful. Organizational climate indicates shared perceptions of the existence and meaning of organizational
practices, policies, and procedures in addition to what behavior is
expected and rewarded (Schneider et al., 2013). Again, many emotions
examined in this book qualify for closer theoretical and empirical
scrutiny in the context of organizational climate. For instance, one
apparent contender here is fear. Prior work suggests that within organizations, a climate of fear can emerge as a result of managerial practice,
such that manager "talk" can lead to fear of repercussion or punishments
for mistakes, and a feeling that it may not be advisable to err or speak up
concerning those errors or other issues at work, including issues of a
sensitive nature. Seen in this light, a climate of fear at work is based on
shared perceptions of what to do and what not to do given a range of
possible (punitive) consequences (see also chapters by Connelly and
Turner, 2018; and Harvey and Dasborough, 2018). Thus, a climate of fear
is one mechanism through which organizational control can be exercised,
at least in the short-term. Future research could examine the longevity of

organizations, together with a range of key indicators (e.g., staff well-being, turnover, performance, profits etc.) vis-à-vis any imposition of fear climates at work, and fluctuations thereof over time. Again, it would be erroneous to presume that a better understanding of the causes and consequences of organizational climate can only be further illuminated through the emotion of fear. Emotions, like schadenfreude, happiness, anger, or shame to name a few, have all been shown in prior studies to be part and parcel of how employees will be socialized into their work roles (Dasborough and Harvey, 2016; Lindebaum, 2017; Sutton, 1991).

Finally, it should be noted there is a superordinate phenomenon located above organizational climate and associated socialization practices. Since this book advances emotion theory in the context of work, we see considerable merit in casting the net a little wider to better understand how socio-economic conditions of the present day influence the talk about emotion at work. Since social-economic conditions have long been recognized to influence what kinds of emotions to display at work (Fromm, 1941/2011; Illouz, 2007), it will be intriguing to ask who has the power to construct, modify or suppress metaphors and emotion-ologies, for what purpose, and to whose benefit, to revert back to Rogers's quote. Consistent with our book's main theme, the question remains – whether, to what extent, and/or how socio-economic conditions can serve as an enabler or inhibiter for the social function of emotion and the talk about it to be at odds, reinforce each other, or perhaps occur simultaneously. But to explore this question, and the questions we raised above, will be the task of future research. To conclude, then, it is our humble hope that this book ignites imagination for creative, if perhaps unorthodox, future theorizing and empirical efforts on this important yet under-explored topic.

NOTES

1. Even within one culture, the talk about emotion can vary over time, suggesting that there also is a chronological element to be considered (see Lindebaum, 2017).
2. We argue that some of this "talk" can be an internal dialogue (i.e., "how dare you, we don't act that way!"), and may or may not be expressed. While Solomon's example may indicate an intra-individual phenomenon (i.e., an "internal conversation"), our position is that this practice may be the product of social programming. In other words, this kind of programming shapes emotion triggers, and how emotion is expressed or suppressed vis-à-vis social norms governing the appropriateness of experiencing and expressing emotion in particular situations. Further, we recognise that psychologists might discern conceptual similarities between the arguments we present here and the central tenets of attribution theory. While we offer occasional references to "attributions", given our focus on how we "talk about" emotion, it is germane to remain faithful to a predominantly sociological perspective.

3. We consider this an intriguing avenue for future research to rigorously design and conduct empirical studies that put these ideas to the test.
4. Studies involving four laboratory sessions of guided practice also confirm this effect. It was found, *inter alia*, that changing initial appraisals through cognitive re-appraisal (i.e., distancing and reinterpretation) lead to a reduction over time in negative affect (for both distancing and reinterpretation) and perceived stress (for distancing only) (Denny and Ochsner, 2014). Hence, changing the initial appraisal led to outcomes that constituted an improvement compared to the original state.
5. Note that we position our work consistent with research by Damasio (2000). He maintains that, while learning and culture can modify the expression of emotions and give them new meanings, emotions themselves are determined by biological processes over a long evolutionary history. Making Damasio's balanced position explicit is highly germane, since, as a topic, the "emotion" and the "talk about the emotion" neither resides exclusively with social constructionism, nor with more biologically-informed perspectives on emotions.
6. Meursault, the protagonist in Camus's masterpiece *The Outsider* (1982) is a powerful example of how "society" retaliates against individuals who do not comply with behavioural expectations in specific situations, such as lack of grief and mourning when a parent has died.
7. These have been identified as West European, Anglo, East-Central European, Orthodox Eastern Europe, South and South-East Asian, Middle East and Sub-Saharan African, Confucian, and Latin American (see Tamir et al., 2016, for more details).

REFERENCES

Anderson, E. (2017). *Private Government How Employers Rule Our Lives (and Why We Don't Talk about It)*. Princeton, NJ, USA: Princeton University Press.
Ashkanasy, N. (2003). Emotions in organizations: a multi-level perspective. In F. Dansereau and F. J. Yammarino (eds), *Multi-Level Issues in Organizational Behaviour and Strategy* (Vol. 2, pp. 9–54). Oxford, UK: Elsevier.
Camus, A. (1982). *The Outsider*. London, UK: Penguin Books.
Connelly, S., and Turner, M. R. (2018). Functional and dysfunctional fear at work: dual perspectives. In D. Lindebaum, D. Geddes, and P. J. Jordan (eds), *Social Functions of Emotion and Talking About Emotion at Work*. Cheltenham, UK and Northampton, MA, USA: Edward Elgar Publishing.
Creed, W. E. D., Hudson, B. A., Okhuysen, G. A., and Smith-Crowe, K. (2014). Swimming in a sea of shame: incorporating emotion into explanations of institutional reproduction and change. *Academy of Management Review, 39*(3), 275–301.
Damasio, A. R. (2000). *The Feeling of What Happens: Body and Emotion in the Making of Consciousness*. London, UK: Vintage.
Dasborough, M., and Harvey, P. (2016). Schadenfreude: the (not so) secret joy of another's misfortune. *Journal of Business Ethics*, 1–15.
de Hooge, I. E., Zeelenberg, M., and Breugelmans, S. M. (2010). A functionalist account of shame-induced behaviour. *Cognition and Emotion, 25*(5), 939–946.
Denny, B. T., and Ochsner, K. N. (2014). Behavioral effects of longitudinal training in cognitive reappraisal. *Emotion, 14*(2), 425–433.
Elfenbein, H. A. (2007). Emotion in organizations: a review and theoretical integration. *The Academy of Management Annals, 1*(1), 315–386.

Fineman, S. (ed.) (1993). *Emotion in Organizations*. London, UK: Sage.

Fineman, S. (ed.) (2008). *The Emotional Organization: Passions and Power.* Oxford, UK: Blackwell Publishing.

Fineman, S. (2010). Emotion in organizations–a critical turn. In B. Sieben and Å. Wettergren (eds), *Emotionalizing Organizations and Organizing Emotions* (pp. 23–41). Basingstoke, UK: Palgrave Macmillan.

Fisher, C. D. (2018). Boredom at work: what, why, and what then? In D. Lindebaum, D. Geddes, and P. J. Jordan (eds), *Social Functions of Emotion and Talking About Emotion at Work*. Cheltenham, UK: Edward Elgar.

Frijda, N. H. (1986). *The Emotions*. Paris, France: Cambridge University Press.

Fromm, E. (1941/2011). *Escape from Freedom*. New York, NY, USA: Ishi Press.

Geddes, D., and Callister, R. R. (2007). Crossing the line(s): a dual threshold model of anger in organizations. *Academy of Management Review, 32*(3), 721–746.

Geddes, D., Callister, R., and Gibson, D. E. (2018). A message in the madness: functions of workplace anger in organizational life. *The Academy of Management Perspectives.*

Gray, H. M., Ishii, K., and Ambady, N. (2011). Misery loves company: when sadness increases the desire for social connectedness. *Personality and Social Psychology Bulletin, 37*(11), 1438–1448.

Harvey, P., and Dasborough, M. (2018). Talking about schadenfreude: sharing versus the social function. In D. Lindebaum, D. Geddes, and P. J. Jordan (eds), *Social Functions of Emotion and Talking About Emotion at Work*. Cheltenham, UK and Northampton, MA, USA: Edward Elgar Publishing.

Hayward, M. L. A., Ashkanasy, N. M., and Baron, R. A. (2018). Employee pride and hubris. In D. Lindebaum, D. Geddes, and P. J. Jordan (eds), *Social Functions of Emotion and Talking About Emotion at Work*. Cheltenham, UK and Northampton, MA, USA: Edward Elgar Publishing.

Illouz, E. (2007). *Cold Intimacies: The Making of Emotional Capitalism*. Cambridge: Polity.

James, W. (1884). What is an emotion? *Mind, 9*, 188–205.

Keltner, D., and Gross, J. J. (1999). Functional accounts of emotions. *Cognition and Emotion, 13*(5), 467–480.

Keltner, D., and Haidt, J. (1999). Social functions of emotions at four levels of analysis. *Cognition and Emotion, 13*(5), 505–521.

Keltner, D., and Kring, A. M. (1998). Emotion, social function, and psychopathology. *Review of General Psychology, 2*, 320–342.

Kiffin-Petersen, S. (2018). Ashamed of your shame? How discrepancy self-talk and social discourse influence individual shame at work. In D. Lindebaum, D. Geddes, and P. J. Jordan (eds), *Social Functions of Emotion and Talking About Emotion at Work*. Cheltenham, UK and Northampton, MA, USA: Edward Elgar Publishing.

Lakoff, G., and Johnson, M. (2006). Metaphors we live by. In J. O'Brien (ed.), *The Production of Reality: Essays and Readings on Social Interaction* (4th ed., pp. 103–114). Thousand Oaks: Pine Forge Press.

Lench, H. C., Bench, S. W., Darbor, K. E., and Moore, M. (2015). A functionalist manifesto: goal-related emotions from an evolutionary perspective. *Emotion Review, 7*(1), 90–98.

Lindebaum, D. (2017). *Emancipation through Emotion Regulation at Work.* Cheltenham, UK and Northampton, MA, USA: Edward Elgar Publishing.

Lindebaum, D., and Courpasson, D. (2017). Becoming the next Charlie Parker: rewriting the role of passions in bureaucracies with whiplash. *Academy of Management Review.*

Lindebaum, D., and Gabriel, Y. (2016). Anger and organization studies: from social disorder to moral order. *Organization Studies, 37*(7), 903–918.

Lindebaum, D., and Geddes, D. (2016a). The emotion, and the talk about the emotion at work. *Symposium presented at the 10th EMONET Conference in Rome, 4–5 July.*

Lindebaum, D., and Geddes, D. (2016b). The place and role of (moral) anger in organizational behavior studies. *Journal of Organizational Behavior, 37*(5), 738–757.

McMurray, R., and Ward, J. (2014). 'Why would you want to do that?': defining emotional dirty work. *Human Relations, 67*(9), 1123–1143.

Moura, K. E., Jordan, P. J., and Troth, A. C. (2018). Inside Out: a receiver's experience of anger in the workplace. In D. Lindebaum, D. Geddes, and P. J. Jordan (eds), *Social Functions of Emotion and Talking About Emotion at Work.* Cheltenham, UK and Northampton, MA, USA: Edward Elgar Publishing.

Nesse, R. M., and Ellsworth, P. C. (2009). Evolution, emotions, and emotional disorders. *American Psychologist, 64*(2), 129–139.

Parrott, W. G., and Harré, R. (1996). Some complexities in the study of emotion. In R. Harré and W. G. Parrott (eds), *The Emotions: Social, Cultural and Biological Dimensions.* London, UK: Sage.

Perez, K. A., and Lench, H. C. (2018). Benefits of awe in the workplace. In D. Lindebaum, D. Geddes, and P. J. Jordan (eds), *Social Functions of Emotion and Talking About Emotion at Work.* Cheltenham, UK and Northampton, MA, USA: Edward Elgar Publishing.

Rogers, C. R. (1977). *Carl Rogers on Personal Power.* London: Constable and Company Ltd.

Scheff, T. J. (1988). Shame and conformity: the deference-emotion system. *American Sociological Review, 53*(3), 395–406.

Scherer, K. R., Schorr, A., and Johnstone, T. E. (2001). *Appraisal Processes in Emotion: Theory, Methods, Research.* New York, NY, USA: Oxford University Press.

Schneider, B., Ehrhart, M. G., and Macey, W. H. (2013). Organizational climate and culture. *Annual Review of Psychology, 64*(1), 361–388.

Smith, R. K., Wingenbach, T. S. H., and Smith, R. H. (2018). Shaping benign and malicious envy in organizations. In D. Lindebaum, D. Geddes, and P. J. Jordan (eds), *Social Functions of Emotion and Talking About Emotion at Work.* Cheltenham, UK and Northampton, MA, USA: Edward Elgar Publishing.

Solomon, R. (2003). *Not Passion's Slave: Emotions and Choice.* Oxford, UK: Oxford University Press.

Spicer, A., and Cederström, C. (2017). *Desperately Seeking Self-Improvement – A Year Inside the Optimization Movement.* London, UK: OR Books.

Stearns, P. N. (2018). Happiness at work: a tension in contemporary history. In D. Lindebaum, D. Geddes, and P. J. Jordan (eds), *Social Functions of Emotion and Talking About Emotion at Work*. Cheltenham, UK and Northampton, MA, USA: Edward Elgar Publishing.

Stearns, P. N., and Stearns, C. Z. (1985). Emotionology: clarifying the history of emotions and emotional standards. *The American Historical Review, XC*, 813–816.

Sutton, R. I. (1991). Maintaining norms about expressed emotions: the case of bill collectors. *Administrative Science Quarterly, 36*(2), 245–268.

Tamir, M., Schwartz, S. H., Cieciuch, J., Riediger, M., Torres, C., Scollon, C., Dzokoto, V., Zhou, X., and Vishkin, A. (2016). Desired emotions across cultures: a value-based account. *Journal of Personality and Social Psychology, 111*(1), 67–82.

Tyran, K. L. (2018). The deeper side of sadness at work: why being sad is not always bad. In D. Lindebaum, D. Geddes, and P. J. Jordan (eds), *Social Functions of Emotion and Talking About Emotion at Work*. Cheltenham, UK and Northampton, MA, USA: Edward Elgar Publishing.

van Kleef, G. A. (2017). The social effects of emotions are functionally equivalent across expressive modalities. *Psychological Inquiry, 28*(2–3), 211–216.

van Maanen, J., and Kunda, G. (1989). Real feelings: emotional expression and organizational culture. In L. L. Cummings and B. M. Staw (eds), *Research in Organizational Behavior* (Vol. 11, pp. 43–104). Greenwich, CT, USA: JAI Press.

Wright, L. (1973). Functions. *Philosophical Review, 82*, 139–168.

Zeelenberg, M., Nelissen, R., Breugelmans, S. H., and Pieters, R. (2008). On emotion specificity in decision making: why feeling is for doing. *Judgment and Decision Making, 3*(1), 18–27.

2. Inside out: a receiver's experience of anger in the workplace

Kathryn E. Moura, Peter J. Jordan and Ashlea C. Troth[*]

INTRODUCTION

Anger is prevalent in organizations today and therefore the focus of significant research (Callister et al., 2017; Gibson and Callister, 2010; Lindebaum and Gabriel, 2016; Lindebaum et al., 2017). An examination of the extensive research on this topic reveals that the majority of these studies centre on the sender of anger expressions, their triggers, reactions (Booth and Mann, 2005; Fitness, 2000; Moura et al., 2015) and the consequences of these episodes in the workplace (Booth and Mann, 2005; Chen and Spector, 1992; Fitness, 2000). Recently, however, some researchers have addressed the impact and consequences of sender anger expressions on the targets of anger (Axelrod and Harlos, 2008; Callister et al., 2017; Harlos, 2010). Our aim in this chapter is to contribute to this research by examining how receivers (targets and observers) of anger at work perceive and manage workplace anger expressions. More specifically, we examine the attributions made about anger by those who witness anger (as receivers and observers) as well as the emotional regulation strategies they use to manage their response to such emotional displays. Overall, in line with the focus of this book, our research contributes to an increased understanding of how employees and managers use talk to explain their emotional experiences and reactions in the workplace. We then examine this talk in terms of dominant theories of emotion in the field.

Although anger expressions at work are often viewed in a pejorative way (e.g., Meier et al., 2013), Geddes and Callister (2007) identified through the Dual Threshold Model (DTM) that anger expressions can result in both functional and dysfunctional outcomes with the key being how this anger is expressed (Gibson and Callister, 2010). They argue that the functionality of an anger expression is not only determined by personal individual interpretations of the event, but also by the social setting in which both the sender and the target operate (i.e., organizational norms and display rules; Kramer and Hess, 2002). Given anger is a common experience in workplaces, several researchers studying anger have stressed the importance of understanding the impact of anger on the receiver (Axelrod and Harlos, 2008; Gibson and Callister, 2010; Harlos, 2010; Stickney and Geddes, 2016). In this chapter, we contribute to this body of work by specifically examining the receiver's attributions (i.e., how respondents talk about the perceived cause of anger) for anger expressions and the emotional regulation strategies they use (i.e., how the respondents talk about the methods they use to decrease, maintain or increase specific emotional experiences and responses) when dealing with anger expressions directed towards themselves and others. Simply, our aim is to better understand how employees experience and make sense of anger expressions by others.

CURRENT RESEARCH ON THE RECEIVERS OF ANGER EXPRESSIONS

To date, studies on receivers of anger expressions relate mainly to interactions between the sender and the target linked to specific contexts such as when dealing with conflict and negotiation, bullying, victimization and abusive supervision situations (Axelrod and Harlos, 2008; Friedman et al., 2004; Geddes and Stickney, 2012; Kopelman et al., 2006; Totterdell et al., 2012; van Kleef et al., 2004; Walker and Jackson, 2017). Research demonstrates that differences in the interpretation of anger expressions occur depending on who is angry with whom (Fitness, 2000; Sloan, 2004). In other words, an employee's status may affect the way in which an individual experiences and responds to events (Basch and Fisher, 2000), with some arguing that interactions between a co-worker and supervisor are the most powerful source of anger (Kramer and Hess, 2002; Waldron, 2000).

Studies indicate that receivers of anger expressions experience both positive and negative outcomes (Geddes and Callister, 2007; Lindebaum et al., 2016). Positively, anger expressions can act as catalysts for change by highlighting factors at work such as injustice (Geddes and Callister, 2007), problems of individual and organizational efficacy (Gross, 1998), and issues related to group unity and goal accomplishment (Callister et al., 2003). On the other hand, anger expressions have also been linked to employees experiencing reduced job security, lower work satisfaction, less organizational commitment (Axelrod and Harlos, 2008) and increased occupational stress (Glomb, 2002). Research additionally established that when an individual is challenged by an angry adversary during conflict and negotiation they can develop a negative impression of the sender (van Kleef et al., 2004) and avoid interaction with them into the future (Kopelman et al., 2006; van Kleef et al., 2004). Furthermore, when anger is associated to victimization and bullying in the workplace, individuals feel unwell (both psychologically and physically) at work (Kiecolt-Glaser et al., 2002), detached from their organization and dissatisfied in their jobs (Axelrod and Harlos, 2008). Overall, there are significant negative outcomes associated with anger expressions at work. On this basis, a better understanding of how others perceive and react to anger expressions in the workplace may provide an insight into ameliorating these negative outcomes and understanding how positive benefits accrue.

THEORETICAL FRAMEWORKS FOR EXAMINING ANGER AT WORK

A broad range of frameworks exist for examining emotion at work including Affective Events Theory (AET; Weiss and Cropanzano, 1996), Dual Threshold Model of Anger (DTM; Geddes and Callister, 2007), Social Rules Theory (SRT; Domaglaski and Steelman, 2007), Attribution Theory (AT; Keashly and Neuman, 2008; Kelley, 1973), Emotions as Social Information (EASI; van Kleef, 2009) and Emotion Regulation (ER; Gross, 1998). In our study, two frameworks were chosen to explore the receiver's internal processes when confronted with anger: Attribution Theory (AT; Kelley, 1973) and The Process Model of Emotion Regulation (ER; Gross, 1998). Attribution Theory provides a framework for understanding causal explanations (Martinko et al., 2010), more specifically in this case, sender anger. The Process Theory of ER contributes to a greater comprehension of how emotions are generated, felt, and expressed (Gross 1998, 2014) and is an important factor in responding to anger expressions.

Attribution Theory is a theory that explains how people make causal descriptions and respond to questions commencing with 'why?' in relation to other people's behavior (Kelley, 1973). There are a number of different ways in which researchers have considered attributions. For instance, in a relatively early contribution, Kelley (1967) proposed the Covariation model. This model consists of a three dimensional framework to determine causal attributions: (i) consistency – the extent to which the present behavior is consistent with past behaviors; (ii) distinctiveness – the level of contextual difference that surrounds the behavior; and (iii) consensus – the extent to which others behave in a similar fashion when in the same situation. For example, the recipient might attribute anger to the sender's frequent anger (see Lindebaum et al., 2016). Frequent anger can be seen as high in consistency, low in distinctiveness and low in consensus suggesting a dispositional cause/internal attribution.

More recently, Weiner (1979, 1985) argued that attributions can be organized into three causal dimensions: (i) locus of causality – whether the cause is internal (specific to the person) or external (situationally influenced); (ii) stability – whether the cause is constant or variable over time; and (iii) controllability – whether the cause is under the control of the person or not (Weiner, 1979). Although we use Weiner's Attribution Theory (1979) as a framework for our analysis, it is important to make note of a few similarities and differences found between Kelley's (1967) and Weiner's (1979) theories to justify our decision to use one specific theory.

In terms of overlap, 'consistency' in Kelley's theory can be linked to Weiner's dimension of 'stability'. Similarly, both theories explore the context of attributions, but in slightly different ways. The dimension of 'distinctiveness' in Kelley's theory examines the level of contextual difference that surrounds the behavior while 'locus of causality' determines whether the cause is internal to the person or external, attributed to the situation or context. The significant difference between theories is Kelley's 'consensus' dimension which explores the extent to which others behave in a similar fashion when in the same situation, while 'controllability' from Weiner's theory focuses on determining whether the cause is under the control of the person or not (distinct from locus of causality that determines whether the cause of anger is attributed internally or externally to the individual). In our study we use Weiner's (1979) Attribution Theory as it better encompasses our understanding of how anger was assessed by the respondents.

Generally, those witnessing expressions of anger in society and at work view it as appropriate or inappropriate. For example, a demonstration of anger by an employee who is almost involved in a workplace accident as a result of the organization's poor work practices or the negligence of a fellow worker would be seen as quite appropriate (through external, variable, and uncontrollable attributions). On the other hand, a demonstration of anger by a manager in an organization where such displays are discouraged via specific organizational display rules that prescribe that managers should avoid confrontation and display positive emotions

(Ekman, 1992; Rafaeli and Sutton, 1987), would be deemed inappropriate (through internal, stable, and controllable attributions). Interestingly, Lindebaum and his colleagues (2016) conducted a study in the United Kingdom Military on the positive and negative reactions to expressions of anger at work. They noted that the UK's military outlook on anger is altering. Participants in that study saw frequent expressions of anger as emerging from an internal deficiency of the sender that was internal, stable and controllable.

Our aim in this study is to examine recipients ER strategies when observing and experiencing anger. We note that these emotional experiences and responses to someone else's anger are closely linked to attributions made and may involve a range of emotions. Analysing the data from our study, we draw on both Attribution Theory and on the Process Model of Emotion Regulation to frame our insights.

METHOD

Participants

To examine the topic broadly, we undertook purposive sampling across a range of industries. Respondents were drawn from the medical, mining, banking, legal and manufacturing sectors in Australia. A total of 30 participants were interviewed. To be included in our sample, participants needed to have experienced anger directed at them (target) or directed at another person or an object (observer). Twenty participants experienced anger as targets and ten as observers. Sixteen participants were female and fourteen male, with the sample including twelve managers and eighteen employees. Participants described twenty targets of anger as established in their work role while ten were new to their position.

Interview Procedure

Approval was received through a university ethics committee prior to the interviews with participants. Interviews lasted 45 to 60 minutes and were semi-structured, one-on-one interviews (Di Cicco-Bloom and Crabtree, 2006). At the start of the interview, respondents were assured of anonymity and confidentiality and asked to sign a consent form. Participants were asked to select a recent event they experienced, preferably within the last two years. In some instances, participants wanted to describe an older incident and as it was more relevant to them, we allowed some flexibility in this area. Participants identified themselves as

Table 2.1   Study one – participant demographics

	Gender	Industry	Experience of Anger	Position	Target Work Role
1	Female	Mining	Target	Manager	Established
2	Female	Legal	Observer	Employee	Established
3	Female	Legal	Target	Employee	New Worker
4	Female	Legal	Target	Employee	Established
5	Female	Legal	Target	Employee	Established
6	Female	Medical	Observer	Manager	Established
7	Male	Medical	Target	Manager	Established
8	Male	Mining	Target	Employee	Established
9	Male	Banking	Target	Employee	New Worker
10	Male	Banking	Observer	Employee	New Worker
11	Female	Banking	Observer	Employee	New Worker
12	Male	Banking	Target	Manager	Established
13	Female	Banking	Target	Employee	Established
14	Male	Banking	Observer	Employee	Established
15	Female	Banking	Observer	Manager	New Worker
16	Male	Banking	Target	Employee	Established
17	Male	Banking	Target	Employee	Established
18	Male	Banking	Observer	Manager	New Worker
19	Male	Manufacturing	Target	Manager	New Worker
20	Female	Manufacturing	Observer	Employee	Established
21	Female	Medical	Target	Manager	Established
22	Male	Medical	Target	Manager	Established
23	Female	Medical	Observer	Employee	New Worker
24	Female	Medical	Target	Manager	Established
25	Male	Mining	Observer	Employee	Established
26	Female	Mining	Target	Employee	Established
27	Female	Mining	Target	Employee	Established
28	Male	Manufacturing	Target	Employee	Established
29	Male	Manufacturing	Target	Manager	New Worker
30	Female	Medical	Target	Manager	New Worker

the 'target' or 'observer' of that specific anger event. To improve event recall, the Day Reconstruction Method (DRM; Kahneman et al., 2004) was used. Through DRM, participants systematically reconstructed their activities and experiences preceding the event that they were recalling. The process was a guided exercise facilitated by the first author and designed to reduce memory biases and improve recall. DRM is intended to enable a more accurate assessment of thoughts and emotions that occurred in the past (Diener and Tay, 2013). Participants were then given an opportunity to describe their experience in more depth by answering a set of twelve key questions about that event. These questions included 'Why do you think the person was angry?' 'What was going through your head to make sense of the anger?' and 'What was your response to the angry person?'

All interviews were recorded and subsequently transcribed. Interview transcripts were initially analysed by the first author and broad themes and sub-themes around attributions and emotion regulation were established. Themes were then entered into the NVivo Software (Bazeley and Jackson, 2013; Guest et al., 2006). Two other coders further tested themes and sub-themes for consistency, reliability and accuracy (Olson et al., 2016). The unit of analysis chosen for this study was response phrases (Downe-Wamboldt, 1992), or phrases long enough to allow for an understanding of the information being coded. Results are discussed below.

RESULTS

The interviews provide insights into the attributions made by receivers of anger and their ER strategies used in response to this anger expression by others. In outlining our findings, we initially examined the respondent's attribution of sender anger in light of Weiner's (1979) three causal dimensions: locus of causality, stability and controllability. Subsequently, we assess the ER strategies used in response to this anger using the Process Model of Emotion Regulation (Gross, 1998) as a guideline.

ATTRIBUTIONS

Attributions are discussed below in relation to locus of causality (internal or external), stability (stable or unstable) and controllability (controllable or uncontrollable; Weiner, 1979).

Locus of Causality

Locus of causality determines whether the cause is internal (specific to the person) or external (situation dependant; Weiner, 1979). Our participants made a number of internal attributions of anger expressions based on the status or position of the individual expressing the anger. For instance, in terms of the status of individuals, participants talked about the internal locus of causality of leaders and managers of their organization in the following way: '*if you're in a leadership role you can't afford to be childish*' (Six, Observer, Manager), '*it's not appropriate for a senior manager to act in that way and especially in the HR role you're in*' (Eight, Target, Employee). One participant saw a business partner angry at the computer software program and stated: '*... an inappropriate response to something so small ... he did have quite a stature in the company ... you're meant to be quite sophisticated, knowledgeable, intelligent and then this is how you're behaving when your computer isn't working properly!*' (Five, Observer, Employee). We note that the majority of participants who made these internal loci of control leadership observations were employees. For those participants, individuals in senior positions had a set of behavioral norms that their subsequent expression of anger appeared to contravene and on this basis they ascribed internal attributions for the anger.

Other examples of attributions where internal locus of causality was involved infer that the expression emerged from some internal deficiency with responses such as: '*inappropriate responses to staff member's behavior*' (Two, Observer, Employee), '*inappropriate response to something so small*' (Five, Observer, Employee), '*uncalled for*' (Ten, Observer, Employee) and '*wasn't warranted*' (Fifteen, Observer, Manager). These responses emerged when the sender's anger appeared to cross the impropriety threshold as defined by Geddes and Callister (2007). In these cases, sender anger was directly related to organizational and professional norms/expectations, and internal causality established if the anger was seen to contravene those organizational and professional norms. Thus, participants viewed sender anger as internal, originating from the angry person's lack of personal control. Participant Fourteen (Observer, Employee) outlined a situation where a team member who had not delivered his work to the manager [sender] in a timely manner experienced aggressive and inappropriate sender anger: '*I just don't think you should deal with people in that manner in an open forum, there's a certain way you talk to people regardless of what's going on, without belittling or humiliating people or creating a stress level that's effectively unwarranted'*. When behavioral norms were clearly contravened (in-appropriate behavior), our participants in this study generally assessed sender behavior in relation to their own moral behavior: '*I would have probably supervised more appropriately all the way through the project, but when, if I was faced with the situation, like she was faced with, I don't think I would have exploded the way she did*' (Two, Observer, Employee).

On the other hand, when expressed anger behavior fell within the norms of the organization and was within the bounds of the expression and impropriety thresholds of anger as defined by Geddes and Callister (2007), different attributions were made in relation to locus of causality. Specifically, participants described some angry individuals as being justified in their anger, especially when attributions made were around a situational (external) issue. Responses included '*all the right to be angry*' (Twenty, Observer, Employee), '*I don't think she did anything wrong*' (Thirty, Target, Manager) and '*fair enough ... a fair call*' (Nine, Target, Employee). Although eight participants described sender anger as appro-priate to the situation, they generally disapproved of the anger expression itself. This is illustrated by Participant Two (Observer, Employee),

> '*I said, I understand what's happened and ... you are absolutely well within your rights to be absolutely outraged at how this has gone down ... but I'm not happy with the way in which it played out, and I'm not happy with the way in which it played out in front of other team members.*'

Stability

Stability refers to whether the cause is constant or variable over time (Weiner, 1979). During the interviews, when discussing the specific anger incident, participants repeatedly made comments about the past behavior of the angry person. They made sense of the anger on the basis of how frequently the individual expressed anger. In terms of attributions, this is linked to their perceptions of the stability and consistency of the individual's angry behavior and whether they were angry on a frequent basis. All 30 participants made attributions that were linked to the angry person's anger frequency, with 22 participants mentioning it as frequent and eight as a 'once only' single occurrence in response to the event.

Of those who identified frequent sender anger, the comments sup-ported the notion that the anger expression was seen as a stable pattern of behavior. The initiator of the anger was described by participants as having '*a hot temper and a reputation for it around the firm*' (Five, Observer, Employee), '*a bit of a history of doing things like that*' (Ten,

Observer, Employee), '*tendencies to be overly sort of angry*' (Thirteen, Target, Employee) and '*a continuous circle for a while*' (Fourteen, Observer, Employee). Distinctly, participants made attributions around frequent displays of anger as a stable behavior.

Three participants explained that when they were dealing with an individual who had frequent (stable) expressions of anger, they were fearful for their physical and/or psychological safety as illustrated by Participant Twenty-Nine (Target, Manager), '*… it was frightening to see someone change totally when the anger came … I was afraid and I thought he wanted to kill me, he wanted to punch me … I thought he wanted to choke me*'.

On the other hand, those who recalled events where there were 'once only' (situationally generated) anger expressions made unstable attributions. These participants talked about the sender anger as '*… completely out of character*' (Twenty-Six, Target, Employee), '*a one off event*' (Nine, Target, Employee), '*haven't seen him angry*' (Twenty Five, Observer, Employee) and '*I [observer] hadn't seen her [sender] actually scream at her [target] like that …*' (Fifteen, Observer, Manager). These attributions, where the individual's expression of anger was unstable over time, encouraged a greater consideration by the observer/target of why the anger event occurred. This is in line with van Kleef's (2009) arguments around the propensity of emotions to encourage others to seek information. Overall, frequent expressions of anger (stable attributions) tended to encapsulate internal locus of causality while individuals who were seen as being angry less frequently were ascribed unstable attributions which tended to coincide with an external locus of causality. We note that these dimensions also overlap considerably with Kelley's Covariation model (1973) where low distinctiveness (stability) leads to specific dispositional attributions.

Controllability

Controllability differs from locus of causality. Locus of causality determines whether the attribution of anger is internal (stimuli from within) or external (stimuli from outside) to the individual while controllability establishes whether the anger expression (either attributed internally or externally) can be controlled by the individual or not (Weiner, 1979). In our study, all participants viewed anger as controllable, that is, within the volition of the individual. This is illustrated by Participant Five (Observer, Employee) who encountered an angry senior partner who was unable to make a dictation software program work:

'I was thinking, this is ridiculous. Obviously when I looked at his response to that [computer dictation software not working well] it just made me think of a child throwing a big tantrum, obviously because you would think he'd know better. I think there were many solutions available but he was just so focused on making it [the software] work himself, that he wasn't interested in exploring other options.'

Display rules that exist in the workplace in relation to anger – what is acceptable behavior and what is not – are clearly illustrated by participant comments. All participants seemed to agree that the angry person could and should control their anger as described by Participant Twenty-Four (Target, Manager). This participant encountered anger when she approached a new manager to request that the sender take on some work the previous manager had undertaken: *'I was taken aback. I was shocked. I thought it was very unprofessional. I was a little bit disgusted really because there are so many expressions you can use to somebody, if you don't think that's your role, than to say what she said'.*

When anger crossed the impropriety threshold (DTM; Geddes and Callister, 2007) and it was a 'once only' occurrence participants made excuses for the sender's anger as described by Participant Twenty-Six (Target, Employee). She encountered a 'once only' anger expression when she forgot to add an important aspect to the PowerPoint presentation she had designed. Although the anger was controllable by the sender and was seen as crossing the impropriety threshold (DTM; Geddes and Callister, 2007), it was dismissed: *'I think he [sender] was probably annoyed at something else [personal issues] and just took his anger out on me'.*

Controllability was also associated with the regularity and appropriateness of sender anger, rather than only being linked to display rules. When participants encountered 'once off' expressions of anger, they expressed concern and compassion towards the angry person as described by Participant Twenty-Five (Observer, Employee): *'I was worried about him, when he put his hands down on the keyboard I thought, okay, let me make sure he is okay, that he's not going to injure himself'.* This concern for the angry person did not diminish the immediate impact of expressed anger on the target nor lessen the belief of the inappropriateness of sender anger as illustrated by Participant Twenty-Six (Target, Employee): *'I got quite upset, and went to the bathroom and had a cry ... I think it is definitely not appropriate to react in that way.'*

Another important aspect to consider is that when the target was a new worker, they blamed themselves for the sender's anger. Doing this seemingly 'neutralized' the effect of deviant anger, as described by participant Nine (Target, Employee) who was new to the organization and broke a machine due to oversight:

> *'I was new, I'd only been there for about a month or so … you knew the reasons why he was angry and it was probably fair enough … I knew it was my fault, I just really thought, I've got to sit here and cop it … I knew I was wrong so I just sort of sat down and copped it and moved on really.'*

In summary, all participants viewed anger as being within the control of the sender. When anger was a 'once only' occurrence, the aspect of controllability was ignored or downplayed. On the other hand, when anger was regular, controllability was highlighted and anger was more likely to be attributed to internal deficiencies in the individual.

EMERGENT THEMES – ATTRIBUTIONS

Based on our analysis, two broad themes emerged from our data around the appropriateness of the anger expression and the frequency of sender anger. In terms of appropriateness, the data supported the Dual Threshold Model in that many senders described the anger they witnessed as inappropriate (exceeding the impropriety threshold) (Geddes and Callister, 2007). Based on our data, it appears that perceived inappropriate expressions of anger in the workplace are linked to the norms or accepted patterns of behavior for that organization. Our respondents talked about expressions of anger that challenged those norms as being inappropriate. Extending this in a minor way, we also found that there were different norms established for leader behavior by employees, with some indication of a higher standard of behavior being set for those in senior and management positions. On the other hand, appropriate sender anger appears to be directly related to events as opposed to display rules.

The other issue that emerged and is suggested in other research (e.g., Lindebaum et al., 2016) was the overriding impact of frequency. For those participants who described the anger of the sender as being a frequent experience, there was almost a universal view that the anger expression was unwarranted. Indeed, considering the window between the expression and impropriety threshold outlined in the Dual Threshold Model, frequency appeared to cut across the consideration of norms in making attributions about the anger episode. Those who expressed frequent anger, even for what appeared to be a minor episode, were seen as out of control and, on that basis the anger was determined as inappropriate (i.e., the window between expressed and impropriety thresholds for these people is smaller). Participants, on the other hand, seemed to be somewhat forgiving of people who they described as being involved in a 'once only' expression of anger. The attributions they made provided justifiable explanations for those individuals with the anger episode being described as external and unstable and controllable 'once only' anger expressions, that is, the window between expressed and impropriety thresholds for these people is larger. Again this may be indicative of a level of flexibility in the thresholds at which anger is identified as inappropriate (Geddes and Callister, 2007; Lindebaum et al., 2016).

EMOTION REGULATION

The next step in our interviews examined emotional experiences and reactions of targets and observers of the anger episodes. As anger is an emotion that generates a fight (approach) or flight (avoid) response in those witnessing anger (Berkowitz and Harmon-Jones, 2004), we sought to understand the emotional response to anger of our participants, as targets and as observers. To do this we used the Process Model of Emotion Regulation framework (Gross, 1998).

Our respondents identified four main emotion regulation processes: situation selection, cognitive re-appraisal, suppression and expression. Although Gross commonly uses these strategies in the literature when referring to the sender (Gross, 1998), we found these ER strategies to be present in receivers (both targets and observers) of anger expressions when responding to anger. We also note that respondents often talked about multiple responses to witnessing anger incidents and not just a single response. These four themes are described next.

Situation Selection

Situation selection is defined by Gross (1998) as a set of strategies used to approach or evade situations to regulate one's emotions, such as moving away from an offensive incident. Use of this type of strategy was a common occurrence for 21 participants who intentionally distanced themselves, and sometimes others (i.e., team members), from the sender. The following participants exemplify this theme: '*I was very protective of my staff, so I just wanted to get them [the team] out of the way*' (Two, Observer, Employee), and by another participant: '*I just went and made myself a cup of coffee and just ignored him really for the rest of the day*' (Thirteen, Target, Employee).

Cognitive Reappraisal

Cognitive reappraisal entails changing one's interpretation of events. This often took the form of cognitive reframing and reappraisal of a situation (Gross, 1998). In our study, cognitive reappraisal was a common occurrence, used by 19 participants. Recipients noted actions such as taking time to think things through and reviewing one's emotional response as explained by Participant Ten (Observer, Employee): '... *you're sort of, your anger subsides quite quickly when you then go, well hell, this could get a little bit worse, you flick the switch and go along.*' Two other examples also illustrate this strategy: '*I tried to keep reminding myself, this is business ...*' (One, Target, Manager) and, '*Well I thought, I've got better things to do than be angry at this bloke ...*' (Nine, Target, Employee).

Suppression

Twenty-four participants talked about suppressed emotions. Suppression was described in various ways from not arguing, '*not going to start conflict or have an opinion just yet*' (Twenty-Four, Target, Manager) to a lack of response, '*didn't retaliate ... didn't say anything back*' (Fifteen, Observer, Manager). Some did not speak at all, while others tried to hold back tears in an attempt to avoid conflict: '*don't cry, don't cry, don't cry*' (Three, Target, Employee). Other participants who observed the anger interaction viewed recipient suppression as positive. This seems to be an indication of the unspoken organizational display rule that maintaining one's control is more acceptable than not controlling oneself: '*the other girl was very, very good actually, she just took it and didn't retaliate, she just stared*' (Participant Fifteen, Observer, Manager). Participant One (Target, Manager) wanted to react strongly, but instead, suppressed her expression: '*I didn't at any time ever raise my voice, or show that I was incredibly irritated and annoyed by the behavior*'.

Three participants felt intimidated by the anger expression and suppressed out of fear for their safety as described by Participant Nineteen (Target, Manager): '*I thought he was going to hit me, but I tried to be calm ... as it was happening I just stared at him and stood firmly in front of him, with the face that I wasn't scared, as a poker face, but after that I was shaking, scared and I just went to the office, sat down ...*'

Expression

Twenty-three participants expressed their emotions. The expression of emotion took on two forms: maintaining current emotion (by agreeing and/or downplaying the significance of the event) and intensifying (taking charge). The most common type of expression was maintaining emotions as described by Participant Sixteen (Target, Employee). This participant forgot to include a colleague in a dinner invitation and when the co-worker (sender) became angry, he downplayed the significance of the event in an attempt to calm the sender down: '... *next time we'll include you, you know, it wasn't really a big deal, it was only, you know, it wasn't a big team, it was with another team you know, look, there wasn't a lot of us there ... in the future I'll fix it and make sure you're included'.*

Intensifying occurred mainly when participants held a management position. This is clearly illustrated by Participants Nineteen and Twenty-Two (Target, Manager) respectively: *'Well, I just said to him, I said, look, you don't need to be speaking to me like that, go and do what you've been asked to do and we'll talk about it later'* and *'I just told him don't touch me, if you touch me it can be a different scenario'.*

EMERGENT THEMES – EMOTION REGULATION

Our examination of the ER strategies used during participants' experience of the anger episode revealed two consistent themes. The first theme is the significant difference between targets and observers of anger in terms of how they responded to the anger. The second theme to emerge was a difference in the way employees and managers approached such experiences.

Targets of Anger – Managers

Based on our data, it seems being the direct target of anger results in specific reactions around protecting oneself. This was common for those who were the direct targets of anger and who felt threatened by the angry person as described by Participant Nineteen (Target, Manager): *'I thought he was going to hit me ... I was just concerned that he would hurt me'.* ER strategies were used to ensure that the target protected themselves from sender anger as described by Participant Nineteen (Target, Manager): *'I tried to be calm and I just told him, don't touch me, if you touch me it can be a different scenario'.* This pattern of reactions emerged when targets attempted to correct sender behavior by expressing emotions as described by Participant Twenty-Two (Target, Manager): '*I sort of pulled him [sender] aside and said, you need to pull these reins in a little bit*'. When targets felt that the situation had been brought under control and the sender responded and listened to them, communication flowed as described by Participant Twenty-Two (Target, Manager): '*once it all cooled down we sat down in my office and we were having a one on one discussion*'. When the target was not heard and sender anger continued, however, they suppressed their emotions as described by Participant One (Target, Manager): '*I didn't at any time ever raise my voice, or show that I was incredibly irritated and annoyed by the [sender] behavior*'.

Targets of Anger – Employees

Employees responded more by suppressing emotions as illustrated by Participant Three (Target, Employee): '*… my immediate feeling was to make everything okay, smooth the situation over, tell them what they want to hear, don't say anything, don't challenge what they're saying so I responded something like, that's fine.*' When sender anger continued, the employee talked about continuing to suppress their emotion selecting to distance themselves physically and mentally from the sender (e.g., going to get a coffee; situation selection) as described by Participant Thirteen (Target, Employee): '*I just went and made myself a cup of coffee and just ignored him really for the rest of the day*'.

The five target employees who were new to their role expressed the tendency to suppress emotions when confronted with stable or unstable sender anger and to state that it was warranted and appropriate as described by Participant Nine (Target, Employee): '*… it was my fault.*' In these cases, targets blamed themselves for sender anger. Their response was to cognitively reappraise the situation and suppress their emotions, accepting sender anger. This is illustrated by Participant Nine (Target, Employee) who broke an important machine due to lack of knowledge on how it worked: '*Well I thought, I've got better things to do than be angry at this bloke … I knew it was my fault … I've just got to sit here and cop this … so I just sort of sat down and copped it*'. This suggests a taking on of responsibility demonstrating an attribution of internal locus of control.

Observers of Anger – Employees

Whereas targets were generally focused on self-protection, the observers' focus was on how the anger was impacting others who had witnessed the incident. According to Lindebaum and others (2017), morality contains a component that mirrors concern for others, going beyond one's personal interests. This is clearly evidenced in observers of sender anger who aimed to protect team members and clients from the impact of the anger episode. It was a common occurrence for observers who were not in a management position to feel frustrated with their own powerlessness and commonly they expressed uncertainty about the role they played as external observers. This is illustrated by Participant Twenty-Three (Observer, Employee) who observed an altercation between a manager and an employee and cognitively reappraised (i.e., antecedent-focused strategy) and suppressed (i.e., response-focused strategy) their own emotions: *'Should I say something, like mate, you really can't talk to people like that. In the mood he was in at the time I thought he's going to get angry at me … but I sort of thought that it's outside of my [responsibility], cause I'm not a manager you know'.*

Employees generally distanced themselves from the sender. They expressed deep concern for the wellbeing of the target, team members and clients who might be confronted in some way by sender anger. Consequently, they took it upon themselves to work towards removing team members from the locality of sender anger (i.e., situation selection) as illustrated by Participant Two (Observer, Employee): *'I was very protective of my staff, so I just wanted to get them [the team] out of the way'.*

When the observer (manager or employee) established that the team, clients and the target were safe, the anger event lost significance as described by Participant Eleven (Observer, Employee): *'I did speak to the associate later on to see how they were, and that made me feel a little bit better because he didn't take it on board as much. Knowing that, that was okay'.* On the other hand, if observers identified that the target was not okay, they tended to talk to the sender in an attempt to solve the problem as described by Participant Two (Observer, Employee):

> *'I [observer] had a very stern conversation with her [sender] and said that I didn't think she dealt with it appropriately … I understand that you are absolutely, absolutely well within your rights to be absolutely outraged at how this has gone down so I'm not discounting the reason for your anger, but I'm not happy with the way in which it played out.'*

Observers of Anger – Managers

Managers talked about similar behaviors when confronted with anger as an observer but felt more responsibility to engage in approach behaviors. When not in the vicinity of sender anger, observers approached the location of anger to determine what was happening, clearly indicating an approach response (see EASI; van Kleef, 2009). This is illustrated by Participant Fifteen (Observer, Manager): *'What could possibly be going on to have her screaming at her, what could she possibly have said or done … I go over there to see what's going on and ask, "Is everything alright?"'* Observers in general noted that the anger episode attracted their attention and they moved towards the incident to try to make sense of what was happening. The increased 'visibility' of a problematic situation involving anger supports van Kleef (2009) and Geddes and Stickney's (2011) view of anger generating approach behaviors. The response that followed this visibility varied depending on the observer's position in the organization. Managers approached the sender and acted as mediators, addressing the issue immediately and organizing to speak to both sender and target. They expressed concerns specifically related to the anger incident regardless of whether or not anger was stable in an attempt to resolve the issue and bring parties together. This is portrayed by Participant Six (Observer, Manager):

> *'So I had a chat to both of them and didn't tell the other one that I was chatting to them … first of all I spoke to the aggrieved person [target] … and I said, "I noticed that there was a little bit of conflict today and you retaliated back" … and then I went to the other girl and said, "I was a little bit disappointed that I noticed there's conflict and you [sender] deserved what you got, the girl retaliating back."'*

In conclusion, the clear message that arose from the data related to the complexity of responses. There was no one typical response, but rather a mix of ER strategies used to respond to the anger episode. Some of the observers' responses clearly mirrored the EASI (van Kleef, 2009) framework as they approached the situation to better understand what was happening. Overall, main ER strategies used by both targets and observers alike were situation selection (21 participants), cognitive reappraisal (19 participants), expression (23 participants) and suppression (24 participants) of emotions.

DISCUSSION

Given the major impact of expressed anger on individuals and their workplaces, several researchers in the field of anger have stressed the importance of understanding the impact of anger on the receiver (Axelrod and Harlos, 2008; Gibson and Callister, 2010; Harlos, 2010). Overall, this study has outlined how employees attribute anger (linked to position of sender, norms and behaviors) and ER strategies used by receivers of anger – whether targets or observers. Although results align with various Dual Threshold Model propositions (Geddes and Callister, 2007), there are a number of insights we provide about the operationalization of this model in the workplace.

Previous research determined that people express anger differently depending on their status in organizations (Sloan, 2004) and an individual's experience and the specific work events they are reacting to (Basch and Fisher, 2000). By focusing on how employees explain their attributions, we provide a deeper understanding of these phenomena. Our data suggest that when targets are dealing with individuals who express anger frequently (a stable attribution), the target maintains a consistent, generally negative view of that anger. On the other hand, 'once only' sender anger (an unstable attribution) generates target uncertainty and approach behaviors to help them understand how to address the sender's anger. Interestingly, in the case of anger, it appears stability in behavior is not seen as a positive, whereas stable attributions that generally provide more certainty for individuals are seen as a positive when dealing with others. Our data also reveal that when targets were new to their job they often attributed themselves to be the external cause of sender anger. In this case, the uncertainty of how to deal with the sender was neutralized and the response was to suppress emotions, regardless of sender regularity or stability of anger.

Overall, targets talked about expressing as well as suppressing their own emotions (e.g., anger, fear, surprise) in an attempt to control the situation, as they often felt threatened by expressions of anger. When in management, targets talked about modifying the situation by focusing attention on sender behavior or on the task to be completed. They did this by expressing emotions. When their attempt at modifying the situation by expressing failed, they suppressed emotions. Prior research confirms that the suppression of unpleasant emotions can lead to high employee strain (Côté, 2005), stress and serious health issues (Alexander and French, 1946; Friedman, 2010; Glomb and Tews, 2004).

For observers, attributions of sender anger frequency and appropriateness were considered in light of their impact on team members, clients and on the sender themselves and were used more specifically as a parameter to evaluate sender behavior in comparison to their own behavior. The nature of the sender locus of causality did not seem to be of concern to observers although they expressed awareness of it. Similarly, the frequency or stability of anger was not viewed as a personal threat to the observers themselves, but was talked about as a threat to the target and team members or clients around the sender at the time of the anger event. Observers felt unsure of the role they played as external onlookers and described cognitively reappraising and distancing themselves from the sender (i.e., situation selection). This differed when observers were managers. Whether anger was stable or not, managers engaged in approach behaviour attempting to resolve the issue and bring parties together. They generally did this by cognitively reappraising and maintaining emotions.

The Dual Threshold Model establishes that anger expressions can be deemed as functional or dysfunctional depending on how anger is expressed (Geddes and Callister, 2007). Considering the window or space between the expression and impropriety thresholds outlined in the Dual Threshold Model, frequency appeared to mitigate the consideration of norms in making attributions about the anger episode. Those who expressed frequent anger were seen as out of control and their anger was described as inappropriate regardless of the situation. On the other hand, participants seemed to be somewhat forgiving of people who they described as being involved in a 'once only' expression of anger.

In relation to appropriateness, the data suggest that apparent inappropriate expressions of anger in the workplace are linked to the norms for that organization and that in some way these expressions of anger challenged those norms, confirming the Dual Threshold Model. Those using the Dual Threshold Model generally interpret the 'placement' of those thresholds as person and situation-specific to the observer, that they are fluid, depending on who is judging the 'appropriateness' of the display (Geddes and Callister, 2007, p. 733). Our research, however, also identified that a higher standard of behavior was expected of those in senior and management positions suggesting that norms may differ depending on the status of the individual regardless of the situation. These findings concur with Callister, Geddes and Gibson's (2017) research. We also found data suggesting that appropriate sender anger can be directly related to events regardless of display norms. In accordance to 'Proposition 12' of the DTM (Geddes and Callister, 2007, p. 733), one could argue that the observer modifies space between thresholds 'appropriately' when circumstances warrant (i.e., in certain circumstances, we as observers give certain people 'more space'). Although anger was attributed as appropriate or not by both targets and observers, this did not detract from the fact that the anger expression was generally not endorsed. Functionality was not linked to the anger expression itself but to the events surrounding the anger incident.

LIMITATIONS AND FUTURE DIRECTIONS

A few limitations arise in this study. Research quality is closely linked to the researcher's interviewing skills and biases can pose limitations to the research. Semi-structured interviews can also be susceptible to inter- viewee biases. To ensure biases and subjectivity were minimized, we took a number of steps in the design of the data collection. Initially, there is a large reliance on memory of past events, which could lead to oversimplification, rationalization, social desirability and hindsight bias (Dasborough, et al., 2008). To address these limitations, we made use of the Day Reconstruction Method (Kahneman et al., 2004) a method to ensure a better recall of events and experiences by reminding the interviewees of their activities on that day. This method also enables a daily assessment of thoughts and emotions (Diener and Tay, 2013). Any concerns over interpretation of the data were dealt with by using multiple coders to ascertain the reliability of our conclusions (Olson et al., 2016).

Another limitation is related to the timeframe (last two years) of the recalled incident, 'a time' when they were target/observer of an anger incident. This was intended to draw people to recall particularly 'memor- able' (meaning 'over the top') types of displays. However, this might have encouraged interviewees to remember instances of 'deviant' anger where they felt the sender 'crossed the line' versus a selection of more or less appropriate responses at work. To overcome this limitation, we offered some flexibility when participants wanted to focus on an incident older than two years.

Given the focus of many researchers to date has been on the sender of anger, further qualitative research is needed to provide greater depth of understanding about anger, specifically focused on observers of this phenomenon. In addition, further research targeted at analyzing the integration of Attribution Theory and Emotion Regulation theory to explain the Dual Threshold Model might provide deeper insights to anger expressions at work. Finally, we acknowledge our study is not a comprehensive examination of anger at work, and on this basis we encourage researchers to examine the contextual boundaries for the Dual Threshold Model.

CONCLUSION

The aim of our study was to use qualitative interviews in order to establish a better understanding of the mechanisms through which recipients (targets and observers) make sense of and deal with anger expressions. More specifically, our goal was to examine how people talked about the attributions and ER strategies used by them in responding to an anger expression in the workplace. In line with the overall theme of this book, we examined this talk in relation to dominant theories of emotion to gain a deeper insight into the two different ways of examining emotion. The major strength of this study is its setting in the qualitative landscape. By having data originating from real scenarios within organizations, a clearer perspective is gained of the internal processes of receivers of anger derived by the richness of information gained for this study. This level of understanding can often be missed in quantitative research (Strauss and Corbin, 1990). Our research contributes to existing research by providing a better understanding of the internal processes of receivers of anger expressions in the workplace specifically focusing on receivers' attributions for expressed anger and subsequent ER strategies used in response. We trust these findings assist organizations in identifying ways in which to address difficulties and issues arising from anger workplace expressions.

NOTE

* Acknowledgements: This chapter was partially funded by an Australian Research Council grant DP130102625 awarded to the second and third authors.

REFERENCES

Alexander, F., and French, T.M. (1946). Psychoanalytic therapy. *Journal of Clinical Psychology, 2*(4), 401–402.
Axelrod, L. J., and Harlos, K. P. (2008). Work mistreatment and hospital administrative staff: policy implications for healthier workplaces. *Healthcare Policy, 4*(1), 40–50.
Basch, J., and Fisher, C. D. (2000). Affective events-emotions matrix: a classification ofwork events and associated emotions. In N. M. Ashkanasy, C. E. Hartel, and W. J. Zerbe (eds), *Emotions in the Workplace: Research, Theory,*

and Practice, (pp. 36–48). Westport, CT, USA: Quorum Books/Greenwood Publishing Group.

Bazeley, P., and Jackson, K. (2013). *Qualitative Data Analysis with NVivo* (2nd ed.). London, UK: Sage.

Berkowitz, L., and Harmon-Jones, E. (2004). Toward an understanding of the determinants of anger. *Emotion, 4*(2), 107–130.

Booth, J., and Mann, S. (2005). The experience of workplace anger. *Leadership and Organization Development Journal, 26*(3/4), 250–262.

Callister, R. R., Geddes, D., and Gibson, D. F. (2017). When is anger helpful or hurtful? Status and role impact on anger expression and outcomes. *Negotiation and Conflict Management Research, 10*(2), 69–87.

Callister, R. R., Gray, B., Schweitzer, M., Gibson, D., and Tan, J. S. (2003). 'Organizational contexts and outcomes of anger expressions in the workplace', paper presented at the annual meeting of the Academy of Management, Seattle.

Chen, P., and Spector, P. (1992). Relationships of work stressors with aggression, withdrawal, theft and substance abuse: an exploration study. *Journal of Occupational and Organizational Psychology, 65*, 117–184.

Côté, S. (2005). A social interaction model of the effects of emotion regulation on work strain. *The Academy of Management Review, 30*(3), 509–530.

Dasborough, M.T., Sinclair, M., Russell-Bennett, R., and Tombs, A. (2008). Measuring emotion: methodological issues and alternatives. In N. M. Ashakanasy and C. L. Cooper (eds), *Research Companion to Emotion in Organizations* (pp. 197–208). Cheltenham, UK and Northampton, MA, USA: Edward Elgar Publishing.

DiCicco-Bloom, B., and Crabtree, B. F. (2006). The qualitative research interview. *Medical Education, 40*(4), 314–321.

Diener, E., and Tay, L. (2013). Review of the day reconstruction method (DRM). *Social Indicators Research, 116*(1), 255–267.

Domagalski, T. A., and Steelman, L. A. (2007). The impact of gender and organizational status on workplace anger expression. *Management Communication Quarterly, 20*(3), 297–315.

Downe-Wamboldt, B. (1992). Content analysis: method, applications, and issues. *Health Care for Women International, 13*(3), 313–321.

Ekman, P. (1992). An argument for basic emotions. *Cognition and Emotion, 6*(3–4), 169–200.

Fitness, J. (2000). Anger in the workplace: an emotion script approach to anger episodes between workers and their superiors, coworkers, and subordinates. *Journal of Organizational Behavior, 21*(2), 147–162.

Friedman, B. H. (2010). Feelings and the body: the Jamesian perspective on automatic specificity of emotion. *Biological Psychology, 84*(3), 383–393.

Friedman, R., Anderson, C., Brett, J., Olekalns, M., Goates, N., and Lisco, C. C. (2004). The positive and negative effects of anger on dispute resolution: evidence from electronically mediated disputes. *Journal of Applied Psychology, 89*, 369–376.

Geddes, D., and Callister, R. R. (2007). Crossing the line(s): a dual threshold model of anger in organizations. *Academy of Management Review, 32*(3), 721–746.

Geddes, D., and Stickney, L. T. (2011). The trouble with sanctions: organizational responses to deviant anger displays at work. *Human Relations, 64*(2), 201–230.

Geddes, D., and Stickney, L. T. (2012). Muted anger in the workplace: changing the sound of employee emotion through social sharing. In N. M. Ashkanasy, C. E. Hartël, and W. J. Zerbe (eds), *Emotions in the Workplace: Research, Theory, and Practice* (Vol. 8, pp. 85–103). Bingley, UK: Emerald Group Publishing Limited.

Gibson, D., and Callister, R. R. (2010). Anger in organizations: review and integration. *Journal of Management, 36*(1), 66–93.

Glomb, T. M. (2002). Workplace anger and aggression: informing conceptual models with data from specific encounters. *Journal of Occupational Health Psychology, 7*, 20–36.

Glomb, T., and Tews, M. (2004). Emotional labor: a conceptualization and scale development. *Journal of Vocational Development, 64*, 1–23.

Gross, J. J. (1998). Antecedent- and response-focused emotion regulation: divergent consequences for experience, expression, and physiology. *Journal of Personality and Social Psychology, 74*(1), 224–237.

Gross, J. J. (2014). *Handbook of Emotion Regulation* (2nd ed.). New York, NY, USA: Guilford Publications.

Gross, J. J., and Thompson, R. A. (2007). Emotion regulation: conceptual foundations. In J. J. Gross (ed.), *Handbook of Emotion Regulation* (pp. 3–26). New York, NY, USA: Guilford Press.

Guest, G., Bunce, A., and Johnson, L. (2006). How many interviews are enough? *Field Methods, 18*(1), 59–82.

Harlos, K. (2010). Anger-provoking events and intention to turnover in hospital administrators. *Journal of Health Organization and Management, 24*(1), 45–56.

Kahneman, D., Krueger, A. B., Schkade, D. A., Schwarz, N., and Stone, A. A. (2004). A survey method for characterizing daily life experience: the day reconstruction method. *Science, 30*(6), 1776–1780.

Keashly, L., and Neuman, J. (2008). Aggression at the service delivery interface: do you see what I see? *Journal of Management and Organization, 1*(2), 180–192.

Kelley, H. H. (1967). Attribution theory in social psychology. In D. Levine (ed.), *Nebraska Symposium on Motivation* (Vol. 15, pp. 192–238). Lincoln, NE: University of Nebraska Press.

Kelley, H. H. (1973). The processes of causal attribution. *American Psychologist, 28*(2), 107–128.

Kiecolt-Glaser, J. K., McGuire, L., Robles, T. F., and Glaser, R. (2002). Emotions, morbidity, and mortality: new perspectives from psychoneuroimmunology. *Annual Review of Psychology, 53*(1), 83–107.

Kopelman, S., Rosette, A. S., and Thompson, L. (2006). The three faces of Eve: strategic displays of positive, negative, and neutral emotions in negotiations. *Organizational Behavior and Human Decision Processes, 99*(1), 81–101.

Kramer, M. W., and Hess, J. A. (2002). Communication rules for the display of emotions in organizational settings. *Management Communication Quarterly, 16*(1), 66–80.

Lindebaum, D., and Gabriel, Y. (2016). Anger and organization studies: from social disorder to moral order. *Organization Studies, 37*(7), 903–918.

Lindebaum, D., Geddes, D., and Gabriel, Y. (2017) Moral emotions and ethics in organisations: introduction to the special issue. *Journal of Business Ethics, 141*(4), 645–656.

Lindebaum, D., Jordan, P. J., and Morris, L. (2016). Symmetrical and asymmetrical outcomes of leader anger expression: a qualitative study of army personnel. *Human Relations, 69*(2), 277–300.

Martinko M. J., Harvey P., and Dasborough, M. (2010). Attribution theory in the organizational science: a case of unrealized potential. *Journal of Organizational Behavior, 32*(1), 144–149.

Meier, L. L., Gross, S., Spector, P. E., and Semmer, N. K. (2013). Relationship and task conflict at work: interactive short-term effects on angry mood and somatic complaints. *Journal of Occupational Health Psychology, 18*(2), 144–156.

Moura, K., Troth, A. C., and Jordan, P. J. (2015). Crossing the impropriety threshold: a study of excessive anger at work. In C. E. J. Hartël, N. M. Ashkanasy, and W. J. Zerbe (eds), *New Ways of Studying Emotions in Organisations* (Vol. 11, Research on Emotions in Organisations, pp. 369–396). Bingley, UK: Emerald Group Publishing.

Olson, J. D., McAllister, C., Grinnell, L. D., Walters, K. G., and Appunn, F. (2016). Applying constant comparative method with multiple investigators and inter-coder reliability. *The Qualitative Report, 21*(1), 26–42.

Rafaeli, A., and Sutton, R. (1987). Expression of emotion as part of the work role. *Academy of Management Review, 12*(1), 23–37.

Sloan, M. (2004). The effects of occupational characteristics on the experience and expression of anger in the workplace. *Work and Occupations, 31*, 38–72.

Stickney, L. T., and Geddes, D. (2016). More than just 'blowing off steam': the roles of anger and advocacy in promoting positive outcomes at work. *Negotiation and Conflict Management Research, 9*(2), 141–157.

Strauss, A., and Corbin, J. (1990). *Basics of Qualitative Research: Grounded Theory Procedures and Techniques.* Newbury Park, CA: Sage.

Totterdell, P. M., Hershcovis, S., Niven, K., Reich, T. C., and Stride, C. (2012). Can employees be emotionally drained by witnessing unpleasant interactions between coworkers? A diary study of induced emotion regulation. *Work and Stress: An International Journal of Work, Health and Organisations, 26*(2), 112–129.

van Kleef, G. A. (2009). How emotions regulate social life: the emotions as social information (EASI) model. *Current Directions in Psychological Science, 18*(3), 184–188.

van Kleef, G. A., De Dreu, C. K. W., and Manstead, A. S. R. (2004). The interpersonal effects of anger and happiness in negotiations: a motivated information processing approach. *Journal of Personality and Social Psychology, 87*(4), 510–528.

Waldron, V. R. (2000). Relational experiences and emotion at work. In S. Fineman (ed.), *Emotion in Organizations* (Vol. 2, pp. 64–82). Newbury Park, CA, USA: Sage.

Walker, B. R., and Jackson, C. J. (2017). Moral emotions and corporate psychopathy: a review. *Journal of Business Ethics, 141*(4), 797–810.

Weiner, B. (1979). A theory of motivation for some classroom experiences. *Journal of Educational Psychology, 71*(1), 3–25.

Weiner, B. (1985). An attributional theory of achievement motivation and emotion. *Psychological Review, 92*(4), 548–573.

Weiss, H., and Cropanzano, R. (1996). Affective events theory: a theoretical discussion of the structure, causes and consequences of affective work experiences. *Research in Organizational Behavior, 18*, 1–74.

3.   Benefits of awe in the workplace

Kenneth A. Perez and Heather C. Lench

The most beautiful thing we can experience is the mysterious. It is the source of all true art and science. He to whom the emotion is a stranger, who can no longer pause to wonder and stand wrapped in awe, is as good as dead – his eyes are closed.

Albert Einstein (1931)

On occasion, we all experience the feeling that we are in the presence of something extraordinary beyond our typical experiences and perhaps even beyond our ability to understand (Keltner and Haidt, 2003). The emotion that accompanies this experience has been defined as awe. Awe can occur in incredibly unique moments, such as the overwhelming feelings reported in accounts from astronauts of their first look at Earth from the perspective of space (Yaden et al., 2016). Succinctly conveying this moment, the American astronaut Gene Cernan said it was "one of the deepest, most emotional experiences I have ever had" (White, 1987). Awe has been reported in a number of more common contexts, including feeling a religious presence, listening to uplifting music and seeing masterpieces of artwork, viewing magnificent trees or mountain views, and looking at the face of one's newborn child (Fuller, 2006; Keltner and Haidt, 2003; Piff et al., 2015; Silvia et al., 2015). We have all felt awe at some point in our lives. Despite the fact that everyday occurrences can elicit feelings of awe, it is not an emotion that people intuitively connect with the workplace or an office environment. But recent research reveals that there is good reason to expect that the experience of awe could be foundational to the development of a productive, healthy, and integrated organization. Within organizations, awe can promote an inclusive and supportive climate, help workers offset the costs of large stretches of mundane work, prompt employees to generate social and cognitive resources for personal growth and development, and encourage creative solutions. In this chapter, we review evidence about the benefits of awe and address how the way that people think and talk about emotions could limit their ability to experience the benefits of awe and to recognize ways to integrate the experience of awe into their daily and work lives. We also review a number of methods to incorporate the experience of awe into work environments for the benefit of employees and the organization.

THE (OFTEN OVERLOOKED) BENEFITS OF POSITIVE EMOTIONS

Positive emotions are critical for health, cognition, and relationships. Positive emotions, such as love, happiness, and awe, were once considered to be almost irrelevant to people's well-being and success. Research and interventions to improve people's lives instead focused on the impact of negative emotions, which were obvious given how powerful negative emotions can overwhelm people and lead them to seek counseling or supportive care. In the last decade, it has become very clear that positive emotions are critical for the quality of people's lives. Positive emotions do not just make people feel good, they elicit changes in physiology, cognition, and social relationships that promote health and success. Just as importantly, the changes that accompany positive emotions prepare people to better cope with future negative experiences by building cognitive, emotional, and social resources.

THE BENEFITS OF FEELING GOOD

A great deal of research in the last decade has focused on positive emotion and has established what positive emotions are, what causes them, and how positive emotions impact people. Simply put, positive emotions are changes in people's bodies, minds, and behaviors that are experienced when things are going well for people (Lench et al., 2011). And these changes have been shown to have benefits for people. The physical changes that accompany positive emotions have been shown to help people recover from negative experiences (Frederickson et al., 2000; Lambert D'raven et al., 2015). In these studies, researchers monitor participants' physiological responses as they experience an event that causes them to feel negative emotion (such as watching a heart-wrenching movie scene). Typically, experiences like these that cause negative emotion also cause a physical stress response, such as higher heart rates and respiration. Participants are then exposed to something that causes positive emotion (such as watching an amusing video). This positive emotional experience "undoes" the stress response, prompting a physical recovery from the negative experience.

Positive emotions also promote changes in the way that people think, and these changes can result in greater success and well-being. Generally speaking, people engage in broader and more creative thought when they are feeling positive emotions. In these studies, participants experience some event that elicits positive feeling, such as finding an unexpected present of chocolate left on their desk, and then complete tasks that measure attention and creativity. These studies have revealed that, after the experience that makes them feel good, people are better able to attend to global information (i.e., "the big picture"), are better able to process new or conflicting information, and are more creative in their thinking and problem solving (Fredrickson and Losada, 2005). Some findings have further shown that the broad, integrative thinking that accompanies positive emotions also promotes a sense that one's life is meaningful (King et al., 2006) and helps people see the silver lining in routine or negative situations (Folkman and Moskowitz, 2000; Fredrickson, 2001). People who are happy also engage in more play with others, which promotes social bonding and connection (Ellsworth and Smith, 1988; Frijda, 1986).

Science has shown the many benefits of positive emotions, but individuals and organizations continue to focus on the reduction of negative emotion in their lives and in the workplace (Elfenbein, 2007). Traditional workplace programs have targeted the management of stress and conflicts, such as effective coping with negative emotions in the presence of work conflicts (Rispens and Demerouti, 2016). This is beginning to change, as organizations develop programs that are targeted to promote positive emotions in the workplace, such as gratitude, that have been shown to have organizational benefits (e.g., Djikstra et al., 2011; Leon-Perez et al., 2016). The focus on negative emotions is likely because negative emotions capture attention and can be disruptive. But neglecting to consider the importance of positive emotions to functioning can result in people missing out on the benefits of policies, procedures, and opportunities that promote positive emotion.

WHAT'S SPECIAL ABOUT AWE?

Not all positive emotions are the same. Different positive emotions, such as love, joy, and awe, can have very specific and different effects on people (Campos et al., 2013; Fredrickson, 1998). The evidence reviewed above suggests that many positive emotions have benefits, so what is so special about awe? The majority of positive emotions that have been studied extensively, like joy and pride, cause people to focus on themselves and their successes. In contrast, awe is a "self-transcendent emotion," which pushes people to think beyond themselves, their goals, and their daily concerns (Shiota et al., 2007; Van Cappellen et al., 2013). What makes awe special is that it is an emotion that prompts people to focus on others and their environment. People who are experiencing awe feel a sense of their own smallness and openness to the world around them (Campos et al., 2013; Keltner and Haidt, 2003, Shiota et al., 2007). As expressed in the quote from Albert Einstein at the start of this chapter, people often "stand wrapped in awe" – momentarily frozen in the experience of a moment that is beyond their ordinary experience. This reaction appears to be unique to awe and emerging evidence suggests that awe can be uniquely beneficial as a result.

One unique feature of awe is the experience of *vastness* that accompanies the emotion (Keltner and Haidt, 2003). People describe this experience as the sense that the self is diminished in the presence of something larger and more formidable than the self. Although the experience of vastness can be induced through physical perspective, such as the view of Earth from space or majestic mountains on the horizon, it can also result from encountering objects or others that induce a sense of space. For example, viewing slow motion videos of water droplets colliding with other liquids can elicit feelings of vastness, presumably due to a sense of temporal space (Piff et al., 2015). The experience of awe and a sense of vastness can also result from interacting with another person who is famous or has great authority or prestige, such as a religious leader or great thinker, presumably due to a sense of social space (Howell and Shamir, 2005). This sense of vastness and a "small self" is considered a defining and unique feature of the emotion of awe and, as we review below, is likely to have unique benefits in that it should promote a sense of connection with others and concern for others.

Another unique feature of awe is the sense of the need for *accommodation* (Keltner and Haidt, 2003). People report this as feeling a desire to integrate the experience into their understanding of the world and themselves. The concept of accommodation originates from Jean Piaget's research on adjustment of mental structures in order to provide a sense of consistency in external reality (Piaget and Inhelder, 1966/1969). His work showed that when children grasp new information, such as that objects out of sight are still physically present, they must change or expand their current understanding of how the world works. The mental shift that is required to make sense of the new information is called accommodation. The experiences that elicit awe similarly provide new information about the world that requires people to change the way that they think about themselves or the world around them. Staring into the face of a newborn child and experiencing awe, for example, is likely to be accompanied by the need to accommodate to a world that contains an infant that is dependent for all of their needs. This "stretching" of the self to accommodate new experiences and information could partially explain why awe promotes openness to incredibly positive experiences and frightening experiences, such as exploding volcanoes and twisting tornados (McDougall, 1921; Piff et al., 2015; Shiota et al., 2007). All of these experiences are outside ordinary events and require processing and accommodation in order to make sense of the world.

BENEFITS OF EXPERIENCING AWE

Emotions are complicated and powerful. Part of what makes emotions so complex is that they organize cognitive, experiential, behavioral, and physiological reactions (Ekman, 1992; Frijda, 1987; Izard et al., 1998; Lench et al., 2011; Mauss et al., 2005). Like other emotions, the experience of awe has been shown to affect all of these reactions. In the sections below, we review evidence regarding how awe changes physiology, cognition, and behavior, and also explore the potential benefits of these changes for the individual in the workplace and organizational behavior.

PHYSICAL CHANGES WITH AWE

When people stand rapt before a grand work of art or an extraordinary landscape, they have physical reactions during the emotion of awe. Their heart rate will increase, they will sweat and their breathing will speed up (Shiota et al., 2011). All of these changes are associated with the activation of the autonomic nervous system, which regulates nonconscious bodily functions such as digestion, heart rate and breathing activity. Despite the increase in physiological activity, the body typically "freezes" when experiencing a state of awe. This suppression of gross motor activity is thought to occur because of the need for accommodation that accompanies awe. Being physically still permits people to stop and evaluate what is occurring that elicited awe, which should promote better understanding and accommodation (Fuller, 2008; Haidt and Keltner, 2002; Joye and Dewitte, 2016; Keltner and Haidt, 2003; Solomon, 2002; Shiota et al., 2011). Another physiological reaction that appears to be unique to the experience of awe is goose bumps – hair standing on its end (Schurtz et al., 2012). Goose bumps reflect stimulation of the autonomic nervous system (Jänig, 2007), and are commonly experienced when people are cold or afraid. The experience of goosebumps that accompanies awe has been described as a submissive response to a powerful presence or experience (Keltner and Haidt, 2003). Researchers theorize that this response could result from an initial evaluation that the awe-inducing event has the potential to harm precisely because it is outside of ordinary experience (Schurtz et al., 2012), and that this response should reduce once people determine that harm is unlikely and they appraise the awe-eliciting experience as positive (Huron, 2006). Extended autonomic activation can be harmful to people in multiple ways, but short bursts of high activity appear to have benefits. Brief autonomic nervous system activity has been linked with mental outcomes such as improved creativity (Jausovec and Bakracevic, 1995) and openness to experience which can improve productivity, learning, and interacting with others (Čukić and Bates, 2014). These findings suggest that experiencing awe could energize people in the workplace, enabling them and motivating them to find creative solutions and to engage with their coworkers and their projects.

There is emerging evidence that the experience of awe can also promote long-term physical health, and in particular that it could reduce the likelihood of chronic disease. Stellar and colleagues (2015) conducted a study comparing the effects of various positive emotions on levels of proinflammatory cytokines. These are immune system cells that address infections or tissue damage. These cells are beneficial when there is an infection, but high levels of cytokines when there is no physical infection or damage can be harmful, resulting in the development of chronic diseases such as diabetes, cardiovascular disease, and depression (Cesari et al., 2003; Dowlati et al., 2010; Wellen and Hotamisligil, 2005). The idea that emotions can influence the immune system is fairly well established with negative emotions. Highly stressful situations and negative emotions can increase cytokine levels and place people at risk for chronic disease (Kiecolt-Glaser et al., 2002). A particular cytokine – Interleukin 6 (IL-6) – has been of particular interest because of its relation to symptoms of depression. IL-6 is released when people or animals are injured or sick, and elevated levels encourage physical and social withdrawal (Maier and Watkins, 1998). When injured or ill, this withdrawal would protect the organism from further harm and promote low activity during the healing process. When not injured or ill, this withdrawal could isolate the individual unnecessarily. The results of the study comparing the effects of different positive emotions revealed that the emotion of awe reduces IL-6 levels (Stellar et al., 2015). More critically, awe reduced IL-6 levels more than the experience of any other positive emotion. The findings reviewed above suggest that promoting the experience of awe in the workplace could improve physical health and reduce development of chronic conditions.

BEHAVIOR CHANGES WITH AWE

When people experience awe, they orient away from themselves and tend to feel connected with others (Shiota et al., 2007). In a description of his experience of viewing Earth from space, astronaut Gene Cernan said, "You don't see the barriers of color and religion and politics that divide this world" (White, 1987). Experimental studies that induce awe and study the effects in a laboratory or controlled setting have shown that awe causes people to engage in altruistic behaviors, be humbler, and show less entitlement in their demeanors (Joye and Bolderdijk, 2015; Piff et al., 2015; Prade and Saroglou, 2016; Rudd et al., 2012; Zhang et al., 2014). In one study, people were brought to a grove of towering eucalyptus trees and spent one minute looking upwards at the majestic trees (Piff et al., 2015). As a control group, other students were taken to the area but asked to look at a tall building. The experimenter then "accidentally" dropped a load of pens in front of the participant. Researchers use this method to measure how many pens the participant will help pick up – an indication of how altruistic or prosocial they are. The awe group, that had viewed the trees, helped pick up more pens than the control group that looked at the building, suggesting more prosocial helping behavior. Those who viewed the trees also responded to hypothetical scenarios that presented an ethical quandary with more moral responses. For example, they were more likely to state that they would bring a grading error that resulted in a higher grade for them to the attention of a professor, or give back money that had been accidentally given to them. In another study, participants watched an awe-inducing video clip depicting panoramic scenes of nature (Piff et al., 2015). They then played a game with another person, during which they could allocate points to themselves or their partner. Each point represented a ticket for a $100 post-study raffle reward and so was valuable to the participants. People who had experienced awe gave away more to the other person, keeping less for themselves. Similarly, people who had experienced awe were more likely to indicate an interest in volunteering their time for charitable causes. Thus awe promotes a prosocial helping orientation to others that is likely to result in a more integrative and supportive work environment. Importantly, many of the tasks used to induce awe in these studies were the type of task that can be implemented in the workplace, such as viewing landscapes or thinking about past awe-inspiring experiences.

The research findings reviewed above suggest that employees who have recently experienced awe would focus less on themselves and more on others and the group (Keltner et al., 2014; Nowak, 2006; Sober and Wilson, 1998). Employees who promote a humble and prosocial orientation have been shown to benefit their organizations (Cohen et al., 2014). Some of these benefits include engaging in organizational citizenship behaviors that support other employees and the organization, and being less likely to take advantage of or steal from companies. These benefits could be particularly useful when employees function as part of work teams, as an other-orientation should promote open and polite communication among team members. Although there is no direct evidence, having employees who are other-focused and supportive could also promote a positive public image of the organization. Consider Microsoft CEO Bill Gates, who, in addition to being an innovative technological genius, is also a world-renowned philanthropist and respected for his contributions to improving the world. Gates's philanthropy likely gives a more positive public image of Microsoft than would otherwise be the case.

CHANGES IN THINKING WITH AWE

Like other emotions, awe also changes the way that people think. Many positive emotions, such as happiness, cause people to be less analytic in their thinking and promote reliance on stereotypes and preconceptions. For example, participants who were made happy were more likely than others to falsely remember stereotypical information in a story (Bless et al., 1996). Happy people are also more likely to use stereotypes about others to make judgments about them (Bodenhausen et al., 1994). In one study, participants completed an emotion induction and then were presented with cases where university students had committed a crime or harmful action. They reviewed the case file and then made recommendations about the disciplinary action the university should take against the student. The case files presented information about the crime or action, as well as a description of the background of the student. Participants in the happy condition assigned harsher punishments to students whose backgrounds were stereotypically associated with the crime, such as a minority name for a physical assault case. Participants feeling negative emotions were less likely to be influenced by information related to stereotypes. Unlike most positive emotions, awe reduces people's tendency to rely on these stereotypes when encoding new memories (Danvers and Shiota, 2017). Reduced reliance on stereotypes is likely the result of the need for accommodation that accompanies experiences of awe. When they experience awe, people seek to embrace the unfamiliar, grand experience in front of them and at least temporarily set aside most of their assumptions about the world in order to accommodate this new experience. In fact, awe appears to result in more analytic and effortful thinking, as reflected in the use of more complex and esoteric language when relating experiences that elicited awe (Darbor et al., 2016). The reduced use of stereotypes in thinking can promote the discovery of more novel solutions to problems and openness to different perspectives from others. More broadly, employees who are more open to others' perspectives can promote a workplace climate that is inclusive and better able to represent diverse views and ideologies.

Awe is also associated with thinking that is present-focused. When people stand wrapped in awe, time is almost irrelevant because the present moment is the most important experience. Support for this notion stems from studies related to extended-now theory, which states that people who focus on the present also experience an expanded sense of time in general (Vohs and Schmeichel, 2003). In one study, participants who recently experienced awe felt that time was more plentiful and available for them, agreeing with statements such as "time is boundless" and "I have lots of time in which I can get things done" (Rudd et al., 2012). Even writing about a past experience of awe caused people to feel less impatient and to be more willing to donate their time to a charitable cause (Rudd et al., 2012). The perception of increased time that accompanies awe could potentially be beneficial in the workplace, particularly among employees who have multiple tasks to juggle or who must fully invest attention in the task or person that they are currently assigned. An expanded sense of time could have broader benefits as well, as people who feel short on time are more likely to eat unhealthy foods (Darian and Cohen, 1995; Neumark-Sztainer et al., 2003) and forego leisure activities (Mannell and Zuzanek, 1991).

CHANGES IN WELL-BEING WITH AWE

Awe is associated with a sense of connection with the self, others, and the world around them (Mitroff and Denton, 1999). Spiritual mindsets appear to benefit people's ability to cope with negative events and experiences, in part because a spiritual focus encourages people to find the silver lining in bad experiences (Pargament, 1997; Van Cappellen et al., 2013). Although spirituality is often manifested in religious affiliation or beliefs, this is not necessarily the case for all individuals (see Saroglou et al., 2008; Van Cappellen et al., 2016; Van Cappellen and Saroglou, 2012). People who do not affiliate with a particular religion can value spirituality and hold spiritual mindsets (Van Cappellen et al., 2013). Within organizations, spiritual mindsets among employees and leaders can make it more likely that decisions and interactions will be congruent with deeply held values of the individuals and the organization as a whole (for a review see Karakas, 2010). An increase in spirituality also seems to have benefits for people's well-being, broadly defined. Prior research has linked religiosity and spirituality with increases in several important outcomes related to well-being including life satisfaction (Ellison and Fan, 2008), meaning in life (Martos et al., 2010) and hope (Ai et al., 2007). Recent evidence has revealed that these well-being outcomes associated with spirituality result in part because people with spiritual mindsets are more prone to experiencing self-transcendent emotions like awe (Krause and Hayward, 2015; Van Cappellen et al., 2016).

Interventions that promote awe experiences have also been demonstrated to improve well-being outcomes over time. As an example, in one study, participants were assigned to write every week about nine beautiful things that they observed that week. These nine beautiful observations were to include three experiences with nature, three experiences with art, and three observations of others' moral behavior every week. Another group of participants (the control group) completed a similar writing experience every week, but with an assignment to focus on their early memories (Proyer et al., 2016). Participants who wrote about awe-inspiring experiences were happier and had fewer depressive symptoms over the month of the intervention. Another study demonstrated that awe can lead people to make decisions that promote happiness (Rudd et al., 2012). Some participants read and immersed themselves into a story designed to invoke awe while others read a neutral story. They then chose to either purchase Broadway show tickets or a watch of equivalent value. Participants in the awe condition were more likely to choose Broadway tickets over the watch. This is important because experiences (like a Broadway show) make people happier than material goods (like a watch) (Carter and Gilovich, 2010; Rosenzweig and Gilovich, 2012; Van Boven and Gilovich, 2003; though see Nicolao et al., 2009; Weidman and Dunn, 2016). Findings such as these suggest that experiencing awe, including by intentionally thinking about awe-inducing moments, can benefit well-being.

ORGANIZATIONAL CHANGES TO EVOKE AWE

The emotion of awe is often associated with momentous occasions that move us beyond all description, but everyday experiences can also evoke (milder) awe and relatively small changes in infrastructure can promote these experiences. It is difficult to estimate how long awe might last after these types of experiences or if people might habituate to awe-inspiring stimuli over time. Given the fact that people tend to surround themselves with images that inspire awe (e.g., screensavers of natural landscapes, pictures of important social moments), we suspect that people do not habituate to awe-inspiring experiences. Research by Verduyn and others (2009) suggest that the duration of emotional experiences depends on a number of factors related to the person and situation that they are placed. These factors include how important the situation is to the individual, how intense the emotion is being felt at the time, and whether or not the situation eliciting the emotion reappears in the future. As each of these factors increase, the predicted duration of the emotion elicited, regardless of it is a positive or negative experience, tends to be longer. In regards to awe, as with other emotions, how long these experiences last after the eliciting experience will depend on these factors. Considering that experiences of awe come from extraordinary moments (which in turn create intense reactions), it should be predicted that it has a relatively long duration in comparison to other emotions. Given the multiple benefits of experiencing awe to employee health, success, and well-being, it is in the best interest of companies to consider ways to promote awe experiences in the workplace. The existing studies on awe give several indications of the types of changes that are likely to be effective in promoting an organization that evokes awe.

REDESIGNING INFRASTRUCTURE TO EVOKE AWE

One of the most widely effective methods to induce awe is to expose people to the natural environment. The reason people may particularly drawn to these experiences can in part be explained by instinctual processes. Edward O. Wilson (1984) describes that people are born with a deep, complex desire to affiliate with and interact with nature, a phenomenon he calls the *biophilia hypothesis*. Environmental psychology research indicates that these interactions with nature may hold psycho-logically restorative properties, assisting with mentally recovering throughout the day in order to facilitate well-being (e.g., van den Berg et al., 2007). The notion of a human preference for natural environments over urbanized, constructed environments has been supported in several studies that directly measure people's preferences (e.g., Kaplan, 1993, 2001; Félonneau, 2004). However, these preferences can also have indirect economic implications. The housing market shows that access to open natural views can greatly increase the value of some houses (Luttik, 2000). These findings have informed a new approach to organizing workspaces called biophilic design (Kellert et al., 2008). The central goal of this approach is to integrate natural elements into workplace design, with an aim to improve employee productivity, well-being, and creativity.

What exactly are the elements that employees desire in their work-space? Of course, it is not feasible or practical for every organization to move away from urban-based offices into a naturally thrilling or exotic location. According to a report on biophilic design conducted by Inter-face (2015), the five things employees across the globe rated as most important were: access to natural light, indoor plants, quiet working spaces, views of the sea, and bright colors. Interestingly, 47% of respondents reported not having any natural light and 58% reported not having any plants in their work environments.

Consider the stereotypical corporate office setting: offices efficiently spaced apart using cubicles and color schemes of gray, beige and white. On the other hand, one that integrates a biophilic design would have open floor spaces and schemes of green, blue, and brown. Companies like Google and Apple both have received significant media attention for their efforts to create elaborate and unique workspaces, which tend to foster positivity amongst the employees (e.g., Hardy, 2014). A significant part of the appeal in these designs comes from open areas that create a sense of community and collaboration rather than isolation. These companies believe that how employees are feeling along the way of engaging with their work is just as important as how quickly or efficiently that work is done. This value to employee engagement can also make the organization more attractive to potential employees, recruiting the top talent in a field (Backhaus and Tikoo, 2004).

Given the high demand for natural lighting in the office, another line of research indicates that people value having access to windows in their workspaces. People use the time spent viewing through windows to help recover from sustained work and maintain their optimal performance (Kaplan and Kaplan, 1989; Kaplan, 1995). Natural views through win-dows have been shown to enhance people's ability to pay attention to tasks and reduce stress (e.g., Hartig et al., 2003; Kaplan, 2001; Tennessen and Cimprich, 1995). Views also increase patience and work engagement (Kaplan, 1993). A question that may arise for organizations is where best to place windows in the design of the workspace. Considering the approach of biophilic design, they would be best placed where greenery or any bodies of water can be visible.

Many of the workplace benefits associated with windows can also be obtained by viewing pictures of nature or scenes that are personally meaningful (Berto, 2005; Hartig et al., 1996; Parsons et al., 1998; Ulrich et al., 1991; van den Berg et al., 2003). Organizations that are unable to provide access to windows with views of nature could therefore incorporate images, pictures, or other decorative items that evoke a sense of nature. People report using a number of substitutes when windows are unavailable, including sculptures, plants, trees, terrariums, and aquariums (Bringslimark et al., 2011). Although the benefits of these items has not been directly assessed, the fact that people identify them as substitutes for views of nature suggest that they meet the same need and could provide similar benefits.

MINDFULNESS INTERVENTIONS IN ORGANIZATIONS

Research on mindfulness has grown exponentially in the last decade, increasing from 28 articles in 2001 to 397 in 2011 (Segal et al., 2013). This research has revealed numerous benefits of mindfulness and has resulted in organizations beginning to develop and implement mindfulness interventions or practices. Although awe and mindfulness are not synonymous, there is overlap in the associated experiences and benefits between the emotion and the cognitive state. Mindfulness is defined as a psychological state that lets individuals relax their thinking, focusing solely on present events and thoughts (Brown et al., 2007; Brown and Ryan, 2003; Vago and Silbersweig, 2012). The practices that accompany mindfulness training, such as focusing on a present moment, are likely to engender a sense of awe.

Several variations of mindfulness interventions have been created to develop people's abilities to engage in a present-focused, relaxed state. Some are based on several broader therapeutic techniques used with mental health disorders, and include present-focus and awareness (Hayes et al., 2006). To date, most workplace interventions have utilized all or parts of a program called Mindfulness Based Stress Reduction (MBSR; Jamieson and Tuckey, 2017; Kabat-Zinn, 2009). This is a lengthy and intensive program, lasting eight weeks in total. The complete program includes multiple practices intended to evoke mindfulness, including meditation, body scanning, yoga, and breathing exercises. These practices are intended to promote a relaxed state and to improve participants' ability to be present-focused over time. The MBSR program is lengthy, because it is designed to change lifestyle patterns and give participants opportunities to practice mindfulness every day as part of the program. This extended program requires a high level of commitment from the organization to permit time and resources for implementation. The benefit to the extended program is that the results are more likely to last beyond the scope of the program, as employees develop the skills necessary to continue mindfulness practices in their lives. Companies who are interested in a shorter version of the program can target specific known issues that employees face given the nature of the job, such as stress reduction and connection with others among customer service agents.

These types of programs have been successful with employees who experience significant stressors in their jobs and lives. For example, an intervention was designed for a sample of 34 United States Marines reservists bound for deployment abroad (Stanley et al., 2011). Military service members typically experience high stress from deployment and are at risk for multiple negative health outcomes as a result. Common health issues include irregular sleep, low energy, headaches, chronic pain, cardiopulmonary symptoms, and gastrointestinal difficulties (Hoge et al., 2007). Service members also experience relatively high rates of psychological disorders during and after deployment, including posttraumatic stress disorder, traumatic brain injuries, depression, and anxiety (Milliken et al., 2007; Tanielian and Jaycox, 2008). In order to assess the effects of the mindfulness intervention, participants were split into two groups, with one group completing a mindfulness intervention and the other group completing a traditional support intervention. In the mindfulness group, personnel underwent a total of 24 hours of mindfulness training spread over eight weeks as part of a course led by an instructor. In addition to this course time, participants were required to practice mindfulness in 30-minute sessions every day. The mindfulness practice consisted of developing the ability to concentrate attention on one object while excluding all thoughts beyond that object. This practice began with concentration for 5 minutes at a time and extended to 30 minutes through the course of the program. In the group that received the mindfulness training, personnel who followed the instructions to practice frequently also reported experiencing mindful states and reductions in stress. More research is needed about the potential connections between mindfulness and states of awe. But it seems clear that focusing on the present moment, which is likely to evoke feelings of awe, has multiple benefits for individuals and organizations.

CONCLUSIONS

People come across special moments that leave unforgettable impressions for the rest of their lives. These experiences evoke awe. The emotional experience of awe prompts people to think beyond themselves and their daily concerns and goals, instead focusing on the bigger picture and connecting with other people. At first glance, this emotion seems to hold little relevance to the day-to-day experience of employees. This view is misleading, and could result in organizations and employees missing out on the important benefits conveyed by the experience of awe. Even though employees might not be circling the earth from space or hiking through majestic vistas, more common experiences such as viewing pictures of landscapes can induce a mild form of awe that has been shown to benefit people. Taken as a whole, the studies reviewed in this chapter suggest that building experiences of awe into a workplace can promote a more productive, healthy and unified organization.

We outlined several approaches that can evoke awe or awe-related states. Infrastructure can be designed to include views of nature. If it is not possible to make such views directly accessible, organizations can permit employees to customize their workspace to include items that substitute for natural views. At the organizational level, management and administrative leaders can benefit from adopting values consistent with ethical leadership, which can create a value-driven orientation that results in more pro-organization behaviors among employees and greater employee satisfaction. Organizations can further offer or promote engagement in programs that invoke mindfulness within employees, which shares many of the benefits associated with awe, including stress reduction and improved coping. Organizations and employees would benefit from, at least occasionally, standing wrapped in awe.

REFERENCES

Ai, A. L., Park, C. L., Huang, B., Rodgers, W., and Tice, T. N. (2007). Psycho-social mediation of religious coping styles: a study of short-term psychological distress following cardiac surgery. *Personality and Social Psychology Bulletin, 33*, 867–882.

Backhaus, K., and Tikoo, S. (2004). Conceptualizing and researching employer branding. *Career Development International, 9*(5), 501–517.

Berto, R. (2005). Exposure to restorative environments helps restore attentional capacity. *Journal of Environmental Psychology, 25*, 249–259.

Bless, H., Clore, G. L., Schwarz, N., Golisano, V., Rabe, C., and Wölk, M. (1996). Mood and the use of scripts: does a happy mood really lead to mindlessness? *Journal of Personality and Social Psychology, 71*, 665–679.

Bodenhausen, G. V., Kramer, G. P., and Süsser, K. (1994). Happiness and stereotypic thinking in social judgment. *Journal of Personality and Social Psychology, 66*, 621–632.

Bringslimark, T., Hartig, T., and Patil, G. G. (2011). Adaptation to windowlessness: do office workers compensate for a lack of visual access to the outdoors? *Environment and Behavior, 43*, 469–487.

Brown, K. W., and Ryan, R. M. (2003). The benefits of being present: mindfulness and its role in psychological well-being. *Journal of Personality and Social Psychology, 84*, 822–848.

Brown, K. W., Ryan, R. M., and Creswell, J. D. (2007). Addressing fundamental questions about mindfulness. *Psychological Inquiry, 18*, 272–281.

Campos, B., Shiota, M. N., Keltner, D., Gonzaga, G. C., and Goetz, J. L. (2013). What is shared, what is different? Core relational themes and expressive displays of eight positive emotions. *Cognition and Emotion, 27*, 37–52.

Carter, T. J., and Gilovich, T. (2010). The relative relativity of material and experiential purchases. *Journal of Personality and Social Psychology, 98*, 146–159.

Cesari, M., Penninx, B. W., Newman, A. B., Kritchevsky, S. B., Nicklas, B. J., Sutton-Tyrrell, K., Rubin, S. M., Ding, J., Simonsick, E. M., Harris, T. B., and Pahor, M. (2003). Inflammatory markers and onset of cardiovascular events: results from the Health ABC study. *Circulation, 108*, 2317–2322.

Cohen, T. R., Panter, A. T., Turan, N., Morse, L., and Kim, Y. (2014). Moral character in the workplace. *Journal of Personality and Social Psychology, 107*, 943–963.

Čukić, I., and Bates, T. C. (2014). Openness to experience and aesthetic chills: links to heart rate sympathetic activity. *Personality and Individual Differences, 64*, 152–156.

Danvers, A. F., and Shiota, M. N. (2017). Going off script: effects of awe on memory for script-typical and -irrelevant narrative detail. *Emotion*. Advance online publication.

Darbor, K. E., Lench, H. C., Davis, W. E., and Hicks, J. A. (2016). Experiencing versus contemplating: language use during descriptions of awe and wonder. *Cognition and Emotion, 30*, 1188–1196.

Darian, J. C., and Cohen, J. (1995). Segmenting by consumer time shortage. *Journal of Consumer Marketing, 12*, 32–44.

Dijkstra, M. M., Beersma, B., and Evers, A. (2011). Reducing conflict-related employee strain: the benefits of an internal locus of control and a problem-solving conflict management strategy. *Work and Stress, 25*, 167–184.

Dowlati, Y., Herrmann, N., Swardfager, W., Liu, H., Sham, L., Reim, E. K., and Lanctôt, K. L. (2010). A meta-analysis of cytokines in major depression. *Biological Psychiatry, 67*, 446–457.

Einstein, A. (1931). *Living Philosophies*. New York, NY, US: Simon and Schuster.

Ekman, P. (1992). Are there basic emotions? *Psychological Review, 99,* 550–553.

Elfenbein, H. A. (2007). Emotion in organizations: a review and theoretical integration. *The Academy of Management Annals, 1*, 315–386.

Ellison, C. G., and Fan, D. (2008). Daily spiritual experiences and psychological well-being among us adults. *Social Indicators Research, 88*, 247–271.

Ellsworth, P. C., and Smith, C. A. (1988). Shade of joy: patterns of appraisal differentiating pleasant emotions. *Cognition and Emotion, 2*, 301–331.

Félonneau, M. L. (2004). Love and loathing of the city: urbanophilia and urbanophobia, topological identity and perceived incivilities. *Journal of Environmental Psychology, 24*, 43–52.

Folkman, S., and Moskowitz, J. T. (2000). Positive affect and the other side of coping. *American Psychologist, 55*, 647–654.

Fredrickson, B. L. (1998). What good are positive emotions? *Review of General Psychology, 2*, 300–319.

Fredrickson, B. L. (2001). The role of positive emotions in positive psychology: the broaden-and-build theory of positive emotions. *American Psychologist, 56*, 218–226.

Fredrickson, B. L., and Losada, M. F. (2005). Positive affect and the complex dynamics of human flourishing. *American Psychologist, 60*, 678–686.

Fredrickson, B. L., Mancuso, R. A., Branigan, C., and Tugade, M. M. (2000). The undoing effect of positive emotions. *Motivation and Emotion, 24*, 237–258.

Frijda, N. H. (1986). *The Emotions*. Cambridge, UK: Cambridge University Press.

Frijda, N. H. (1987). Emotion, cognitive structure, and action tendency. *Cognition and Emotion, 1*, 115–143.

Fuller, R. C. (2006). *Wonder: From Emotion to Spirituality*. Chapel Hill, NC, US: University of North Carolina Press.

Fuller, R. C. (2008). *Spirituality in the Flesh: Bodily Sources of Religious Experiences*. Oxford, UK: Oxford University Press.

Haidt, J., and Keltner, D. (2002). Awe/responsiveness to beauty and excellence. In C. Peterson and M. E. P. Seligman (eds), *The VIA Taxonomy of Strengths*. Cincinnati, OH, US: Values in Action Institute.

Hardy, Q. (2014, March 1). The monument of tech. *New York Times*.

Hartig, T., Böök, A., Garvill, J., Olsson, T., and Garling, T. (1996). Environmental influences on psychological restoration. *Scandinavian Journal of Psychology, 37*, 378–393.

Hartig, T., Evans, G. W., Jamner, L. D., Davis, D. S., and Gärling, T. (2003). Tracking restoration in natural and urban field settings. *Journal of Environmental Psychology, 23*, 109–123.

Hayes, S. C., Luoma, J. B., Bond, F. W., Masuda, A., and Lillis, J. (2006). Acceptance and commitment therapy: model, processes and outcomes. *Behaviour Research and Therapy, 44*, 1–25.

Hoge, C. W., Terhakopian, A., Castro, C. A., Messer, S. C., and Engel, C. C. (2007). Association of post traumatic stress disorder with somatic symptoms, health care visits, and absenteeism among Iraq war veterans. *American Journal of Psychiatry, 164*, 150–153.

Howell, J. M., and Shamir, B. (2005). The role of followers in the charismatic leadership process: relationships and their consequences. *The Academy of Management Review, 30,* 96–112.

Huron, D. (2006). *Sweet Anticipation: Music and the Psychology of Expectation.* Cambridge, MA, US: MIT Press.

Interface (2015). *Human Spaces: The Global Impact of Biophilic Design in the Workplace.* Report retrieved from https://interfaceinc.scene7.com/is/content/InterfaceInc/Interface/EMEA/eCatalogs/Brochures/Human%20Spaces%20report/English/ec_eu-globalhumanspacesreport-enpdf.pdf, accessed on 23 August 2018.

Izard, C. E., Levinson, K. L., Ackerman, B. P., Kogos, J. L., and Blumberg, S. H. (1998). Children's emotional memories: an analysis in terms of differential emotions theory. *Imagination, Cognition and Personality, 18,* 173–188.

Jamieson, S. D., and Tuckey, M. R. (2017). Mindfulness interventions in the workplace: a critique of the current state of the literature. *Journal of Occupational Health Psychology, 22,* 180–193.

Jänig, W. (2007). Pain associated with the autonomic nervous system. *Neurobiology of Disease, 93,* 1021–1030.

Jausovec, N., and Bakracevic, K. (1995). What can heart rate tell us about the creative process? *Creativity Research Journal, 8,* 11–24.

Joye, Y., and Bolderdijk, J. W. (2015). An exploratory study into the effects of extraordinary nature on emotions, mood, and prosociality. *Frontiers in Psychology, 5,* 1577.

Joye, Y., and Dewitte, S. (2016). Up speeds you down. Awe-evoking monumental buildings trigger behavioral and perceived freezing. *Journal of Environmental Psychology, 47,* 112–125.

Kabat-Zinn, J. (2009). *Full Catastrophe Living: Using the Wisdom of Your Body and Mind to Face Stress, Pain, and Illness.* New York, NY, US: Random House.

Kaplan, R. (1993). The role of nature in the context of the workplace. *Landscape and Urban Planning, 26,* 193–201.

Kaplan, R. (2001). The nature of the view from home: psychological benefits. *Environment and Behavior, 33,* 507–542.

Kaplan, R., and Kaplan, S. (1989). *The Experience of Nature: A Psychological Perspective.* New York, NY, US: Cambridge University Press.

Kaplan, S. (1995). The restorative benefits of nature: toward an integrative framework. *Journal of Environmental Psychology, 15,* 169–182.

Karakas, F. (2010). Spirituality and performance in organizations: a literature review. *Journal of Business Ethics, 94,* 89–106.

Kellert, S. R., Heerwagen, J., and Mador, M. (2008). *Biophilic Design: The Theory, Science, and Practice of Bringing Buildings to Life.* Hoboken, NJ, US: Wiley.

Keltner, D., and Haidt, J. (2003). Approaching awe, a moral, spiritual, and aesthetic emotion. *Cognition and Emotion, 17,* 297–314.

Keltner, D., Kogan, A., Piff, P. K., and Saturn, S. R. (2014). The sociocultural appraisals, values, and emotions (SAVE) framework of prosociality: core processes from gene to meme. *Annual Review of Psychology, 65,* 425–460.

Kiecolt-Glaser, J. K., McGuire, L., Robles, T. F., and Glaser, R. (2002). Emotions, morbidity, and mortality: new perspectives from psychoneuro-immunology. *Annual Review of Psychology, 53,* 83–107.

King, L. A., Hicks, J. A., Krull, J. L., and Del Gaiso, A. K. (2006). Positive affect and the experience of meaning in life. *Journal of Personality and Social Psychology, 90,* 179–196.

Krause, N., and Hayward, R. D. (2015). Assessing whether practical wisdom and awe of God are associated with life satisfaction. *Psychology of Religion and Spirituality, 7,* 51–59.

Lambert D'raven, L. T., Moliver, N., and Thompson, D. (2015). Happiness intervention decreases pain and depression, boosts happiness among primary care patients. *Primary Health Care Research and Development, 16,* 114–126.

Lench, H. C., Flores, S. A., and Bench, S. W. (2011). Discrete emotions predict changes in cognition, judgment, experience, behavior, and physiology: a meta-analysis of experimental emotion elicitations. *Psychological Bulletin, 137*(5), 834–855.

Leon-Perez, J. M., Notelaers, G., and Leon-Rubio, J. M. (2016). Assessing the effectiveness of conflict management training in a health sector organization: evidence from subjective and objective indicators. *European Journal of Work and Organizational Psychology, 25*(1), 1–12.

Luttik, J. (2000). The value of trees, water and open space as reflected by house prices in the Netherlands. *Landscape and Urban Planning, 48,* 161–167.

Maier, S. F., and Watkins, L. R. (1998). Cytokines for psychologists: implications of bidirectional immune-to-brain communication for understanding behavior, mood, and cognition. *Psychological Review, 105,* 83–107.

Mannell, R. C., and Zuzanek, J. (1991). The nature and variability of leisure constraints in daily life: the case of the physically active leisure of older adults. *Leisure Sciences, 13,* 337–351.

Martos, T., Thege, B. K., and Steger, M. F. (2010). It's not only what you hold, it's how you hold it: dimensions of religiosity and meaning in life. *Personality and Individual Differences, 49,* 863–868.

Mauss, I. B., Levenson, R. W., McCarter, L., Wilhelm, F. H., and Gross, J. J. (2005). The tie that binds? Coherence among emotion experience, behavior, and physiology. *Emotion, 5,* 175–190.

McDougall, W. (1921). *An Introduction to Social Psychology* (14th ed.). Boston, MA, US: John W. Luce and Company.

Milliken, C. S., Auchterlonie, J. L., and Hoge, C. W. (2007). Longitudinal assessment of mental health problems among active and reserve component soldiers returning from the Iraq war. *Journal of the American Medical Association, 298,* 2141–2148.

Mitroff, I., and Denton, E. (1999). A study of spirituality in the workplace. *Sloan Management Review, 40,* 83–92.

Neumark-Sztainer, D., Hannan, P. J., Story, M., Croll, J., and Perry, C. (2003). Family meal patterns: associations with sociodemographic characteristics and improved dietary intake among adolescents. *Journal of the American Dietetic Association, 103,* 317–322.

Nicolao, L., Irwin, J. R., and Goodman, J. K. (2009). Happiness for sale: do experiential purchases make consumers happier than material purchases? *Journal of Consumer Research, 36*, 188–198.

Nowak, M. A. (2006). Five rules for the evolution of cooperation. *Science, 314*, 1560–1563.

Pargament, K. I. (1997). *The Psychology of Religion and Coping: Theory, Research, Practice.* New York, NY, US: Guilford Press.

Parsons, R., Tassinary, L. G., Ulrich, R. S., Hebl, M. R., and Grossman-Alexander, M. (1998). The view from the road: implications for stress recovery and immunization. *Journal of Environmental Psychology, 18*, 113–139.

Piaget, J., and Inhelder, B. (1969). *The Psychology of the Child* (H. Weaver, Trans.) New York, NY, US: Basic Books. (Original work published 1966).

Piff, P. K., Dietze, P., Feinberg, M., Stancato, D. M., and Keltner, D. (2015). Awe, the small self, and prosocial behavior. *Journal of Personality and Social Psychology, 108*, 883–899.

Prade, C., and Saroglou, V. (2016). Awe's effects on generosity and helping. *The Journal of Positive Psychology, 11*, 522–530.

Proyer, R. T., Gander, F., Wellenzohn, S., and Ruch, W. (2016). Addressing the role of personality, ability, and positive and negative affect in positive psychology interventions: findings from a randomized intervention based on the authentic happiness theory and extensions. *The Journal of Positive Psychology, 11*, 609–621.

Rispens, S., and Demerouti, E. (2016). Conflict at work, negative emotions, and performance: a diary study. *Negotiation and Conflict Management Research, 9*, 103–119.

Rosenzweig, E., and Gilovich, T. (2012). Buyer's remorse or missed opportunity? Differential regrets for material and experiential purchases. *Journal of Personality and Social Psychology, 102*, 215–223.

Rudd, M., Vohs, K. D., and Aaker, J. (2012). Awe expands people's perception of time, alters decision making, and enhances well-being. *Psychological Science, 23*, 1130–1136.

Saroglou, V., Buxant, C., and Tilquin, J. (2008). Positive emotions as leading to religion and spirituality. *The Journal of Positive Psychology, 3*, 165–173.

Schurtz, D. R., Blincoe, S., Smith, R. H., Powell, C. J., Combs, D. Y., and Kim, S. H. (2012). Exploring the social aspects of goose bumps and their role in awe and envy. *Motivation and Emotion, 36*, 205–217.

Segal, Z. V., Williams, J. G., and Teasdale, J. D. (2013). *Mindfulness-based Cognitive Therapy for Depression* (2nd ed.). New York, NY, US: Guilford Press.

Shiota, M. N., Keltner, D., and Mossman, A. (2007). The nature of awe: elicitors, appraisals, and effects on self-concept. *Cognition and Emotion, 21*, 944–963.

Shiota, M. N., Neufeld, S. L., Yeung, W. H., Moser, S. E., and Perea, E. F. (2011). Feeling good: autonomic nervous system responding in five positive emotions. *Emotion, 11*, 1368–1378.

Silvia, P. J., Fayn, K., Nusbaum, E. C., and Beaty, R. E. (2015). Openness to experience and awe in response to nature and music: personality and profound aesthetic experiences. *Psychology of Aesthetics, Creativity, and the Arts, 9*, 376–384.

Sober, E., and Wilson, D. S. (1998). *Unto Others: The Evolution and Psychology of Unselfish Behavior*. Cambridge, MA, US: Harvard University Press.

Solomon, R. C. (2002). *Spirituality for the Skeptic: The Thoughtful Love of Life*. New York, NY, US: Oxford University Press.

Stanley, E. A., Schaldach, J. M., Kiyonaga, A., and Jha, A. P. (2011). Mindfulness-based mind fitness training: a case study of a high-stress pre-deployment military cohort. *Cognitive and Behavioral Practice, 18*, 566–576.

Stellar, J. E., John-Henderson, N., Anderson, C. L., Gordon, A. M., McNeil, G. D., and Keltner, D. (2015). Positive affect and markers of inflammation: discrete positive emotions predict lower levels of inflammatory cytokines. *Emotion, 15*, 129–133.

Tanielian, T., and Jaycox, L. H. (eds) (2008). *Invisible Wounds of War: Psychological and Cognitive Injuries, Their Consequences, and Services to Assist Recovery*. Santa Monica, CA, US: RAND Corporation.

Tennessen, C. M., and Cimprich, B. (1995). Views to nature: effects on attention. *Journal of Environmental Psychology, 15*, 77–85.

Ulrich, R. S., Simons, R., Losito, B. D., Fiorito, E., Miles, M. A., and Zelson, M. (1991). Stress recovery during exposure to natural and urban environments. *Journal of Environmental Psychology, 11*, 201–230.

Vago, D. R., and Silbersweig, D. A. (2012). Self-awareness, self-regulation, and self-transcendence (S-ART): a framework for understanding the neuro-biological mechanisms of mindfulness. *Frontiers in Human Neuroscience, 6*, 296.

Van Boven, L., and Gilovich, T. (2003). To do or to have? That is the question. *Journal of Personality and Social Psychology, 85*, 1193–1202.

Van Cappellen, P., and Saroglou, V. (2012). Awe activates religious and spiritual feelings and behavioral intentions. *Psychology of Religion and Spirituality, 4*, 223–236.

Van Cappellen, P., Saroglou, V., Iweins, C., Piovesana, M., and Fredrickson, B. L. (2013). Self- transcendent positive emotions increase spirituality through basic world assumptions. *Cognition and Emotion, 27*, 1378–1394.

Van Cappellen, P., Toth-Gauthier, M., Saroglou, V., and Fredrickson, B. L. (2016). Religion and well-being: the mediating role of positive emotions. *Journal of Happiness Studies, 17*, 485–505.

van den Berg, A. E., Hartig, T., and Staats, H. (2007). Preference for nature in urbanized societies: stress, restoration, and the pursuit of sustainability. *Journal of Social Issues, 63*, 79–96.

van den Berg, A. E., Koole, S. L., and van der Wulp, N. Y. (2003). Environmental preference and restoration: (how) are they related? *Journal of Environmental Psychology, 23*, 135–146.

Verduyn, P., Van Mechelen, I., Tuerlinckx, F., Meers, K., and Van Coillie, H. (2009). Intensity profiles of emotional experience over time. *Cognition and Emotion, 23*, 1427–1443.

Vohs, K. D., and Schmeichel, B. J. (2003). Self-regulation and extended now: controlling the self alters the subjective experience of time. *Journal of Personality and Social Psychology, 85*, 217–230.

Weidman, A. C., and Dunn, E. W. (2016). The unsung benefits of material things: material purchases provide more frequent momentary happiness than experiential purchases. *Social Psychological and Personality Science, 7*, 390–399.

Wellen, K. E., and Hotamisligil, G. S. (2005). Inflammation, stress, and diabetes. *The Journal of Clinical Investigation, 115*, 1111–1119.

White, F. (1987). *The Overview Effect: Space Exploration and Human Evolution.* Boston, MA, US: Houghton Mifflin.

Wilson, E. O. (1984). *Biophilia: The Human Bond with other Species.* Cambridge, MA, US: Harvard University Press.

Yaden, D. B., Iwry, J., Slack, K. J., Eichstaedt, J. C., Zhao, Y., Vaillant, G. E., and Newberg, A. B. (2016). The overview effect: awe and self-transcendent experience in space flight. *Psychology of Consciousness: Theory, Research, and Practice, 3*, 1–11.

Zhang, J. W., Piff, P. K., Iyer, R., Koleva, S., and Keltner, D. (2014). An occasion for unselfing: beautiful nature leads to prosociality. *Journal of Environmental Psychology, 37*, 61–72.

4. Boredom at work: what, why, and what then?

Cynthia D. Fisher

In 1993, I wrote that boredom at work was a neglected concept (Fisher, 1993), a conclusion reinforced in a 2009 review by Loukidou, Loan-Clarke, and Daniels. The entire psychology literature featured on average less than one article per year on any aspect of boredom between 1926 and 1980 (Smith, 1981). The lack of talk about boredom has changed dramatically over the last few years. Van Tilburg and Igou (2017) report that 1422 articles related to boredom were published in the psychology literature between 2010 and the end of 2015. They conclude that, "boredom research is gradually moving from the fringes of psychological science toward the mainstream" (van Tilburg and Igou, 2017, p. 309). Boredom has been discussed by scholars from many disciplines, including philosophy (e.g., O'Brien, 2014; Svendsen, 2005), theology (e.g., Wardley, 2012), sociology (e.g., Barbalet, 1999), human factors engineering (e.g., Cummings, et al., 2016; Casner and Schooler, 2015), critical management theory (e.g., Johnsen, 2016; Paulsen, 2015), and educational, social, cognitive, clinical, and organizational psychology. I will take a predominantly psychological approach in this chapter.

Toohey (2011) would label the phenomenon explored in this chapter "simple boredom," in contrast to "existential boredom" (also known as acedia or melancholia). He views existential boredom as an academic concept rather than an emotion, and notes that this supposed chronic state of extreme meaningless and ennui has attracted rather self-indulgent writing and discussion by theologians, philosophers, and literary figures for centuries (e.g., Svendsen, 2005). In contrast, the simple emotional state of boredom has been dismissed as childish and not worth discussion until relatively recently. Toohey introduces his book on boredom by stating that, "Boredom is one of the most unexpectedly common of all human emotions, and for that reason it shouldn't be ignored, or trivialized. It is part and parcel of ordinary life" (Toohey, 2011, p. 1). This chapter explores the simple boredom that is part and parcel of the experience of work, often drawing on literature that is not specific to the employment context. This broader literature is highly relevant and may often inform the understanding of boredom at work. The first task is to clarify what boredom is. I will then consider why people are bored at work, and then explore what they do in response, discussing an expanding range of both positive and negative consequences of boredom in the workplace and the ways we talk about it.

CHARACTERIZING BOREDOM

Boredom has been conceptualized and measured in a variety of time frames. The most long-term and stable conceptualization is at trait level, as *boredom proneness* (Farmer and Sundberg, 1986) or *boredom susceptibility* as a component of sensation seeking (Zuckerman, 1979). The shortest term is as a transient affective state, more specifically, as an emotion (Fisher, 1993). The literature and measures of boredom quite conveniently divide into trait vs state approaches (Vodanovich and Watt, 2016). In practice, however, most of the non-laboratory research on state boredom has been based on self-reports of the extent to which respondents typically feel bored in a particular context (e.g., work, leisure) – arguably closer to an attitude than a relatively short-lived emotional state. The primary focus of this paper will be state boredom, whether measured in real time or as a typical state at work, with more general trait boredom propensity acknowledged as a likely contributor to the experience of state boredom.

Everyone knows what it feels like to be bored, though a range of academic definitions exist. Vogel-Walcutt, Fiorella, Carper, and Schatz (2012) reviewed the literature on boredom in educational settings and found 109 papers that defined state boredom. Table 4.1 presents a representative set of definitions from a variety of disciplines to demonstrate both variety and communality in views. Early definitions of boredom tended to confound the subjective experience of boredom with antecedent task characteristics such as repetitiveness or lack of stimulation (e.g., Davies et al., 1983). More recently, the subjective experience of boredom has taken center stage and state boredom is now almost universally viewed as an emotion (e.g., Fahlman et al., 2013; O'Brien, 2014).

Table 4.1   Definitions of boredom

Source	Definition	Context
Barbalet (1999, p. 631)	Absence of meaning leads to a restless, irritable feeling that the subject's current activity or situation holds no appeal, and that there is a need to get on with something interesting	General, Sociology
Davies et al. (1983, p. 1)	An emotional response to an environment which is unchanging or which changes in a repetitive and highly predictable fashion	Human Factors
Eastwood et al. (2012, p. 484)	The aversive state that occurs when we (a) are not able to successfully engage attention with internal (e.g., thoughts or feelings) or external (e.g., environmental stimuli) information required for participating in satisfying activity; (b) are aware of the fact that we are not able to engage attention and participate in satisfying activity, which can take the form of either awareness of a high degree of mental effort expended in an attempt to engage with the task at hand or awareness of engagement with task-unrelated concerns (e.g., mind wandering); and (c) attribute the cause of our aversive state to the environment (e.g., "this task is boring", "there is nothing to do")	General
Fahlman and others (2013, p. 80)	The aversive experience of having an unfulfilled desire to be engaged in a satisfying activity	General

Source	Definition	Context
Fisher (1993, p. 397)	An unpleasant, transient affective state in which the individual feels a pervasive lack of interest in and difficulty concentrating on the current activity. When a specific activity is to be performed, individuals experiencing boredom feel that it takes conscious effort to maintain or return attention to the activity	Workplace
Mikulas and Vodanovich (1993, p. 3)	A state of relatively low arousal and dissatisfaction which is attributed to an inadequately stimulating environment	General
O'Brien (2014, p. 237)	A mental state of weariness, restlessness, and lack of interest in something to which one is subjected, which is unpleasant and undesirable, and in which the weariness and restlessness are causally related to the lack of interest	General, analytical philosophy
van Tilburg and Igou (2012)	Feeling unchallenged and perceiving one's activities as meaningless	General
Vogel-Walcutt and others (2012, p. 102)	State boredom occurs when an individual experiences both the (objective) neurological state of low arousal and the (subjective) psychological state of dissatisfaction, frustration, or disinterest in response to the low arousal	Education

State boredom meets all the criteria for being considered an emotion. First, it varies substantially within person over time. In a diary study of boredom at work, 61% of the variance in daily boredom was within person (van Hooff and van Hooft, 2017). A weekly study of boredom in a university class reported that 66% of the variation in boredom during lectures over the semester was within person (Tanaka and Murayama, 2014). Second, boredom, like all emotions, can be described by characteristic cognitive appraisal, affective, somatic, and motivational/action tendency components. Table 4.2 displays what is known about boredom in terms of these components, with a sample of citations for each.

Table 4.2 Summary of qualities of boredom as an emotion

Affective Tone	Mildly to highly negative/unpleasant	van Tilburg and Igou, 2017
Cognitive Appraisals		
Goal relevance	Low	van Tilburg and Igou, 2017; Eastwood et al., 2012; Fisher, 1993; Russell, 1980; Smith and Ellsworth, 1985
Goal congruence	Low	
Coping potential	Low OR very high	
Novelty/complexity/ ambiguity	Low OR too high	
Effort	Low (or occasionally high)	
Attention	Low	
Meaningfulness	Low	
Perceived challenge	Low	
Action Tendency	Escape, disengage, distract, change tasks (or apathy/learned helplessness)	Goetz et al., 2014; van Tilburg and Igou, 2012
Somatic State		
Arousal/physiological response	Deactivated OR activated	Fahlman et al., 2013; Merrifield and Danckert, 2014
Body posture	Upper body collapsed, head backwards, low movement activity, stare, slump, head on arms/hands, yawn OR restless fidgeting	Toohey, 2011; Wallbott, 1998
Psychophysical signature	Relative to sadness, increasing heart rate, decreasing skin conductance, increasing cortisol	Merrifield and Danckert, 2014
Function	Motivate pursuit of more rewarding/meaningful goals/activities	Barbalet, 1999; Bench and Lench, 2013; Elpidorou, 2014

In terms of cognitive appraisals, boredom is very low in attention, meaningfulness, challenge, goal relevance, and goal congruence. Boredom has been shown to have a different pattern of appraisals from other negative emotions including sadness, anger, frustration, fear, disgust, guilt, shame, regret, and disappointment (van Tilburg and Igou, 2012, 2017) and is empirically distinct from apathy, anhedonia, depression, and anxiety (Fahlman et al., 2009; Goldberg et al., 2011). In the workplace, Reijseger and others (2013) have shown that boredom can be empirically distinguished from burnout and engagement, though the states are correlated.

In terms of affective tone, there is agreement that boredom is almost always affectively unpleasant, though intensity may vary considerably. In terms of arousal, boredom is unique among emotions in that arousal level may vary from very low (passive resignation, drowsiness) to quite high. A few of the definitions in Table 4.1 explicitly include low arousal, while many other authors have noted the frequent occurrence of high arousal (e.g., Bench and Lench, 2013; Fahlman et al., 2013; Goetz et al., 2014; Merrifield and Danckert, 2014). In the latter case, bored individuals experience high levels of restless agitation as they increase their efforts to forcibly maintain attention on the current task or to escape the boring situation either physically or psychologically.

In terms of adaptive purpose (Keltner and Gross, 1999; Lench et al., 2015), the function of the emotion of boredom is to stimulate exploration and the pursuit of new and more rewarding opportunities. Elpidorou (2014, p. 2) notes that "boredom is informative" and that it "motivates the pursuit of a new goal when the current goal ceases to be satisfactory, attractive, or meaningful." The autonomic arousal that can accompany boredom prepares the individual for such action (Bench and Lench, 2013). In general, a tendency to abandon pointless pursuits and seek more rewarding and goal-congruent activities is likely to be adaptive and facilitate survival. However, the demands and constraints of many work settings limit choices of alternative goals and activities, and the efforts of employees to down-regulate boredom may sometimes produce undesirable outcomes for organizations. Specific employee responses to feeling bored at work will be discussed in more detail later in this chapter.

Further, emotions have objects – they are felt about/because of/in response to a specific stimulus, event or situation. In the case of boredom, the object is described well by O'Brien (2014, p. 241) as "something repetitive, monotonous, predictable and all-too familiar; something too far above or too far below one's level; or something compulsory; or something to which one is confined." A definition of the emotion of state boredom, which combines key elements of the above discussion, is: *An aversive feeling of 1. being trapped in a situation, 2. with an undesirably low or high level of challenge or stimulation, 3. low relative meaning, and 4. the experience of restlessness and attentional difficulties in consequence.*

One might wonder whether state boredom has types or dimensions. Working in the educational field, Goetz and others (2014) suggest that there are five types of boredom in academic settings, distinguished by their degree of unpleasantness and arousal. The first type is *indifferent boredom*, which is low in arousal, relaxed, mellow and slightly positive in hedonic tone. *Calibrating boredom* is relatively low in arousal and slightly negative in valence. Attention may wander and the individual is willing to change the boring situation though they are not actively working to do so. *Searching boredom* is higher in both arousal and negative valence, featuring restlessness and a more active search for alternative activities to relieve the boredom. *Reactant boredom* is very high in arousal and negative valence, with a very strong desire to escape the situation. Finally, *apathetic boredom* is low in arousal but very negative in hedonic tone, resembling learned helplessness or depression, and may occur when efforts to escape have failed. It has been suggested, though not tested, that individuals may progress from mild to more intense types of boredom as exposure to a boring situation continues over time.

Boredom is often conceptualized and measured as a unidimensional construct (e.g., Reijseger et al., 2013), though the Multidimensional State Boredom Scale has five dimensions which load on a higher order general boredom factor (Fahlman et al., 2013). The dimensions are lack of engagement, high arousal, low arousal, difficulty focusing attention, and perceived slow passage of time. Baratta and Spence (2015) recommend treating these as multiple correlated dimensions rather than combining them into a single composite score for analysis purposes.

Finally, one might ask, who experiences boredom? The short answer is probably almost everyone, from time to time. Boredom has been described as one of the most common of all human emotions (Toohey, 2011) and was reported by 63% of respondents on at least one occasion in a ten-day experience sampling study (Chin et al., 2017). Chin and others found that boredom was most often reported while individuals were studying, doing nothing in particular, or at work. Historically, boredom at work was considered most common and problematic in routine and monotonous tasks such as factory assembly work, long-haul driving, and inspection tasks. With the advent of more automatic systems in the modern workplace, boredom is now a problem in supervisory control situations in which humans monitor automated systems for the rare occasions on which intervention is needed (Casner and Schooler, 2014; Cummings et al., 2016). However, boredom can also be experienced by white collar and professional employees who might appear to hold enriched and stimulating jobs (Costas and Kärreman, 2016; Harju and Hakanen, 2016; van der Heijden et al., 2012). At the other end of the evolutionary scale, it is possible that an affective experience similar to boredom occurs in captive animals housed in unenriched environments in laboratories, farms, or zoos. "Bored" animals may develop self-harm behaviors, stereotypies, helplessness, and other indicators of low well-being. Serious conversations about animal boredom, how to measure it, and animal welfare implications are beginning to occur (Burn, 2017; Williams, 2015).

CAUSES OF BOREDOM

The definition of state boredom adopted in this chapter points to several categories of causes:

(1) being trapped in a situation with little autonomy;
(2) with an undesirably low or high level of challenge or stimulation;
(3) with low relative meaning; and
(4) experiencing attentional difficulties in consequence.

Each of these will be explored in more detail below.

BEING TRAPPED/LACK OF AUTONOMY

One work environment contributor to boredom is lack of autonomy, which may operate in several ways. First, individuals may attribute their task activity to external control and discount potential intrinsically interesting aspects of the task, as suggested by Cognitive Evaluation and Self Determination Theories (Deci and Ryan, 1985; Ryan and Deci, 2017). Jang (2008) has shown that providing an autonomy-supportive rational for continued work on an uninteresting task was effective in engaging students in learning and that an increase in identified regulation accounted for this effect (Ryan and Deci, 2000). Second, when a task is performed solely for external reasons, it is likely to be seen as having low personal meaning, as described below. Third, strong external controls such as detailed work rules, close supervision, and the requirement to remain on task or at one's workstation may reduce opportunities to escape, avoid, or modify boring activities to be more interesting (Fisher, 1993).

UNDESIRABLY LOW OR HIGH LEVEL OF CHALLENGE OR STIMULATION

Both under- and over-challenging tasks, relative to the performer's capabilities, can result in boredom (Acee et al., 2010; Fisher, 1993). Tasks that are repetitive, simple, or require continuous attention in a search for intermittent targets often induce boredom. These tasks either can be performed with very little attention or require a high level of sustained attention without providing stimulation in return (e.g., vigilance tasks). Jobs which feature periods of waiting to act while having nothing to do, as may be the case for many service provider jobs, can also be boring due to inadequate challenge (Fisher, 1993). An optimal level of relatively high challenge and relatively high performer skill may provide the least boring situation (Csikszentmihalyi and LeFevre, 1989). Job characteristics theory suggests that jobs that are chronically low on skill variety, task identity, task significance, autonomy, and feedback are unlikely to sustain interest or intrinsic motivation (Hackman and Oldham, 1980). However, prolonged performance and repetition may lead to satiation and boredom even on tasks that ordinarily have the potential to be interesting.

On the other side of the scale, work tasks that are too complex for performers are also often perceived as boring and create attentional difficulties (Acee et al., 2010; Fisher, 1993). Pekrun's (2006) well-known Control-Value Model of emotions in academic achievement settings suggests that students will be bored when they experience low subjective control over outcomes in the form of weak self-efficacy, as is more likely when tasks are too difficult. Considerable evidence supports this assertion (e.g., Pekrun et al., 2010; Tanaka and Murayama, 2014). More directly, there is evidence that student boredom in classes is positively related to the perceived difficulty of the material (Acee et al., 2010; Tanaka and Murayama, 2014) at both between- and within-person levels. Difficult material has high attention demands but failure to understand means that attention is unrewarding. There is evidence that performance and boredom are linked by feedback loops and reciprocal causation – boredom contributes to later poor performance through attentional failures and low motivation to engage with the task, and poor performance leads to future boredom, presumably through reduced subjective control (Pekrun et al., 2014).

LOW RELATIVE MEANING

Humans are meaning-seeking beings, and meaninglessness has been identified by a number of scholars as a key cause of boredom (e.g., Barbalet, 1999; van Tilburg and Igou, 2012). What is or is not meaning-ful is an idiosyncratic judgment by individuals. Klinger's (1999, 2013) work on the content of everyday thought shows that thoughts often turn to current concerns or goals to which the individual is committed. When required to attend to a task that is not relevant to salient current concerns or goals, individuals experience frustration and find paying attention to the task effortful and the task boring (Critcher and Gilovich, 2010). Even a work task which is enriched and would normally be engaging can be perceived as boring and lacking in relative meaning when other concerns are more pressing.

In education, Pekrun's (2006) Control-Value Model addresses meaning via the value component of the model – whether students believe that a learning activity has immediate or long-term benefits. A host of studies show that when value is higher, boredom is lower, motivation is higher, and learning is more likely (e.g., Jang, 2008; Pekrun et al., 2010). In the literature on job design, job characteristics such as task identity, task significance, and prosocial impact are likely to provide meaning and motivation and thus reduce boredom (Grant, 2008a, 2008b; Hackman and Oldham, 1980).

The literature on interests contains considerable research on the concept of stable *individual interests*, how they develop, and the effects they have on motivation and learning (e.g., Hidi and Renninger, 2006; Renninger and Hidi, 2016; Rotgans and Schmidt, 2017). For instance, one may develop a sustained individual interest in dog training, in mathematics, in medieval history, or in web design. Working in an area of individual interest is usually meaningful, enjoyable, stimulating, and undertaken for reasons that feel relatively autonomous. Surprisingly, there is no analogous construct in the boredom literature, though surely people do develop active aversions to particular topics or activities that are consistently disliked and meaningless to their concerns. Activities related to these idiosyncratic *individual boredoms* would almost immedi-ately induce state boredom, attentional difficulties, and the urge to escape. Introspection suggests, for instance, that my individual boredoms include anything to do with sports involving men and balls, all discus-sions of higher education research policy, and anecdotes about the antics of other people's children. Individual boredoms are ignored by generic approaches to work design and may require focus on a much more customised view of person–job fit.

Alternative views on lack of meaning as a cause of boredom are provided by European critical management theorists, with worker alien- ation, a concept similar to boredom, seen as a near-inevitable conse- quence of capitalism. Johnsen (2016) suggests that boredom is a relatively new construct which emerged in connection with the rise of modern organizations and their imposition of artificial time regimes which strip meaning from human activities. Costas and Kärreman (2016) conducted a qualitative study of boredom among management consult- ants in two large firms. They found that many of these highly qualified individuals reported being bored and saw their work as repetitive, standardised, clerical, and unimportant – essentially, lacking in meaning. This created an identity clash with their employers' discourses about the autonomous, creative, and highly varied nature of the elite consultant role. The root cause of boredom in this situation was attributed to unfulfilled expectations about what the work would be like (high vs low in meaning) and subsequent arrested identity. Similarly, Bailey, Madden, Alfes, Shantz, and Soane (2017) caution that heavy-handed or inauthentic efforts by organizations to manage meaning may create disengagement and "existential labor" for employees.

ATTENTIONAL DIFFICULTIES AND OTHER METACOGNITIVE CUES

While attention to a boring task may wane due to low autonomy, too much or too little challenge or stimulation, and/or low relative meaning, there is evidence that the experience of attentional difficulty itself, as well as perceptions of the slow passage of time and high subjective effort, may directly contribute to the inference that one is bored (East- wood et al., 2012). Damrad-Frye and Laird (1989, p. 320) state that "boredom seems to represent a metacognitive judgment about one's attentional activity." Boredom is felt when the current activity fails to capture and hold the performer's attention, or it takes conscious and continuous effort to sustain attention, or the performer is acutely aware of wishing to direct attention elsewhere. Internal awareness of mind wan- dering, feelings about the slow passage of time, and subjective effort in focusing attention are all metacognitive cues that boredom is being experienced.

People have implicit theories of what mind wandering signals about their feelings toward the current activity. The content as well as the occurrence of mind wandering is relevant to inferences of boredom (Critcher and Gilovich, 2010). Fisher (1998) showed that individuals believed that frequent mind wandering at work indicated boredom and dissatisfaction with the job, especially when the mind wandering was to unimportant and non-urgent topics. Critcher and Gilovich (2010) found that when performers' minds wandered to other pleasant activities they could be doing at the moment, or to several such things, and there was no obvious reason why it should do so, they inferred that they were bored with their current task. If their minds wandered to an unpleasant, single, or past event (out of the many past events potentially available to think about), then mind wandering was attributed to the "reverie's irresistible pull" rather than to boredom with the current task.

Altered perceptions of the passage of time are associated with both boredom and interest, probably as a side effect of the low versus high amount of attention absorbed by the task. Time seems to drag when one is bored, yet fly when one is engrossed in an interesting activity. The German word for boredom, *langeweile*, literally means "long time" (Belton and Priyadharshini, 2007), and time perception is one of five dimensions in Fahlman et al.'s (2013) measure of state boredom. Conti (2001, p. 3) notes that, "The 'watched pot' feeling of time inching slowly along contrasts sharply with the pleasant, absorbed feeling that comes with 'losing track of time.'" With few exceptions, conscious attention to the slow passage of time seems to be aversive.

There is evidence that individuals use their perception of the passage of time as input into judgments about whether or not they are bored. Several laboratory studies have manipulated the apparent passage of time by displaying clocks that ran faster or slower than real time, or told participants that their 15-minute work period was completed when actually either 10 or 20 minutes had passed. Unless given an alternative explanation for altered time perception, individuals led to believe that time passed slowly concluded that they were more bored with the task, and those led to believe that time passed swiftly concluded that they enjoyed the task more (London and Monell, 1974; Sackett et al., 2010; Sucala et al., 2010).

Another metacognitive cue that one is feeling bored is the perception of subjective effort. In Bruya's (2010) book on effortless attention, he points out that normally one would expect subjective cognitive effort to increase as task demands and concentration increase, but there is sometimes a paradoxical reduction in perceived effort, despite very high levels of concentration, when individuals enter a state of flow while engaged in performance of an optimally challenging task. The perception of the amount of effort required to continue to concentrate on a task appears to be a key cue in appraisals of boredom versus interest, with effortful attention suggesting boredom. Damrad-Frye and Laird (1989) created high and low volume auditory distractions from a task. They found that when individuals were distracted by low background noise, they attributed their difficulty in attending to the task to boredom with the activity itself. When the noise was louder, they correctly attributed their attentional difficulties to the noise rather than to boredom with the task.

In sum, individuals are likely to feel bored when they feel trapped in a low autonomy situation on a task that is too simple or too challenging for them, that has little meaning (or less personal meaning than competing current concerns), and when they are aware of mind wandering, the slow passage of time, and the large amount of effort required to maintain attention to the task. We will now consider how individuals react when in such a situation.

RESPONSES TO AND CONSEQUENCES OF BOREDOM

Individuals often attempt to regulate their emotions, and in particular, to reduce their experience of negative emotions (Koole, 2009). The most common and effective approaches to down-regulating negative emotions in general include distraction and reappraisal (Augustine and Hemenover, 2009; Webb et al., 2012), and these approaches are used in the case of boredom as well. Negative emotions signal that something is wrong, that progress toward a goal is unsatisfactory (Carver and Scheier, 1990). Boredom specifically signals "there is nothing here for you; try something different." The adaptive purpose or function of boredom is to stimulate movement, exploration, and seeking a more rewarding and meaningful environment (Bench and Lench, 2013). However, it is sometimes beneficial long term to the individual to persist on a task even though it is experienced as boring (e.g., to concentrate on a classroom lecture or read a dense report or complete an essential task). In the work setting, employees have performance expectations and are often constrained to situations that greatly restrict their ability to escape a boring task for something more satisfying. Pilots cannot leave the cockpit unattended and autopilot unsupervised on long flights, anaesthesiologists cannot doze off during surgery, and factory workers must continue to produce products at the required rate. Boredom in these situations is sometimes detrimental for well-being and performance. The negative affective consequences (or at least correlates) of boredom will be discussed below. I will then discuss behavioral and cognitive responses to boredom that may occur either while continuing to work on the boring task or escaping to alternative off-task activities. Finally, the performance-related consequences of boredom and employees' attempts to cope with it will be discussed.

AFFECTIVE RESPONSES TO BOREDOM

At trait level, boredom proneness is associated with depression, hostility, anger, impulsivity, aggression, low life satisfaction, and negative affect (e.g., Kass et al., 2001; Vodanovich, 2003; Vodanovich and Watt, 2016). A large number of correlational studies have confirmed that typical/chronic boredom at work is negatively related to attitudinal outcomes such as job satisfaction, engagement and organizational commitment (e.g., Reijseger et al., 2013). Boredom positively predicts burnout and experienced stress and subsequent physical and mental health sequelae (Harju et al., 2014; Reijseger et al., 2013). In one of the very few within-person daily field studies of boredom, van Hooff and van Hooft (2016) found that daily boredom was positively related to depressed mood at the end of the workday for employees who were high on work centrality. In a second daily study, they found that boredom one day negatively predicted intrinsic motivation and job attitudes the next day (van Hooff and van Hooft, 2017). An experience sampling study involving reports of emotions every 30 minutes found that boredom often co-occurred with other negative emotions such as loneliness, anger, sadness, and worry (Chin et al., 2017). Clearly, boredom is an unpleasant affective state that is associated with other negative states. It is therefore not surprising that bored individuals attempt to self-regulate this unpleasant emotion in a variety of ways.

COGNITIVE AND BEHAVIORAL RESPONSES TO BOREDOM

Cognitive and behavioral responses to boredom should include attempts to address its causes in the form of lack of autonomy, too much or too little challenge or stimulation, and low relative meaning (van Tilburg and Igou, 2012). Such attempts may feature reappraisal and other strategies to exert control or enhance interest, challenge, and meaning while continuing to work on the original task. Alternatively, these attempts may utilise distraction, either by dividing one's attention while working on the original task, or by escaping from the boring task to another activity

(Nett et al., 2011; Skowronski, 2012). Table 4.3 lists responses to boredom which have been documented in the workplace and/or the classroom.

Table 4.3 Cognitive and behavioral responses to boredom

	Increase meaning or challenge or variety on-task	Increase meaning, challenge, or variety off-task	Distract or escape
Behavioral Responses			
Increase or vary pace of work	x		
Ask for more work or to learn new skills	x		
Switch between tasks	x		
Suggest ways to improve the work	x		
Change or vary methods of work	x		
Perform additional (work or non-work) tasks concurrently	x		
Do boring task first to get it over with	x		
Job crafting	x		
Horseplay, sabotage, risky behavior	x	x	
Fidget	x		
Prosocial/organizational citizenship behavior		x	x
Counterproductive work behavior		x	x
Socialize, gossip		x	x
Cyberloaf or other forms of time banditry		x	x
Absence, tardiness, long breaks			x
Sleep			x
Quit, retire early			x
Eat, drink, snack			x
Procrastinate			x

	Increase meaning or challenge or variety on-task	Increase meaning, challenge, or variety off-task	Distract or escape
Cognitive Responses			
Exert effort to concentrate	x		
Set task goals	x		
Reappraise task importance	x		
Mind wandering	x		x
Increase social identity	x	x	

ON-TASK RESPONSES

Some responses to boredom are efforts to increase engagement with the current task. Sansone and her colleagues have written extensively about their Self-Regulation of Motivation Model (e.g., Sansone and Harac-kiewicz, 1996; Sansone and Thoman, 2005; Sansone et al., 1992). When a task is boring but individuals believe they will benefit from continuing to perform it, self-regulation of interest is helpful to sustain effort and persistence. They suggest that individuals monitor their motivation and enact strategies to create or maintain motivation toward a boring task when needed. Their research has identified a number of Interest Enhancing Strategies (IES) spontaneously adopted by individuals who wish to persist on a task initially found boring. Some IES include deepening involvement with the task by setting challenging goals or introducing extra demands or variety to the task to make it harder, and generating self-relevant rationales for why the activity is desirable and beneficial to personal goals.

Green-Demers, Pelletier, Stewart, and Gushue (1998) investigated the effectiveness of a number of IES in enhancing motivation toward the less interesting aspects of training among ice skaters. They found that generating self-relevant rationales for the task (reappraisal), increasing challenge by varying the way the task was performed, and setting difficult goals were effective in enhancing motivation. Smith, Wagaman, and Handley (2009) hypothesized and found that IES were more likely to be used and were more effective in enhancing intrinsic motivation when individuals were working under a promotion (gain) focus than a prevention (avoidance of loss) focus. The playful inventiveness permitted in a promotion focus is a good regulatory fit with IES, whereas careful performance of the task exactly as instructed is a better regulatory fit with prevention focus. Aside from generating more interest in the task itself, some individuals report simply applying will power to complete the boring task as quickly as possible, or undertaking the boring task first to get it over with (Sansone, 2009).

There is evidence that IES are also used in the workplace by employees seeking to cope with or ameliorate boredom. Game (2007) described boredom coping strategies involving *engagement* (extend the task, make it more complex, build one's task-related skills, learn new things, do extra work, cognitively reframe the task to enhance its importance to one's goals), *partial engagement* (set task goals or promise oneself rewards for persistence), or *disengagement* (seek off task stimulation, avoid the task, procrastinate, switch to another task, daydream). Game (2007) called the on-task engagement strategies "a personalised form of job enrichment" and found that use of engagement strategies was associated with greater employee well-being, higher job satisfaction, and better compliance with safety regulations.

In a similar vein, two recent articles have explored the engagement strategy of job crafting (Wrzesniewski and Dutton, 2001) as a response to or means of coping with boredom. Harju, Hakanen, and Schaufeli (2016) found that job crafting in the form of seeking challenges predicted future increases in engagement and reductions in boredom, though high initial job boredom impeded crafting. Van Hooff and van Hooft (2014) found that bored employees who engaged in job crafting (seeking challenges and increasing structural resources) were less likely to perform dysfunctional "bored behaviors" such as daydreaming, taking breaks, or shifting to non-work activities. Job crafting seems likely to enhance perceptions of autonomy and meaning as well as providing more stimulating work, probably in areas of individual interest.

Other IES involve seeking additional stimulation or meaning during performance of a boring task by distracting oneself from the task with concurrent physical or mental activities. These may include actions such as fidgeting, talking to others, listening to music, horseplay, or performing a second task while continuing to work on the primary task (Fisher, 1993). Green-Demers and others (1998) found that seeking additional stimulation from the surrounding environment rather than from deeper interaction with the task itself was not effective in enhancing either intrinsic or extrinsic motivation for the task.

There is some evidence that any stimulation, even unpleasant stimulation, may be preferable to unrelieved boredom. Havermans, Vancleef, Kalamatianos, and Nederkoorn (2015) gave university students a choice to administer an electrocutaneous shock of varying intensities to their own forearms while they watched a one-hour documentary or one hour of continuous repetitions of the same 85-second segment of the documentary. They shocked themselves ten times as often on average, and up to 3.5 times as intensely, while watching the repetitive (boring) video. This has some analogies to the behavior of mink kept in an unenriched environment. They were quicker to orient to novel stimuli of all valences, and engaged with them for longer, than mink kept in an enriched environment (Meagher and Mason, 2012).

Perhaps the most common response to boredom while working on a task is mind wandering, also called task un-related thought, daydreaming, stimulus-independent thought, self-generated thought, and spontaneous thought (Baars, 2010; Cummings et al., 2016; Smallwood, 2013). Experience sampling studies show that up to half of all waking human thought is not related to the immediate task or the external environment (Killingsworth and Gilbert, 2010; Klinger, 1999). Mind wandering may represent an attempt to use distraction, employ excess cognitive capacity, and establish meaning by focusing on more personally relevant thoughts during the performance of a boring task (Kane et al., 2007; Stawarczyk et al., 2011). Even airline pilots report frequent mind wandering while flying (Casner and Schooler, 2014, 2015). Such stimulus-independent thought should not be regarded merely as a form of cognitive failure, but instead as a uniquely human adaptation which assists individuals in successfully navigating the challenges of their lives (Baird et al., 2011). Baars (2010, p. 208) notes that, "The stream of spontaneous thought is remarkably rich and self-relevant, reflecting one's greatest personal concerns, interpersonal feelings, unfulfilled goals and unresolved challenges, worries and hopes, inner debates, self-monitoring, feelings of knowing, visual imagery, imaginary social interactions, recurrent beliefs, coping reactions, intrusive memories, daydreams and fantasies, future plans, and more." Most of these topics would have more meaning and relevance to individuals than an unchallenging and unimportant work task.

Seli and colleagues (Seli et al., 2016a, 2016b) have discovered that while mind wandering may occur unintentionally as the brain attempts to re-establish an optimal level of arousal, one third or more of mind wandering may be intentional. Unintentional mind wandering seems more common on difficult tasks, whereas intentional mind wandering is likely on easy tasks which require less attention. A great deal of the content of mind wandering is about planning for future goals and actions (Baird et al., 2011), though nostalgic thoughts about the past have also been shown to reduce boredom, mediated by the strength of the motive to search for meaning (van Tilburg et al., 2013). Who among us hasn't planned their weekend or written a grocery list to stave off the painful restlessness of being trapped in a boring meeting or seminar? While Killingsworth and Gilbert (2010) titled their large-scale experience sampling article, "A Wandering Mind is an Unhappy Mind" (compared to one that isn't wandering), it is likely that intentionally wandering minds are less unhappy than those trapped in single-minded focus on an unchallenging and meaningless task. The performance-related consequences of mind wandering will be discussed further in a later section of this chapter.

OFF-TASK RESPONSES

Given that the action tendency of boredom is to escape the current situation to one that offers more challenge or meaning, it is not surprising that bored employees avoid or abandon boring tasks when possible. Long-term responses to boredom include avoidance options such as turnover, absenteeism, and intention to retire early (Harju et al., 2014; Kass et al., 2001). A short-term avoidance response is procrastination. There is evidence that boredom proneness and anticipated boringness of a task are related to procrastination, with tasks perceived as likely to be boring put off rather than undertaken in a timely manner (Ferrari, 2000; Senécal et al., 1997; Steel, 2007; Vodanovich and Rupp, 1999; Wan et al., 2014).

Van Hooff and van Hooft (2014) found, following Affective Events Theory (Weiss and Cropanzano, 1996), that boredom produces affect-driven bored behavior such as working slowly, taking long breaks, pretending to be busy, and doing non-work-related tasks as well as engaging in counterproductive work behavior. Additional evidence for counterproductive work behavior as an outcome of boredom comes from Bruursema, Kessler, and Spector (2011). They found that trait boredom proneness was positively related to all six dimensions of counterproductive work behavior (abuse against others, production deviance, sabotage, withdrawal, theft, and horseplay). Employee reports of the amount of objective repetition and monotony in their jobs also predicted counterproductive work behavior in this study. Finally, boredom proneness and repetition interacted, with those high on dispositional boredom proneness being especially likely to commit counterproductive work behaviors when their jobs were repetitive (Bruursema et al., 2011).

Bored employees may also engage in more interesting or personally relevant non-work tasks such as cyberloafing and other forms of time banditry while they are supposed to be working (Brock et al., 2013; Eddy et al., 2010; Martin et al., 2010; van der Heijden et al., 2012; Wan et al., 2014). Critical management theorist Paulsen (2015) notes the very high rate of *empty labor* or *time appropriation* (doing non-work activities during work time) in modern organizations, often enabled by internet access. This may be cast as not just an attempt to relieve boredom by an individual, but as an emancipatory act of resistance to management. Successfully stealing time from the employer may be an enjoyable game and a way to re-establish autonomy.

A potential off-task response to boredom, which may be increasingly important, is eating, drinking, or snacking. These activities provide oral stimulation, a break from the current task, the opportunity to move around, and possibly a chance to interact with others. Roy's (1959) classic participant observation study of work group social life on a repetitive factory job noted that the work day was punctuated with ritualized interactions involving food – banana time, peach time, lunch time, coffee time, fish time, and Coke time. Research in health psychology confirms that eating is a common response to boredom (e.g., Crockett et al., 2015; Havermans et al., 2015; Koball et al., 2012). The phenomenon extends to animals too, with mink caged in an un-enriched environment eating more mink treats than those kept in an enriched environment (Meagher and Mason, 2012). Recently, Sonnentag, Pundt, and Venz (2017) explored between and within-person predictors of eating sweet vs healthy snacks at work. Self-control demands such as keeping one's attention on a task even though bored or performing emotional labor were associated with stronger affect-regulation motives, which in turn predicted choice of sweet treats. Given societal concern with obesity and unhealthy eating, organizations may wish to consider whether their job designs increase this risk among employees, as well as other means they might use to encourage healthy choices when employees snack (Sonnentag et al., 2017).

When bored, individuals attempt to re-establish meaning in what they are doing (Barbalet, 1999; van Tilburg and Igou, 2011). This might be done either on or off task, and by redefining and enhancing the meaningfulness of the entire job or by performing single meaningful acts during acute episodes of boredom. At job level, Isaksen (2000) explored how incumbents in repetitive food preparation jobs used self-talk or reappraisal to create meaning around their very mundane work. Qualitative analyses revealed eight types of meaning: seeing work as central to one's self-identity and self-respect, valuing social relationships at work, appreciating that pay or other outcomes of work facilitate satisfying activities outside of work (family well-being, future projects), learning new things which provides satisfaction, working hard to produce a high quality product one can be proud of, contributing to the well-being of others, creating ways to improve the job, and experiencing freedom through control of one's own work tasks. All 28 interviewees mentioned at least two forms of meaning making, with some using as many as six. Those who endorsed more forms of meaning were less likely to complain about the meaningless of the job as a whole.

Van Tilburg and Igou (2011) pointed out that social identification is a source of personal meaning, so that one way to increase meaning would be to identify more strongly with an in-group. In five laboratory studies, they showed that induced boredom increased positive evaluation of in-group features, preferential treatment of an in-group member, and punitive behavior toward an out-group member. They further demonstrated that these effects were mediated by the strength of motivation to engage in meaningful behavior. These findings are consistent with a suggestion by Barbalet (1999) that intergroup conflict might be a means by which individuals reduce boredom through increased meaning and in-group cohesion. Johnsen (2016) suggests that bored workers can create meaning and identity though shared anti-management activities, as demonstrated by Roy's (1959) factory workers and the daily food rituals they created.

On a more positive note, another way to increase meaning at a moment in time is to perform a prosocial behavior, and there is some evidence that boredom can increase this propensity. Van Tilburg and Igou (2017) showed that induced boredom resulted in the intention to donate more to a charity, especially when the charity was seen as highly effective. Perceived meaninglessness mediated the relationship between felt boredom and intention to give. Skowronski (2012) suggested that organizational citizenship behaviors may reduce boredom by providing variety as well as meaning, and that this response would be more likely to be used by employees who are autonomously motivated and who identify with the organization's goals. Likewise, any discretionary proactive behavior (Bindl and Parker, 2011) would be a way that bored individuals could increase autonomy, meaning, and variety for themselves while improving organizational outcomes at the same time.

PERFORMANCE

I have discussed how bored employees may respond cognitively and/or behaviorally to manage their own experience of boredom. However, in the work context, organizationally defined performance matters too. In some cases, employees' boredom management efforts compromise performance or safety, as when individuals miss work altogether, procrastinate or avoid essential tasks, mind wander to the point that performance deteriorates, challenge themselves with risky horseplay, or engage in extensive personal behavior on company time (Eddy et al., 2010). The cost of many of these behaviors is not obvious or easy to calculate, so the true cost of boredom at work may not be fully appreciated.

There is not a great deal of recent research on the relationship between experienced boredom and externally measured job performance, though one study found that trait boredom proneness was associated with lower supervisor performance ratings (Watt and Hargis, 2010), and boredom has been found to predict accidents (e.g., Drory, 1982; Frone, 1998). The largest bodies of research on boredom and objective performance are in the areas of education and human factors. Educational researchers have reported extensive evidence that student boredom predicts poor academic outcomes, misbehavior in the classroom, and dropping out of school (e.g., Goetz and Hall, 2014; Pekrun et al., 2014; Renninger and Hidi, 2016). Human factors psychologists and engineers have generated a great deal of research on cognitive fatigue and decrements in vigilance performance in occupations such as radar operator, pilot, and driver (e.g., Ackerman, 2011; Larue et al., 2011). They have found that experienced boredom is implicated in the vigilance decrements that begin to manifest after about 30 minutes on signal detection tasks (Pattyn et al., 2008). Given limited attentional capacity, the mind wandering which often accompanies boredom may result in "perceptual decoupling from sensory input" such that external information is less likely to be noticed (Smallwood, 2015). This makes it more likely that important signals from the primary task will be missed, resulting in slower or less consistent responding, increased error rates, and accidents (e.g., Casner and Schooler, 2014, 2015; Cummings et al., 2016; Finomore et al., 2009; McVay and Kane, 2009; Sawin and Scerbo, 1995; Stawarczyk et al., 2011).

Boredom may also be good for performance. As mentioned above, employee responses to boredom may include setting challenging goals, learning new things, suggesting task improvements, multi-tasking, or performing organizational citizenship behavior. There have also been suggestions that occasional periods of routine work and state boredom in the midst of an otherwise demanding job may facilitate creative performance (Baars, 2010; Elsbach and Hargadon, 2006; Ohly et al., 2006). Steve Jobs famously said, "I'm a big believer in boredom. Boredom allows one to indulge in curiosity, and out of curiosity comes everything."

Chronic high workload, especially with interruptions and low control, has been shown to hinder the creativity of professionals (Perlow, 1999).

These individuals may need time away from stressful job duties for incubation, and a period of mindless work on simple well-understood tasks with low performance pressure or time pressure may be effective. These are the types of tasks that might induce boredom if prolonged, but also provide temporary respite from persistent high attention demands. Employees might experience what Goetz and others (2014) called "indifferent boredom" – a relaxed low arousal state of slightly positive affective tone in which their spare mental capacity can subconsciously work on problem solutions. Laboratory evidence shows that creativity is enhanced more by an incubation period of work on a low cognitive demand task than an equally long period of rest (Baird et al., 2012; Sio and Ormerod, 2009). The idea that boredom (in small doses) may be good for performance has implications for the design of high-pressure jobs with creative demands (Elsbach and Hargadon, 2006; Ohly et al., 2006).

A recent popular book by Zomorodi (2017) is entitled *Bored and brilliant: How spacing out can unlock your most productive and creative self*. The author suggests that mental down-time and mind wandering are important enablers of creativity, yet our addiction to mobile phones means that we are seldom bored enough for this to occur. She recommends a multi-day phone and social media detox to make space for creative boredom.

CONCLUDING THOUGHTS

The emotion of state boredom is attracting increased attention from scholars in many disciplines, across a variety of settings, and using a wide range of research methods. We know that boredom is an unpleasant state which is associated with other negative emotions both concurrently and in the near term (e.g., Chin et al., 2017; van Hooff and van Hooft, 2016, 2017). Typical or chronic boredom at work is negatively correlated with the attitudinal outcomes generally considered most important to organizations, including job satisfaction, organizational commitment, and engagement (Harrison et al., 2006; Reijseger et al., 2013), and chronic boredom proneness is associated with many indicators of poor well-being and destructive behavior both on and off the job (Vodanovich and Watt, 2016). Employee responses to boredom are many and varied, cognitive and behavioral, and sometimes productive but often destructive for organizations.

Most of the research on boredom at work has been at the stable person level, measuring typical or chronic boredom as an attitude toward the job as a whole or boredom proneness as a disposition, rather than state boredom as a transient emotional experience in connection with the immediate task and setting. The recent application of experience sampling methodology in the field and experimentation using boredom inductions in the laboratory have permitted more fine-grained examination of the near-term antecedents and consequences of boredom, but there is much yet to be learned. For instance, it is likely that time on task is relevant to the development and impact of boredom in the workplace, as it is in the extreme case of vigilance tasks. The impact of breaks and interest-enhancing strategies on boredom could also be examined. The concept of stable *individual boredoms* and how they are developed, paralleling the research on individual interests, is also worth pursuing. Job crafting or strengths-based job design may offer the possibility of avoiding or minimizing exposure to tasks which are deeply loathed and meaningless to a particular individual, when the person in the next office may find the same tasks fascinating and rich in meaning.

Organizational interventions in the form of traditional job redesign are likely to reduce boredom (Hackman and Oldham, 1980). Autonomy-supportive leadership may also help (Jang, 2008). Relational job design in which employees have contact with or see the beneficial impact of their activities on others may reduce the incidence of boredom through reappraisal mechanisms that enhance meaning and perhaps stimulate self-set goals (Grant, 2007, 2008a). Attempts by organizations to imbue a sense of meaning in employees through job design, ethical leadership, and culture and shared values may help, though run the risk of backfiring if seen as inauthentic (Bailey et al., 2017).

Understanding state as well as chronic boredom may become more important in the future as the workplace is increasingly populated by Millennials and their successors Generation Z. While good research is lacking, the popular press have publicized reports of decreasing attention spans among digital natives (McSpadden, 2015). Mael and Jex (2015) suggest that boredom on the job is on the rise in the West, although repetitive and simple work is increasingly being automated or off-shored. They ask why boredom should be increasing at the same time that jobs are becoming more complex. Their answer is that the ubiquitous presence of information and communication technology has greatly increased the amount and continuous availability of many forms of stimulation. Individuals who have habituated to multi-tasking and constant entertainment may suffer boredom when required to concentrate on one thing at a time or to forego continuous access to mobile phones, internet entertainment, and social media while at work. This situation fits neatly into the definition of boredom developed in this chapter – these workers may feel trapped in a low autonomy situation, with less variety and stimulation than they are accustomed to, without access to personally meaningful social media, to which their mind wanders frequently, making it difficult to concentrate on their work tasks. Come to think of it, this describes most inhabitants of today's college classrooms.

Consistent with the thrust of this book, my final points address the ways people talk, or fail to talk, about boredom. Boredom is not (usually) a social emotion. It is inherently an internal experience rather than one that must be discussed or displayed to others. While there may be visible physiological manifestations such as yawning or fidgeting, often there is no one present to witness these signs or talk to about the experience of boredom. In fact, the presence of others may relieve boredom by providing welcome distraction or variety, although another's banal or ego-centric speech may be a proximal cause of boredom (Leary et al., 1986).

Talking about boredom may be dangerous in several ways. First, it may prime others to feel bored as well. Certainly the last thing any speaker or teacher should do at the start of a presentation or lecture is to apologize in advance to the audience that it may be boring! Toohey (2011) notes that simple boredom is often seen as childish. Indeed, "I'm bored!" brings to mind a whining child or teenager too lazy or uncreative to find something useful or engaging to do, and who thinks that the world owes them nonstop entertainment. This may be one reason that individuals are reluctant to publicly admit to boredom at work. In addition, boredom proneness, with its many unpleasant correlates (Vodanovich and Watt, 2016), sounds very much like a character flaw, perhaps indicating arrested development. Lack of interest can be seen as an indicator of lack of mature self-discipline. But is feeling trapped in a situation one doesn't like an example of childish reactance, or of a normal adult's desire to exercise autonomy?

In many interpersonal roles, expressing boredom is contrary to organizational or professional display rules. Consider the case of a call center agent delivering a cold call script for the 100th time of the day or a psychiatrist listening to a client complain repetitively about his or her life. Emotional labor is required to avoid showing boredom to clients and to instead provide (or simulate) full and solicitous attention.

Perhaps simple boredom at work attracted little attention until recently because it was not acceptable to talk about feeling bored except in obvious cases such as extremely repetitive blue-collar work. Dedicated professionals in enriched jobs would not normally give voice to their feelings of boredom, particularly if these feelings conflicted with organizational or professional discourses about the nature of the work and the passion that should be felt toward it (Costas and Kärreman, 2016). For instance, while it's quite acceptable for my academic colleagues to complain about how bored they feel while marking large numbers of exam scripts or project papers, describing their feeling toward research in the same terms invites disapproval, violates professional norms, and is likely to be avoided (Lindebaum, 2017). Admitting even to one's self that one is bored with research may cause feeling of inauthenticity, fraud, self-doubt, and shame as no one else seems to be bored. However, the ability to acknowledge and express emotions may be essential to benefiting from them. For instance, Lindebaum and Geddes (2016) note that a world without anger expression would be a world in which injustices were not redressed. Similarly, it is possible that a world without boredom and the freedom to acknowledge and act on it would be a stagnant and unsatisfying world, given that boredom can be a stimulus to productive exploration and change. It may also be a world where mind wandering and hence creativity are much less likely to occur.

REFERENCES

Acee, T. W., Kim, H., Kim, H. J., Kim, J., Chu, H. R., Kim, M., Choo, Y., and Wicker, F. W. (2010). Academic boredom in under- and over-challenging situations. *Contemporary Educational Psychology, 35,* 17–27, doi:10.1016/j.cedpsych.2009.08.002.

Ackerman, P. L. (ed.) (2011). *Cognitive Fatigue: Multidisciplinary Perspectives on Current Research and Future Applications.* Washington, DC, USA: American Psychological Association.

Augustine, A. A., and Hemenover, S. H. (2009). On the relative effectiveness of affect regulation strategies: a meta-analysis. *Cognition and Emotion, 23,* 1181–1220, doi:10.1080/02699930802396556.

Baars, B. J. (2010). Spontaneous repetitive thoughts can be adaptive: postscript on "mind wandering". *Psychological Bulletin, 136,* 208–210, doi:10.1037/a0018726.

Bailey, K., Madden, A., Alfes, K., Shantz, A., and Soane, E. (2017). The mismanaged soul: existential labor and the erosion of meaningful work. *Human Resource Management Review, 27,* 416–430.

Baird, B., Smallwood, J., Mrazek, M. D., Kam, J. W. Y., Franklin, M. S., and Schooler, J. W. (2012). Inspired by distraction: mind wandering facilitates creative incubation. *Psychological Science, 23,* 1117–1122, doi:10.1177/0956797612446024.

Baird, B., Smallwood, J., and Schooler, J. W. (2011). Back to the future: autobiographical planning and the functionality of mind-wandering. *Consciousness and Cognition, 20,* 1604–1611, doi:10.1016/j.concog.2011.08.007.

Baratta, P. L., and Spence, J. R. (2015). A riddle, wrapped in a mystery, inside an enigma … or just multidimensional? Testing the multidimensional structure of boredom. In N. M. Ashkanasy, W. J. Zerbe and C. E. J. Härtel (eds), *New Ways of Studying Emotions in Organizations (Research on Emotion in Organizations, Vol. 11)* (pp. 139–172). Emerald Group Publishing Limited.

Barbalet, J. M. (1999). Boredom and social meaning. *British Journal of Sociology, 50,* 631–646, doi:10.1111/j.1468-4446.1999.00631.x.

Belton, T., and Priyadharshini, E. (2007). Boredom and schooling: a cross-disciplinary exploration. *Cambridge Journal of Education, 37,* 579–595, doi:10.1080/03057640701706227.

Bench, S. W., and Lench, H. C. (2013). On the function of boredom. *Behavioral Sciences, 3,* 459–472, doi://dx.doi.org/10.3390/bs3030459.

Bindl, U. K., and Parker, S. K. (2011). Proactive work behavior: forward-thinking and change-oriented action in organizations. In S. Zedeck (ed.), *APA Handbook of Industrial and Organizational Psychology, Vol. 2: Selecting and Developing Members for the Organization* (pp. 567–598). Washington, DC, USA: American Psychological Association, doi:10.1037/12170-019.

Brock, M. E., Martin, L. E., and Buckley, M. R. (2013). Time theft in organizations: the development of the time banditry questionnaire. *International Journal of Selection and Assessment, 21,* 309–321, doi:10.1111/ijsa.12040.

Bruursema, K., Kessler, S. R., and Spector, P. E. (2011). Bored employees misbehaving: the relationship between boredom and counterproductive work behaviour. *Work and Stress, 25,* 93–107, doi:10.1080/02678373.2011.596670.

Bruya, B. (ed.) (2010). *Effortless Attention: A New Perspective in the Cognitive Science of Attention and Action.* Cambridge, MA, USA: MIT Press.

Burn, C. C. (2017). Bestial boredom: a biological perspective on animal boredom and suggestions for its scientific investigation. *Animal Behaviour, 130,* 141–151, doi.org/10.1016/j.anbehav.2017.06.006.

Carver, C. S., and Scheier, M. F. (1990). Origins and functions of positive and negative affect: a control-process view. *Psychological Review, 97,* 19–35.

Casner, S. M., and Schooler, J. W. (2014). Thoughts in flight: Automation use and pilots' task-related and task-unrelated thought. *Human Factors, 56,* 433–442, doi:10.1177/0018720813501550.

Casner, S. M., and Schooler, J. W. (2015). Vigilance impossible: diligence, distraction, and daydreaming all lead to failures in a practical monitoring task. *Consciousness and Cognition, 35,* 33–41, doi:10.1016/j.concog.2015.04.019.

Chin, A., Markey, A., Bhargava, S., Kassam, K. S., and Loewenstein, G. (2017). Bored in the USA: experience sampling and boredom in everyday life. *Emotion, 17,* 359–368, doi:10.1037/emo0000232.

Conti, R. (2001). Time flies: investigating the connection between intrinsic motivation and the experience of time. *Journal of Personality, 69,* 1–26, doi:10.1111/1467-6494.00134.

Costas, J., and Kärreman, D. (2016). The bored self in knowledge work. *Human Relations, 69,* 61–83, doi:10.1177/0018726715579736.

Critcher, C. R., and Gilovich, T. (2010). Inferring attitudes from mindwandering. *Personality and Social Psychology Bulletin, 36,* 1255–1266, doi:10.1177/0146167210375434.

Crockett, A. C., Myhre, S. K., and Rokke, P. D. (2015). Boredom proneness and emotion regulation predict emotional eating. *Journal of Health Psychology, 20*, 670–680, doi:10.1177/1359105315573439.

Csikszentmihalyi, M., and LeFevre, J. (1989). Optimal experience in work and leisure. *Journal of Personality and Social Psychology, 56*, 815–822, doi:10.1037/0022-3514.56.5.815.

Cummings, M. L., Gao, F., and Thornburg, K. M. (2016). Boredom in the workplace: a new look at an old problem. *Human Factors, 58*, 279–300, doi:10.1177/0018720815609503.

Damrad-Frye, R., and Laird, J. D. (1989). The experience of boredom: the role of the self-perception of attention. *Journal of Personality and Social Psychology, 57*, 315–320, doi:10.1037/0022-3514.57.2.315.

Davies, D. R., Shackleton, V. J., and Parasuraman, R. (1983). Monotony and boredom. In R. Hockey (ed.), *Stress and Fatigue in Human Performance.* Chichester, UK: Wiley.

Deci, E. L., and Ryan, R. M. (1985). *Intrinsic Motivation and Self-determination in Human Behavior.* New York, NY, USA: Plenum.

Drory, A. (1982). Individual differences in boredom proneness and task effectiveness at work. *Personnel Psychology, 35*, 141–151, doi:10.1111/j.1744-6570.1982.tb02190.x.

Eastwood, J. D., Frischen, A., Fenske, M. J., and Smilek, D. (2012). The unengaged mind: defining boredom in terms of attention. *Perspectives on Psychological Science, 7*, 482–495, doi:10.1177/1745691612456044.

Eddy, E. R., D'Abate, C. P., and Thurston Jr., P. W. (2010). Explaining engagement in personal activities on company time. *Personnel Review, 39*, 639–654, doi:10.1108/00483481011064181.

Elpidorou, A. (2014). The bright side of boredom. *Frontiers in Psychology, 5*, 1–5, doi:10.3389/fpsyg.2014.01245.

Elsbach, K. D., and Hargadon, A. B. (2006). Enhancing creativity through "mindless" work: a framework of workday design. *Organization Science, 17*, 470–483, doi:10.1287/orsc.1060.0193.

Fahlman, S. A., Mercer, K. B., Gaskovski, P., Eastwood, A. E., and Eastwood, J. D. (2009). Does a lack of life meaning cause boredom? Results from psychometric, longitudinal, and experimental analyses. *Journal of Social and Clinical Psychology, 28*, 307–340, doi:10.1521/jscp.2009.28.3.307.

Fahlman, S. A., Mercer-Lynn, K., Flora, D. B., and Eastwood, J. D. (2013). Development and validation of the multidimensional state boredom scale. *Assessment, 20*, 68–85, doi:10.1177/1073191111421303.

Farmer, R., and Sundberg, N. D. (1986). Boredom proneness – the development and correlates of a new scale. *Journal of Personality Assessment, 50*, 4–17, doi:10.1207/s15327752jpa5001_2.

Ferrari, J. R. (2000). Procrastination and attention: factor analysis of attention deficit, boredomness, intelligence, self-esteem, and task delay frequencies. *Journal of Social Behavior and Personality, 15*, 185–196.

Finomore, V., Matthews, G., Shaw, T., and Warm, J. (2009). Predicting vigilance: a fresh look at an old problem. *Ergonomics, 52*, 791–808, doi:10.1080/00140130802641627.

Fisher, C. D. (1993). Boredom at work: a neglected concept. *Human Relations, 46*, 395–417, doi:10.1177/001872679304600305.

Fisher, C. D. (1998). Effects of external and internal interruptions on boredom at work: two studies. *Journal of Organizational Behavior, 19*, 503–522, doi:AID-JOB854>3.0.CO;2-9.

Frone, M. R. (1998). Predictors of work injuries among employed adolescents. *Journal of Applied Psychology, 83*, 565–576, doi:10.1037/0021-9010.83.4.565.

Game, A. M. (2007). Workplace boredom coping: health, safety, and HR implications. *Personnel Review, 36*, 701–721, doi:10.1108/004834807 10774007.

Goetz, T., and Hall, N. C. (2014). Academic boredom. In R. Pekrun and L. Linnenbrink-Garcia (eds), *International Handbook of Emotions in Education* (pp. 311–347). New York, NY, USA: Routledge/Taylor and Francis Group.

Goetz, T., Frenzel, A. C., Hall, N. C., Nett, U. E., Pekrun, R., and Lipnevich, A. A. (2014). Types of boredom: an experience sampling approach. *Motivation and Emotion, 38*, 401–419, doi://dx.doi.org/10.1007/s11031-013-9385-y.

Goldberg, Y. K., Eastwood, J. D., LaGuardia, J., and Danckert, J. (2011). Boredom: an emotional experience distinct from apathy, anhedonia, or depression. *Journal of Social and Clinical Psychology, 30*, 647–666, doi://dx.doi.org/10.1521/jscp.2011.30.6.647.

Grant, A. M. (2007). Relational job design and the motivation to make a prosocial difference. *Academy of Management Review, 32*, 393–417.

Grant, A. M. (2008a). The significance of task significance: job performance effects, relational mechanisms, and boundary conditions. *Journal of Applied Psychology, 93*, 108–124, doi:10.1037/0021-9010.93.1.108.

Grant, A. M. (2008b). Designing jobs to do good: dimensions and psychological consequences of prosocial job characteristics. *The Journal of Positive Psychology, 3*, 19–39, doi:10.1080/17439760701751012.

Green-Demers, I., Pelletier, L. G., Stewart, D. G., and Gushue, N. R. (1998). Coping with the less interesting aspects of training: toward a model of interest and motivation enhancement in individual sports. *Basic and Applied Social Psychology, 20*, 251–261, doi:10.1207/s15324834basp2004_2.

Hackman, J. R., and Oldham, G. R. (1980). *Work Redesign*. Reading, MA, USA: Addison-Wesley, doi:10.1037/0735-7028.11.3.445.

Harju, L. K., and Hakanen, J. J. (2016). An employee who was not there: a study of job boredom in white-collar work. *Personnel Review, 45*, 374–391, doi:10.1108/PR-05-2015-0125.

Harju, L. K., Hakanen, J. J., and Schaufeli, W. B. (2014). Job boredom and its correlates in 87 Finnish organizations. *Journal of Occupational and Environmental Medicine, 56*, 911–918, doi:10.1097/JOM.0000000000000248.

Harju, L. K., Hakanen, J. J., and Schaufeli, W. B. (2016). Can job crafting reduce job boredom and increase work engagement? A three-year cross-lagged panel study. *Journal of Vocational Behavior, 95–96*, 11–20, doi://doi.org/10.1016/j.jvb.2016.07.001.

Harrison, D. A., Newman, D. A., and Roth. P. L. (2006). How important are job attitudes? Meta-analytic comparisons of integrative behavioral outcomes and time sequences. *Academy of Management Journal, 49*, 305–325, doi:10.5465/AMJ.2006.20786077.

Havermans, R. C., Vancleef, L., Kalamatianos, A., and Nederkoorn, C. (2015). Eating and inflicting pain out of boredom. *Appetite, 85*, 52–57, doi:10.1016/j.appet.2014.11.007.

Hidi, S., and Renninger, K. A. (2006). The four-phase model of interest development. *Educational Psychologist, 41*, 111–127, doi:10.1207/s15326985ep4102_4.

Isaksen, J. (2000). Constructing meaning despite the drudgery of repetitive work. *Journal of Humanistic Psychology, 40*, 84–107, doi:10.1177/0022167800403008.

Jang, H. (2008). Supporting students' motivation, engagement, and learning during an uninteresting activity. *Journal of Educational Psychology, 100*, 798–811, doi:10.1037/a0012841.

Johnsen, R. (2016). Boredom and organization studies. *Organization Studies, 37*, 1403–1415, doi:10.1177/0170840616640849.

Kane, M. J., Brown, L. H., McVay, J. C., Silvia, P. J., Myin-Germeys, I., and Kwapil, T. R. (2007). For whom the mind wanders, and when: an experience-sampling study of working memory and executive control in daily life. *Psychological Science, 18*, 614–621, doi:10.1111/j.1467-9280.2007.01948.x.

Kass, S. J., Vodanovich, S. J., and Callender, A. (2001). State-trait boredom: relationship to absenteeism, tenure, and job satisfaction. *Journal of Business and Psychology, 16*, 317–327, doi:1011121503118.

Keltner, D., and Gross, J. J. (1999). Functional accounts of emotions. *Cognition and Emotion, 13*, 467–480, doi:10.1080/026999399379140.

Killingsworth, M. A., and Gilbert, D. T. (2010). A wandering mind is an unhappy mind. *Science, 330*, 932, doi:10.1126/science.1192439.

Klinger, E. (1999). Thought flow: properties and mechanisms underlying shifts in content. In J. A. Singer and P. Salovey (eds), *At Play in the Fields of Consciousness: Essays in the Honour of Jerome L. Singer* (pp. 29–50). Mahwah, NJ, USA: Lawrence Erlbaum Associates, Inc.

Klinger, E. (2013). Goal commitments and the content of thoughts and dreams: basic principles. *Frontiers in Psychology, 4*, 415, doi:10.3389/fpsyg.2013.00415.

Koball, A. M., Meers, M. R., Storfer-Isser, A., Domoff, S. E., and Musher-Eizenman, D. R. (2012). Eating when bored: revision of the emotional eating scale with a focus on boredom. *Health Psychology, 31*, 521–524, doi:10.1037/a0025893.

Koole, S. L. (2009). The psychology of emotion regulation: an integrative review. *Cognition and Emotion, 23*, 4–41, doi:10.1080/02699930802619031.

Larue, G. S., Rakotonirainy, A., and Pettitt, A. N. (2011). Driving performance impairments due to hypovigilance on monotonous roads. *Accident Analysis and Prevention, 43*, 2037–2046, doi:10.1016/j.aap.2011.05.023.

Leary, M. R., Rogers, P. A., Canfield, R. W., and Coe, C. (1986). Boredom in interpersonal encounters. *Journal of Personality and Social Psychology, 51*(5), 968–975.

Lench, H. C., Bench, S. W., Darbor, K. E., and Moore, M. (2015). A functionalist manifesto: goal-related emotions from an evolutionary perspective. *Emotion Review, 7,* 90–98, doi:10.1177/1754073914553001.

Lindebaum, D. (2017). *Emancipation Through Emotion Regulation at Work.* Cheltenham, UK and Northampton, MA, USA: Edward Elgar Publishing.

Lindebaum, D., and Geddes, D. (2016). The place and role of (moral) anger in organizational behavior studies. *Journal of Organizational Behavior, 37,* 738–757, doi: 10.1002/job.2065.

London, H., and Monell, L. (1974). Cognitive manipulations of boredom. In H. London, and R. Nisbett (eds), *Thought and Feeling* (pp. 44–59). Chicago, IL, USA: Aldine.

Loukidou, L., Loan-Clarke, J., and Daniels, K. (2009). Boredom in the workplace: more than monotonous tasks. *International Journal of Management Reviews, 11,* 381–405, doi:10.1111/j.1468-2370.2009.00267.x.

Mael, F., and Jex, S. (2015). Workplace boredom: an integrative model of traditional and contemporary approaches. *Group and Organization Management, 40,* 131–159, doi:10.1177/1059601115575148.

Martin, L. E., Brock, M. E., Buckley, M. R., and Ketchen, D. J. (2010). Time banditry: examining the purloining of time in organizations. *Human Resource Management Review, 20,* 26–34, doi:10.1016/j.hrmr.2009.03.013.

McSpadden, K. (2015, May 14). You now have a shorter attention span than a goldfish. *Time,* retrieved from http://time.com/3858309/attention-spans-goldfish/.

McVay, J. C., and Kane, M. J. (2009). Conducting the train of thought: working memory capacity, goal neglect, and mind wandering in an executive-control task. *Journal of Experimental Psychology: Learning, Memory, and Cognition, 35,* 196–204, doi:10.1037/a0014104.

Meagher, R. K., and Mason, G. J. (2012). Environmental enrichment reduces signs of boredom in caged mink. *PLoS ONE, 7,* e49180, http://doi.org/10.1371/journal.pone.0049180.

Merrifield, C., and Danckert, J. (2014). Characterizing the psychophysiological signature of boredom. *Experimental Brain Research, 232,* 481–91, doi://dx.doi.org/10.1007/s00221-013-3755-2.

Mikulas, W. L., and Vodanovich, S. J. (1993). The essence of boredom. *Psychological Record, 43,* 3–12.

Nett, U. E., Goetz, T., and Hall, N. C. (2011). Coping with boredom in school: an experience sampling perspective. *Contemporary Educational Psychology, 36,* 49–59, doi:10.1016/j.cedpsych.2010.10.003.

O'Brien, W. (2014). Boredom. *Analysis, 74,* 236–244, doi:10.1093/analys/anu041.

Ohly, S., Sonnentag, S., and Pluntke, F. (2006). Routinization, work characteristics and their relationships with creative and proactive behaviors. *Journal of Organizational Behavior, 27,* 257–279, doi:10.1002/job.376.

Pattyn, N., Neyt, X., Henderickx, D., and Soetens, E. (2008). Psychophysiological investigation of vigilance decrement: boredom or cognitive fatigue? *Physiology and Behavior, 93,* 369–378, doi:10.1016/j.physbeh.2007.09.016.

Paulsen, R. (2015). Non-work at work: resistance or what? *Organization, 22*, 351–367, doi:10.1177/1350508413515541.

Pekrun, R. (2006). The control-value theory of achievement emotions: assumptions, corollaries, and implications for educational research and practice. *Educational Psychology Review, 18*, 315–341, doi:10.1007/s10648-006-9029-9.

Pekrun, R., Goetz, T., Daniels, L. M., Stupnisky, R. H., and Perry, R. P. (2010). Boredom in achievement settings: exploring control-value antecedents and performance outcomes of a neglected emotion. *Journal of Educational Psychology, 102*, 531–549, doi:10.1037/a0019243.

Pekrun, R., Hall, N. C., Goetz, T., and Perry, R. P. (2014). Boredom and academic achievement: testing a model of reciprocal causation. *Journal of Educational Psychology, 106*, 696–710, doi:10.1037/a0036006.

Perlow, L. A. (1999). The time famine: toward a sociology of work time. *Administrative Science Quarterly, 44*, 57–81, doi:10.2307/2667031.

Reijseger, G., Schaufeli, W. B., Peeters, M. C., Taris, T. W., van Beek, I., and Ouweneel, E. (2013). Watching the paint dry at work: psychometric examination of the Dutch boredom scale. *Anxiety, Stress and Coping, 26*, 508–525, doi:10.1080/10615806.2012.720676.

Renninger, K. A., and Hidi, S. E. (2016). *The Power of Interest for Motivation and Engagement.* New York, NY, USA: Routledge/Taylor and Francis Group.

Rotgans, J. I., and Schmidt, H. G. (2017). Interest development: arousing situational interest affects the growth trajectory of individual interest. *Contemporary Educational Psychology, 49*, 175–184, doi:10.1016/j.cedpsych.2017.02.003.

Roy, D. (1959). "Banana time": job satisfaction and informal interaction. *Human Organization, 18*, 158–168, doi:10.17730/humo.18.4.07j88hr1p4074605.

Russell, J. A. (1980). A circumplex model of affect. *Journal of Personality and Social Psychology, 39*, 1161–1178, doi:10.1037/h0077714.

Ryan, R. M., and Deci, E. L. (2000). Self-determination theory and the facilitation of intrinsic motivation, social development, and well-being. *American Psychologist, 55*, 68–78, doi:10.1037/0003-066X.55.1.68.

Ryan, R. M., and Deci, E. L. (2017). *Self-determination Theory: Basic Psychological Needs in Motivation, Development, and Wellness.* New York, NY, USA: Guilford Publications.

Sackett, A. M., Meyvis, T., Nelson, L. D., Converse, B. A., and Sackett, A. L. (2010). You're having fun when time flies: the hedonic consequences of subjective time progression. *Psychological Science, 21*, 111–117, doi:10.1177/0956797609354832.

Sansone, C. (2009). What's interest got to do with it? Potential trade-offs in the self-regulation of motivation. In J. P. Forgas, R. F. Baumeister, and D. M. Tice (eds), *Psychology of Self-regulation: Cognitive, Affective, and Motivational Processes* (pp. 35–51). New York, NY, USA: Psychology Press.

Sansone, C., and Harackiewicz, J. M. (1996). "I don't feel like it": the function of interest in self-regulation. In L. L. Martin, and A. Tesser (eds), *Striving and Feeling: Interactions Among Goals, Affect, and Self-regulation* (pp. 203–228). Hillsdale, NJ, USA: Lawrence Erlbaum Associates, Inc.

Sansone, C., and Thoman, D. B. (2005). Interest as the missing motivator in self-regulation. *European Psychologist, 10*, 175–186.

Sansone, C., Weir, C., Harpster, L., and Morgan, C. (1992). Once a boring task always a boring task? Interest as a self-regulatory mechanism. *Journal of Personality and Social Psychology, 63*, 379–390, doi:10.1037/0022-3514.63.3.379.

Sawin, D. A., and Scerbo, M. W. (1995). Effects of instruction type and boredom proneness in vigilance: implications for boredom and workload. *Human Factors, 37*, 752–765, doi:10.1518/001872095778995616.

Seli, P., Risko, E. F., and Smilek, D. (2016a). On the necessity of distinguishing between unintentional and intentional mind wandering. *Psychological Science, 27*, 685–691, doi:10.1177/0956797616634068.

Seli, P., Risko, E. F., Smilek, D., and Schacter, D. L. (2016b). Mind-wandering with and without intention. *Trends in Cognitive Sciences, 20*, 605–617, doi:10.1016/j.tics.2016.05.010.

Senécal, C., Lavoie, K., and Koestner, R. (1997). Trait and situational factors in procrastination: an interactional model. *Journal of Social Behavior and Personality, 12*, 889–903.

Sio, U. N., and Ormerod, T. C. (2009). Does incubation enhance problem solving? A meta-analytic review. *Psychological Bulletin, 135*, 94–120, doi:10.1037/a0014212.

Skowronski, M. (2012). When the bored behave badly (or exceptionally). *Personnel Review, 41*, 143–159, doi:10.1108/00483481211200006.

Smallwood, J. (2013). Distinguishing how from why the mind wanders: a process-occurrence framework for self-generated mental activity. *Psychological Bulletin, 139*, 519–535, doi:10.1037/a0030010.

Smallwood, J. (2015). Mind wandering and attention. In J. M. Fawcett, E. F. Risko, and A. Kingston (eds), *The Handbook of Attention* (pp. 233–255). Cambridge, MA, USA: MIT Press.

Smith, C. A., and Ellsworth, P. C. (1985). Patterns of cognitive appraisal in emotion. *Journal of Personality and Social Psychology, 48*, 813–838, doi:10.1037/0022-3514.48.4.813.

Smith, J. L., Wagaman, J., and Handley, I. M. (2009). Keeping it dull or making it fun: task variation as a function of promotion versus prevention focus. *Motivation and Emotion, 33*, 150–160, doi:10.1007/s11031-008-9118-9.

Smith, R. P. (1981). Boredom: a review. *Human Factors, 23*, 329–340, doi:10.1177/001872088102300308.

Sonnentag, S., Pundt, A., and Venz, L. (2017). Distal and proximal predictors of snacking at work: a daily-survey study. *Journal of Applied Psychology, 102*, 151–162, doi:10.1037/apl0000162.

Stawarczyk, D., Majerus, S., Maj, M., Van der Linden, M., and D'Argembeau, A. (2011). Mind-wandering: phenomenology and function as assessed with a novel experience sampling method. *Acta Psychologica, 136*, 370–381, doi:10.1016/j.actpsy.2011.01.002.

Steel, P. (2007). The nature of procrastination: a meta-analytic and theoretical review of quintessential self-regulatory failure. *Psychological Bulletin, 133*, 65–94, doi:10.1037/0033-2909.133.1.65.

Sucala, M. L., Stefan, S., Szentagotai-Tatar, A., and David, D. (2010). Time flies when you expect to have fun: an experimental investigation of the relationship between expectancies and the perception of time progression. *Cognition, Brain, Behavior: An Interdisciplinary Journal, 14*, 231–241.

Svendsen, L. (2005). *A Philosophy of Boredom*. London, UK: Reaktion Books.

Tanaka, A., and Murayama, K. (2014). Within-person analyses of situational interest and boredom: interactions between task-specific perceptions and achievement goals. *Journal of Educational Psychology, 106*, 1122–1134, doi:10.1037/a0036659.

Toohey, P. (2011). *Boredom: A Lively History*. London, UK: Yale University Press.

van der Heijden, G., Schepers, J., and Nijssen, E. (2012). Understanding workplace boredom among white collar employees: temporary reactions and individual differences. *European Journal of Work and Organizational Psychology, 21*, 349–375, doi:10.1080/1359432X.2011.578824.

van Hooff, M. L., and van Hooft, E. A. (2014). Boredom at work: proximal and distal consequences of affective work-related boredom. *Journal of Occupational Health Psychology, 19*, 348–259, doi:10.1037/a0036821.

van Hooff, M. L., and van Hooft, E. A. (2016). Work-related boredom and depressed mood from a daily perspective: the moderating roles of work centrality and need satisfaction. *Work and Stress, 30*, 209–227.

van Hooff, M. L., and van Hooft, E. A. (2017). Boredom at work: towards a dynamic spillover model of need satisfaction, work motivation, and work-related boredom. *European Journal of Work and Organizational Psychology, 26*, 133–148, doi:10.1080/1359432X.2016.1241769.

van Tilburg, W. A., and Igou, E. R. (2011). On boredom and social identity: a pragmatic meaning-regulation approach. *Personality and Social Psychology Bulletin, 37*, 1679–1691, doi:10.1177/0146167211418530.

van Tilburg, W. A., and Igou, E. R. (2012). On boredom: lack of challenge and meaning as distinct boredom experiences. *Motivation and Emotion, 36*, 181–194, doi://dx.doi.org/10.1007/s11031-011-9234-9.

van Tilburg, W. A., and Igou, E. R. (2017). Can boredom help? Increased prosocial intentions in response to boredom. *Self and Identity, 16*, 82–96, doi:10.1080/15298868.2016.1218925.

van Tilburg, W. A., Igou, E. R., and Sedikides, C. (2013). In search of meaningfulness: nostalgia as an antidote to boredom. *Emotion, 13*, 450–461, doi:10.1037/a0030442.

Vodanovich, S. J. (2003). Psychometric measures of boredom: a review of the literature. *The Journal of Psychology, 137*, 569–595, doi:10.1080/00223980309600636.

Vodanovich, S. J., and Rupp, D. E. (1999). Are procrastinators prone to boredom? *Social Behavior and Personality, 27*, 11–16, http://doi:dx.doi.org/10.2224/sbp.1999.27.1.11.

Vodanovich, S. J., and Watt, J. D. (2016). Self-report measures of boredom: an updated review of the literature. *The Journal of Psychology, 150*, 196–228, doi:10.1080/00223980.2015.1074531.

Vogel-Walcutt, J. J., Fiorella, L., Carper, T., and Schatz, S. (2012). The definition, assessment, and mitigation of state boredom within educational settings: a comprehensive review. *Educational Psychology Review, 24*, 89–111, doi:10.1007/s10648-011-9182-7.

Wallbott, H. G. (1998). Bodily expression of emotion. *European Journal of Social Psychology, 28*, 879–896, doi:AID-EJSP901>3.0.CO;2-W.

Wan, H. C., Downey, L. A., and Stough, C. (2014). Understanding non-work presenteeism: relationships between emotional intelligence, boredom, procrastination and job stress. *Personality and Individual Differences, 65*, 86–90, doi:10.1016/j.paid.2014.01.018.

Wardley, K. J. (2012). "A weariness of the flesh": towards a theology of boredom and fatigue. In K. S. Moody and S. Shakespeare (eds), *Intensities: Philosophy, Religion and the Affirmation of Life* (pp. 117–136). Farnham, UK and Burlington, VT, USA: Ashgate Publishing.

Watt, J. D., and Hargis, M. B. (2010). Boredom proneness: its relationship with subjective underemployment, perceived organizational support, and job performance. *Journal of Business and Psychology, 25*, 163–174, doi://dx.doi.org/10.1007/s10869-009-9138-9.

Webb, T. L., Miles, E., and Sheeran, P. (2012). Dealing with feeling: a meta-analysis of the effectiveness of strategies derived from the process model of emotion regulation. *Psychological Bulletin, 138*, 775–808, doi:10.1037/a0027600.

Weiss, H. M., and Cropanzano, R. (1996). Affective events theory: a theoretical discussion of the structure, causes and consequences of affective experiences at work. *Research in Organizational Behavior, 18*, 1–74.

Williams, C. (2015). Bored? Well, don't be. *New Scientist, 227*, 36–41, doi:10.1016/S0262-4079(15)31081-2.

Wrzesniewski, A., and Dutton, J. E. (2001). Crafting a job: revisioning employees as active crafters of their work. *Academy of Management Review, 26*, 179–201, doi:10.5465/AMR.2001.4378011.

Zomorodi, M. (2017). *Bored and Brilliant: How Spacing Out Can Unlock Your Most Productive and Creative Self*. New York, NY, USA: St. Martin's Press.

Zuckerman, M. (1979). *Sensation Seeking: Beyond the Optimal Level of Arousal*. Hillsdale, NJ, USA: Lawrence Erlbaum Associates, Inc, doi:10.1016/0191-8869(80)90044-6.

5. Shaping benign and malicious envy in organizations

Rosanna K. Smith, Tanja S. H. Wingenbach and Richard H. Smith

Life throws us together into organizations in which we typically compete for status, rewards, and recognition. Social comparisons permeate this evolving process from beginning to end, often determining whether we rise or fall relative to others, giving rise to many strong emotions (e.g., Brickman and Bulman, 1977; Smith, 2000). While most organizations try to foster positively-valenced emotions, like an individual's sense of healthy pride in their role in the organization (for instance, through recognition mechanisms such as employee of the month, sales rankings, etc.), the strains created by competition may frequently take over, creating experiences of failure and inferiority—breeding negatively-valenced emotions such as envy, rather than pride (see Smith et al., 2016, for a review).

Consider the unfortunate experience of Sinedu Tadesse, a student at Harvard, who developed intense envy toward another student, Trang Phuong Ho. Although both women entered Harvard in the fall of 1991 with sterling academic records, only Trang was able to thrive once there. Trang maintained a solid GPA, displayed an engaging personality, had a wide network of friends, kept frequent contact with her family, and participated in many activities. Sinedu had mediocre grades, which precluded her chances of getting into medical school, attracted little attention from others despite a deep desire for intimate friendships, was aloof from her family, and engaged in few activities besides her school-work. Sinedu's envy toward Trang unfolded in the intricate, multi-layered competitive backdrop of a complex organization, Harvard, where Sinedu ultimately decided to kill Trang and then to end her own life.

Envy and its role in organizations are our main concerns in this chapter. We will use examples from this well-documented case (Thernstrom, 1998) to illustrate many of our points. Despite its extreme and heart-wrenching nature, the circumstances and situations experienced by

Sinedu provide a useful framework for understanding the elements of envy experienced at the individual level. Further, Harvard, as a complex organization with competitive elements, encapsulates many of the organizational processes examined in this chapter. Overall, however, we hope to show that envy is a natural part of life and that of organizations, and if dealt with constructively, envy can have positive outcomes. This is in keeping with the more general notion that an emotion can be positive or negative in its effects independent of the emotion's valence (e.g., Lindebaum and Jordan, 2012), with the negatively-valenced emotion of envy as a case in point (e.g., Sterling et al., 2016; Sterling and Labianca, 2015, for a review in the organization context).

In this chapter we: (1) review theoretical accounts of why people experience envy, (2) describe two types of envy: benign and malicious, (3) outline how organizations can shape appraisals of deservingness and control which can lead to envy of either the benign or malicious kind, and (4) address how the unwillingness to admit feelings of malicious envy can lead to particularly negative outcomes for organizations.

WHY DO WE FEEL ENVIOUS?

Envy is usually construed as a discrete emotion with distinct features (e.g., Smith and Kim, 2007), though scholars disagree about some of these features (see Smith et al., 2016, for a discussion). However, at its core, envy is a painful recognition of inferiority in reaction to an unflattering social comparison (e.g., Festinger, 1954; Fiske, 2010; Lange et al., in press; Smith, 2000; Tai et al., 2012). It is important to emphasize how *understandable* envy is as a painful reaction to someone else's advantage. Decades of research in psychology provide theoretical and empirical support for the role of social comparison in self-evaluations, upward comparisons creating the conditions for upsetting decreases in self-evaluation (e.g., Festinger, 1954; Goethals and Darley, 1977; Lockwood and Kunda, 1997; Morse and Gergen, 1970; Salovey and Rodin, 1984; Zell and Alicke, 2010; Zell et al., 2017). It is a brute fact of everyday life that another person's relative advantage usually has potent consequences for the likelihood of achieving one's own goals, especially in areas of life of personal relevance and where people compete against others for limited resources—organizations being a common one (see Greenberg et al., 2007 for a review). In an evolutionary sense, envy is a natural response to a thwarting of an important goal (Barrett, 2012; Ellsworth and Smith, 1988; Frijda et al., 1989; Larsen and McGraw,

2014; Russell, 2003), and, to this extent *should* be painful (Barrett, 2012; Tesser, 1988; Tesser et al., 1988).

Evolution is predicated on the fact that people differ in ways that consistently matter in terms of survival and reproductive success (Buss, 1999). Superiority grants individuals better access to resources that lead to adaptive advantage (e.g., Buss, 1999; Frank, 1999; Gilbert, 1992). Since resources are generally limited in competitive situations, comparing one's own standing to that of others can be seen as a sensible strategy to estimate the effort required to gain the desired resource (Hill and Buss, 2008). Without an emotion such as envy, we might find our inferior state *mal*adaptively satisfying. With the experience of envy comes the motivation to seek the valued resource.

Functionalist accounts of emotion assume that each emotion serves the purpose of facilitating goal-directed action (e.g., Keltner and Gross, 1999). Assuming that emotions have a function helps explain why we have emotions. That is, emotions can be seen as solutions to problems and envy can be seen as an adaptive response to disadvantage (Hill and Buss, 2006). From an evolutionary perspective, the envy and the effort that follows from feeling it, should increase the chances of securing survival and reproduction, explaining the adaptive functions of envy. Today, envy might be of particular importance within competitive environments, such as organizations where relative performances may be more salient and on display (e.g., Duffy et al., 2008; Foster, 1972; Obloj and Zenger, 2017; Russell, 1930; Sullivan, 1956; Vecchio, 1997, 2000, 2005). Perhaps just as important in terms of resulting emotions, the raw effects of inferiority (e.g., relative failures with regard to promotion, pay, recognition and praise, etc.) are compounded by, as we noted earlier, the social comparison implications for self-evaluations (e.g., Festinger, 1954; Morse and Gergen, 1970) *based on these relativistic effects*. Not only do social comparisons partially define the meaning of success and failure, but they lead to inferences about abilities—superior relative performance means success (and implies high ability) and inferior performance means failure (and implies low ability) (e.g., Kelley, 1967). The implications for particular self-judgments and overall self-evaluation have been shown to be substantial (e.g., Tesser, 1988), as self-evaluations are shaped by social comparisons.

At Harvard, Sinedu experienced painful failures because others outperformed her both academically and socially. She was turned away from a creative writing class because other students had better sample writings. She gave a poor presentation in a biology class, especially relative to the next presenter who did so brilliantly by contrast. Sinedu also felt that she was boring compared to her many bright and interesting classmates, and as a result, she was ignored. It seemed that every effort she made, whether in forming friendships or pursuing her academic goals, failed in relation to those around her. In other words, these relative comparisons resulted in consequential loss for Sinedu—*because* others were superior at writing, she did not get a chance to take a writing class—*because* others were more engaging, she did not form friendships.

ENVY COMES IN TWO FORMS: MALICIOUS AND BENIGN

Although hostility traditionally has been considered a defining feature of envy proper (e.g., Lange et al., in press; Smith and Kim, 2007), more recent scholarly work give close to equal attention to a non-hostile form of envy (e.g., Falcon, 2015; Sterling et al., 2016; van de Ven et al., 2009). When people use the English term "envy" in everyday life, they may be thinking in terms of *either* the malicious or benign type. Not only do people use the word "envy" in two senses (e.g., Foster, 1972; Neu, 1980; Rawls, 1971; Silver and Sabini, 1978), this distinction is also consistent cross-culturally with many languages having two words for envy, capturing even more cleanly this benign and malicious distinction (van de Ven et al., 2009). Thus, people's sense of the emotion, and how they talk about it, may often diverge from its classic hostile meaning and from how it is assumed to function in social life (see Lindebaum, 2017, for a broad treatment on such divergences more generally). Recent empirical work on envy emphasizes that envy might indeed best be characterized as arising in both of these varieties (but see Cohen-Charash and Larson, 2017). Envy, when it is benign, usually leads to salutary outcomes, such as increased performance, without the negative effects associated with malicious envy (e.g., Belk, 2011; Crusius and Lange, 2014; van de Ven et al., 2009, 2011). Such findings have great practical implications for organizations, which we will return to later in this chapter.

Malicious envy. Classical approaches to envy emphasizing its hostile nature suggest that the awareness of inferiority triggering envy leads to these feelings of ill will as well as a desire to harm the superior individual. In organizations, harm can take many forms, from directly undermining a colleague's performance to simple gossip (Smith et al., 2016). With Sinedu, her sense of inferiority, though emanating from multiple sources, eventually focused on one individual—her roommate, Trang—with Sinedu's hostility becoming so great she concluded that ending Trang's life solved the problem of her inferiority. Many cultural exemplars of the person in the throes of envy, such as Cain in the Bible and Iago in English literature, parallel Sinedu's final actions (e.g., Schoeck, 1969; Smith and Kim, 2007).

While murder is on the extreme end of hostile actions taken because of envy, empirical work confirms in both laboratory (e.g., Salovey and Rodin, 1984; van de Ven et al., 2015) and organizational settings (e.g., Duffy et al., 2012; Schaubroeck and Lam, 2004) that some form of hostility towards the target of envy is common. For example, in a study by Schaubroeck and Lam (2004), employees at a bank who were passed over for promotion came to dislike the coworkers who were promoted, and envy partially mediated this dislike. Other studies provide evidence for a range of negative outcomes, most implying some sort of hostility, from negative gossip (Michelson et al., 2010), social undermining (e.g., Duffy et al., 2012; Eissa and Wyland, 2015), and decreased willingness to help the envied other (Kim et al., 2010) to other undesirable outcomes, such as decreased group performance (Duffy and Shaw, 2000; Khan et al., 2014) and job dissatisfaction (Dogan and Vecchio, 2001; Vecchio, 2005), increased turnover (Duffy and Shaw, 2000) and absenteeism (Duffy and Shaw, 2000).

People who feel envious are usually aware that their strong negative feelings (e.g. resentment, hostility) are not fully legitimate (e.g., Heider, 1958; Silver and Sabini, 1978; Smith and Kim, 2007), however much they would like to be "justified" in their negative feelings towards the envied, especially since norms stress the celebration of other people's successes. Thus, the envying person may harbor additional negative feelings that go unexpressed in direct form, but nonetheless have potent effects—such as fostering actions that undermine the envied person, and, in so doing, harm the organization's goals. However, scholars point out that the motivation to undermine a perceived superior has a certain logic to it (e.g., Foster, 1972; Silver and Sabini, 1978; Sabini and Silver, 1982). Although failing to act submissively to superiors can result in being harmed (e.g., Allan and Gilbert, 2002; Campos et al., 1983), it also makes sense that disadvantaged people should be on the constant lookout for opportunities for self-assertion. While envy is painful, as noted earlier, it may also serve as a kind of adaptive call to action (e.g., Hill and Buss, 2006). Hostility, arguably, gives an edge and focus to this motivation. Possibly, a touch of ill will may break the envying person free of a prevailing submissive frame of mind, override worry about the possible social reprisal, and help focus energy on reducing the feelings of inferiority produced by the presence of the superior other.

Benign envy. As noted earlier, when people use the word envy in the benign sense, they are referring to an unpleasant state but one that is free of hostility. In some ways, it may be close to admiration (e.g., Foster, 1972; Silver and Sabini, 1978; van de Ven, 2017). As a consequence, benign envy tends to have more positive motivational implications for the person feeling it—inspiring the envying person to close the gap between the self and other through self-improvement (Belk, 2011; Crusius and Lange, 2014; van de Ven et al., 2009, 2011), whereas malicious envy tends to motivate the tearing down of the envied person. Thus, while both benign and malicious envy ultimately motivate behavior aimed toward reducing the gap between self and other, benign envy produces more positive outcomes, even leading to increased productivity (Kim et al., 2010; van de Ven et al., 2009).

Envy free of hostility also aligns with common notions of envy (e.g., Fiske, 2010; Parrott, 1991; Rawls, 1971; Smith and Kim, 2007). After all, envy undoubtedly requires recognition that the envied person possesses something of value, and thus, has an aspirational quality. Interestingly, we can look to Sinedu's experience as well to recognize both types of envy. Sinedu initially felt emotions akin to benign envy toward Trang when they first met and became roommates. Sinedu, not yet resigned to failure as a student and as a social being, admired Trang, seeing her as someone to emulate and to aspire to be like. As far as one can glean from her diary entries during this early time, her feelings had little hostile edge to them. She wished dearly to approximate Trang's social ease, and she hoped that they would be the best of friends in the process. However, when Sinedu's emulative strivings proved fruitless, her envy took on a malicious form.

In the next sections, we return at various points to this important distinction between benign and malicious envy within the context of organizations. Specifically, we argue that the experience of envy is in keeping with appraisal theory, in which, cognitive evaluations of a situation play a significant role in the resulting emotional experience (e.g., Frijda et al., 1989; Lazarus, 1991). In particular, we draw from van de Ven and others (2011) who have experimentally demonstrated that the appraisals of "deservingness" and "control" determine the type of envy that is experienced. With Sinedu, her early diary entries document the meticulous efforts she made to copy Trang's and other people's behavior so that she could learn what it takes to be popular and well-liked. The multitude of failed attempts to be and perform more like Trang led to appraisals of comparative deservingness—either that Trang did not seem to deserve her greater popularity or that Sinedu, herself, felt she deserved similar popularity—and lack of control about the situation. Further, these appraisals unfolded within a specific organizational context, namely Harvard, which shaped these comparisons and resulting appraisals. In the following section, we explore how these two elements operate more generally within the organizational context.

APPRAISALS AFFECTING ENVY IN ORGANIZATIONS

Organizations have formal and informal channels in which people compete for resources. The way these channels are structured, and the organizational culture created, can have a profound impact on what social comparisons are made and the nature of their effects on varieties of envy. It is no surprise that Trang provided an especially potent, envy-inducing social comparison for Sinedu. Research shows that people tend to envy those similar to them on comparison-relevant attributes such as age, gender, and aspirational focus (e.g., Festinger, 1954; Goethals and Darley, 1977; Tesser, 1988) as well as those who are "local" and proximal rather than distant and abstract (Alicke et al., 2010; Festinger et al., 1950). Organizations, such as universities, almost ensure such relevant, close-quarters comparisons. Further, the organizational environment influences perceptions of deservingness and control in relation to these comparisons, which subsequently link to whether envy takes on a more benign or malicious form.

PERCEIVED DESERVINGNESS

The awards and resources that organizations provide their members are inevitably distributed unequally. Some people receive more promotions, pay raises, and praise than others. This unequal distribution, in which rewards go to those performing well compared to others, is a ripe environment for feelings of malicious envy to grow (see Floyd et al., 2016, and Sterling and Labianca, 2015, for reviews). One way organizations can minimize the deleterious effects of such unequal distributions is via influencing the extent to which the distributions are perceived to be deserved or fair. For instance, a coworker might receive a promotion over another; however, the extent to which the latter coworker perceives that promotion to be based on merit should play a profound role in the resulting feelings of envy that coworker might hold towards the other.

Indeed, research has shown that appraisal of deservingness (or justice) is one key antecedent to whether an invidious comparison produces benign or malicious envy (e.g., van de Ven et al., 2009). In an earlier study by Smith and others (1994), analysis of accounts of envy showed that feelings of inferiority alone, without some sense of injustice, predicted depressive rather than hostile feelings. In fact, inferiority predicted depressive feelings but not hostility, which indicated that feeling inferior, by itself, is insufficient for the full range of affects often associated with envy. These findings fit in with even earlier empirical work, and broader scholarly thinking, that has largely focused on malicious envy. When we envy, in the malicious sense, we think that the envied person does not quite deserve his or her advantage (e.g., Heider, 1958; Scheler, 1915/1972; Smith, 1991), or at least that our disadvantage is undeserved (Ben-Ze'ev, 2000). Again, one can recognize the resentful flavor of envy in Sinedu's diary entries as she expresses her frustrations over being unable to match the achievements and popularity enjoyed by Trang and others. Sinedu thought she also deserved the things that Trang enjoyed and *resented* Trang's superiority—even though Trang was a well-liked person who had done nothing deliberate to undermine Sinedu's ambitions.

The clear implications for organizations is that they would do well to create conditions where their members believe that decisions are made equitably (e.g., Adams, 1965); using agreed-upon, fair procedures (e.g., Thibaut and Walker, 1975), and in ways that show respect (e.g., Tyler and Blader, 2003). But how easy is it for an organization to achieve the goal of having members believe that they have been fairly treated? Some scholarly work on envy suggests several challenges. Heider (1958) argued that envy contains a sense of injustice, because it will typically occur between people who are similar in terms of background, class, and the like. Psychological "balance" forces require that similar people *should* have similar outcomes, a principle that Heider called an "ought" force in the context of invidious comparisons. Thus, even if objective standards otherwise indicate that another person's advantage is deserved, and despite the presence of fair procedures and dignified treatment, the envious person may feel a sense of injustice, because the envied person's advantage violates what "ought" to be. The expectations driven by similarity, a condition likely to occur in many organizations in which people with similar backgrounds and skills interact with each other, may tend to override efforts by an organization to "justify" variations in outcomes.

The core challenge for organizations may be that disadvantaged members, if they feel envy, can hold a subjectively-held belief that the advantage is unfair, even if normative standards of justice have been met (e.g., Blader et al., 2013; Ng, 2017; Wilkin and Connelly, 2015). Clearly, judgments of subjective fairness will not always follow from unbiased considerations (e.g., van Dijk et al., 2005, 2008). Rather, these judgments can be colored by a number of factors in the workplace, perhaps especially in organizations having a competitive culture (Loden, 1985; Maier, 1999; Walton, 1999). Some evidence suggests that the sense of injustice in envy is qualitatively different from the kind that produces indignation and resentment in their unalloyed forms. It is subjectively derived, and, in many instances of envy, evidence of unfairness is probably nurtured quickly and in a biased manner, increasing over time so that the invidious feelings can seem more legitimate in the privately held views of the envying person (Smith, 1991; Smith et al., 1994).

Given the potential for biased perceptions, organizations probably need to give *extra* attention to creating conditions whereby their members are being fairly treated and that they correctly perceive this fair treatment. Regarding distributive justice, for example, it would be important to make sure that members have accurate perceptions of what type and amount of "inputs" translate into "outcomes" (Adams, 1965), and that members' relative contributions are perceived with minimal bias and distortion (Floyd et al., 2016). Regarding procedural justice, malicious envy might be minimized by steering focus away from raw outcomes and their variability (such as pay, etc.) and instead emphasize the agreed-upon, transparent procedural wisdom employed by the organization to determine these outcomes (Leventhal et al., 1980). With regard to interactional justice, organizations would need to go the extra mile to ensure that members feel they are treated with dignity and respect (Barclay and Kiefer, 2014; Bies and Moag, 1986; Kim et al., 2010; Tyler and Blader, 2003), even if their emotions seem tinged with envy.

In sum, people in organizations can be satisfied (e.g., not maliciously envious) with receiving less than others if they perceive the organizational actions to be fair. Organizations do not have to ensure all people receive equal rewards, but that people perceive the rewards distributed are equitable and just.

PERCEPTIONS OF CONTROL

We thrive in organizations, to the overall benefit of the organization as well, when we have a sense of control. That is, we believe that by working hard, developing skills that help us advance, earn greater pay and success. The research comparing benign and malicious envy highlights perceptions of control as another factor, besides deservingness, that distinguishes the two types of envy (van de Ven et al., 2009). Benign envy, however unpleasant, is associated with a belief that the experienced disadvantage *can be* overcome; malicious envy is associated with a lack of ability and a basic frustration that nothing will change. People feeling malicious envy tend to believe that the desired attribute is beyond their personal reach or power to obtain, feeding into related, self-serving perceptions that the envied person's advantage is undeserved (e.g., Elster, 1998; Neu, 1980; Scheler, 1915/1972; Smith, 1991; Vecchio, 1997). Interestingly, when Sinedu made initial efforts to emulate the successful behavior of Trang and others, she still believed that mastering the intricacies of social interactions was possible for her. This belief probably went a long way to creating benign envy or admiration rather than hostile envy during those early days at Harvard. But as her efforts failed and painful social comparisons took their toll, her emotions turned hostile. Sinedu described "hopelessness of change" and a sense that the situation would never "reverse" while others continued on, "tucked" in their rich lives while she cried "alone in the cold" (Thernstrom, 1998, p. 115).

Perceptions of control are probably related to hostile reactions as well, especially if the lack of control seems unfair. In fact, it is probably the belief in having little control over one's disadvantaged status that tends to go along with a sense of unfairness, if only because it will seem that one should not be blamed for the disadvantage. Thus, the dual effects of perceived low control and perceived unfairness should create especially strong malicious envy (van de Ven et al., 2009) with its signature feature of hostility. In addition, research traditions linking frustration to aggression go back to the monograph by Dollard and others (1939), in which they claimed that all acts of aggression were caused by the blocking of an expected goal, with the resulting frustration leading to aggression. There may be an element of envy-based hostility that has its origin in frustration alone. It is worth noting that Plutchik (1962) argued envy entails a composition of the primary emotions of sadness, surprise, and anger—with frustration being a form of anger and aggression being a way to express anger. Later research by Berkowitz (1989, 1990) argued frustration causes aggression through the eliciting of negative affect that then automatically produces thoughts associated with aggression. Envy would be one such negative affect. Berkowitz also argued that this process need not be a conscious one. Various processes could lead people to see others as causing their frustration and thus encouraging aggression (Fox and Spector, 1999).

Organizations play a key role in their members' sense of control. Specifically, past work shows that how members within an organization interpret the gains, successes, and abilities of the organization's star performers influences whether members feel inspired or defeated (Floyd et al., 2016; Lockwood and Kunda, 1997; van de Ven et al., 2009). At Harvard, channels for development were often limited. For instance, getting into a class was often highly competitive, let alone doing well once in the class. Classes are presumably the place where people of lesser knowledge or ability can learn and grow. But this gateway to development was often closed to those who did not already demonstrate mastery. For example, Thernstrom taught writing at Harvard when Sinedu and Trang attended and was actually the professor who rejected Sinedu from the writing seminar just mentioned (she could choose only 12 from 100 applications!). Thernstrom writes: "The list of successful applicants had been posted on the door. It was an unfortunate system— that is in order to take a writing class to learn you had to prove you were already accomplished—but it was the way many things were done at Harvard" (p. 21). When rewards and resources are distributed unequally in relation to varying levels of performance, it is key that organizations provide ways that those who receive less feel they have control over closing that gap. First, it is essential that organizations are clear on the skills needed to succeed (Molden and Dweck, 2006; van de Ven et al., 2009). This is often an overlooked part of why members become frustrated by the success of others—it is often not clear what exactly is expected of them to similarly succeed. As a result, the only feedback they can reliably see is the success of others, with little sense of the antecedent factors. Second, organizations should provide paths and tools to help members develop those skills. This could be in the form of professional development seminars, training sessions, and formalized mentorship (Dogan and Vecchio 2001; Kluger and DeNisi, 1996). In this way, star performers are more likely to be seen as role models (as opposed to threats) whose path to superior performance can indeed be modeled—thus causing inspiration rather than frustration and resentment in others.

Of course, it might not be possible for organizations to provide the services to develop all their members to achieve equivalent standards of performance. Furthermore, some members might be limited in their ability to attain a certain level of performance even with support from the organization. However, there are several ways that organizations can enhance their members' sense of control over their success even in these cases. The first is to reduce the chances that certain social comparisons will be made, especially between people where the gaps between self and others are large. This strategy has been termed "encapsulation." Encapsulation is the creation of distinct social units (Bedeian, 1995) that reduce contact between individuals of unequal status. For instance, sports teams often have an A and a B team, which bucket people of varying skill levels into groups. In this way, the more likely comparisons are between those with closer differences in ability, skill, and knowledge. These "local" comparisons enhance the likelihood that members of the organization will thrive through their meritorious actions (e.g., Floyd et al., 2016; Sterling and Labianca, 2015). In other words, entry into the "right pond," where one's own relative achievement is more feasible, is one key way people can feel more in control of their outcomes (e.g., Frank, 1985).

Another approach to increasing perceived control is for organizations to maximize the number of ways that any one member can succeed (see Sterling and Labianca, 2015, for suggestions related to social network analysis). For instance, returning to the sports team example, teams often have roles like "social chair," which formalize other dimensions of an organization's functioning beyond just athleticism. In this way, the organization expands its definition of success and value to traits that its members might more naturally possess, and thereby enhance their sense of control and contribution to the organization. In a similar vein, organizational behavior scholars have identified two basic ways that organizations can be structured: vertically or horizontally (Ostroff and Smith, 1992). In a vertical structure, rewards and status exist on a continuum where those in the higher ranks possess more. This promotes a more "zero-sum" logic to the organization—you are at the top or not. In horizontal structure, people are given more equivalent ability to provide input and value, distributed in a more "ecosystem" manner—with each member framed as equally valuable to the whole. This expands the definition of success and allows members of an organizational to feel more in control of their value to the organization.

A CHALLENGE TO MANAGING ENVY: FEW ADMIT TO THE FEELING

While envy is a pervasive emotion in organizations and in life more generally, it is rarely explicitly admitted to or discussed, especially if its malicious form is any way implied (e.g., Foster, 1972; Silver and Sabini, 1978; Sabini and Silver, 1982; Smith and Kim, 2007). Indeed, as noted earlier, envy is an example of an emotion in which everyday conceptions of its function may diverge from how the emotion is understood by those who study it (e.g., Lindebaum, 2017). One of the authors of this chapter (R. H. Smith) attended an international conference on envy in the workplace (International Symposium, 2011) in which many managers, company leaders, as well as therapists addressing workplace issues attended. An informal survey of those attending revealed no evidence that anyone had ever experienced an occasion in which a member, employee, or client presented a personal problem using the term "envy." This was true even though their actual problems were often suffused with the challenges associated with envy. In this section, we discuss why envy is underreported both at the level of the self and the organization, and the consequences of this lack of acknowledgment.

Perhaps more than any other emotion, envy often operates unrecognized (Foster, 1972; Schoeck, 1969; Silver and Sabini, 1978). Further, people do not simply avoid admitting the feeling to others, but they seem loath to acknowledge the feeling in private as well (Smith, 2004; Smith and Kim, 2007). Anthropologist George Foster argued that these tendencies to hide or repress envy may be largely *because* envy is so painful and self-threatening (particularly malicious envy). Foster (1972) writes:

> *"It is probably because of the enormous hold that envy has on us, and a measure of the inner depths to which it stirs us, that we are reluctant to admit to envy, and to discuss it openly. … Yet envy is with us all the time: it surrounds us, and it penetrates to our innermost being. For more often than we consciously realize, we feel some degree of distress either because we recognize that we are fortunate enough to have something desirable not shared by those around us, or because we see that others have something we might also like to have. But, we are reluctant to attribute such feelings to envy because few things are more destructive to our self-image. We can admit to feelings of guilt, shame, false pride, and even momentary greed without necessarily damaging our egos. We can even safely confess to occasional overpowering feelings of anger, our self-image does not necessarily suffer as long as we can justify that anger. … Envy is untenable and unacceptable"* (pp. 165–166).

As far as we can glean from Thernstrom's account, Sinedu initially appeared unaware of her envious feelings. To the extent that she did, she probably construed them as benign. Later, she appeared to recognize her envy, but, ultimately, this awareness faded after Trang rejected her. But, until this later stage, she feared people would believe that she was envious. She was careful to avoid giving any appearance of this feeling. She feared the ridicule that would result. To prevent the leaking of her envious feelings, she tried to present herself as powerful and confident. Revealing her insecurities and any hint of envy would have been to "dishonor" herself. People would have felt "superior" and would have "gloated." Letting others "cross the boundary" would have resulted in her being the "butt" of their jokes (Thernstrom, 1998, pp. 99–100). She largely hid her envy; we are only privy to Sinedu's feelings because of the public records that allowed Thernstrom to access her diary. Even these entries are subject to self-distortions, especially as her experience evolved.

Another way to understand the lengths that people go to hide their envy, to themselves as well as to others, is through the intimate connection between envy and shame. Shame is the "painful feeling of having lost the respect of others because of the improper behavior, incompetence, etc., of oneself" (*Webster's New World Dictionary*, 1982, p. 1308). Shame is similar to envy in the sense that it also involves a sense of inferiority (e.g., Cheung et al., 2004). In moral cases of shame, the inferiority results from wrongful behavior, but shame also results from non-moral failings (see Gilbert, 1998 for a review)—that is, one can be ashamed for a failing or an attribute that is beyond one's control (e.g., shame over a physical deformity or low ability). With shame, the "defective" aspect of the self is often highlighted by public scrutiny (or the implicit evaluation of another person) (e.g., Ausubel, 1955; Smith et al., 2002). Thus, to the extent that one's envy is shameful, it is all the more likely to be denied or hidden.

Foster (1972), along with most other scholars, also emphasizes that another part of the problem with admitting envy stems from societal norms that typically dictate we should rejoice in the good fortunes of others, especially our close friends and colleagues. In most cultures, envy is considered a sin (Schoeck, 1969; Silver and Sabini, 1978). Envious feelings are regarded with extreme disapproval (Heider, 1958; Parrott and Smith, 1993), especially if they reveal ill will. Consequently, when we feel envy, shame often compounds the problem—probably aggravating feelings of inferiority that much more. We feel envy, and then we can feel ashamed of our envy, and, perhaps, further shame as well, particularly if cultural norms run counter to expressing envy.

Because people are unlikely to admit to their envy, malicious envy especially, envious reactions are likely to emerge in defensive ways. Derogating a rival (usually on moral dimensions, e.g., "she's a show-off") may serve as a defense against the threat to the self posed by envy—as negative feelings about the self become projected onto the advantaged person (Schaubroeck and Lam, 2004). This possibility is consistent with research in other domains showing that self-image threats lead people to denigrate others to restore a favorable self-image (e.g., Fein and Spencer, 1997). Perhaps, shame-infused envy might also exacerbate envious hostility. Although one might predict that persistent focus on painful inferiority would create largely depressive reactions in which anger is directed inward (Smith et al., 1994)—and part of the shame response is of this kind—the course that shame takes seems to lead outward as well. People feeling shame can lash out at others (e.g., Tangney and Salovey, 1999; Tangney and Dearing, 2002), creating a "shame-rage" spiral (e.g., Scheff and Retzinger, 1991). The public aspect of shame may aggravate this process. To the extent that inferiority is put on public display by another person, anger can be directed at this agent, redirecting focus away from the inferiority of the self to the hurtful action of the "shamer," who may be construed as engaging in inappropriate humiliation (Combs et al., 2010). While it is unclear if others were explicitly shaming Sinedu, her diaries documented painful feelings of public humiliation in her failed attempts to perform both in social and classroom settings alongside her more competent peers. These feelings of shame eventually transmuted into anger and rage toward those peers.

Certainly, some people will recognize their malicious envy and sense that their private, subjective sense of injustice is an inadequate basis for their hostility and begrudging the envied person's advantage. Although this knowledge is threatening, positive, constructive responses are possible. Envying persons may sometimes use the emotion as a motivation to improve (Schaubroeck and Lam, 2004) or, alternatively, select other domains upon which to focus their energies and then to link with their self-worth (e.g., Tesser, 1988). Although efforts to improve the self may lead to a chronic focus on one's inferiority, which might create depressive outcomes, at least the general response will lack destructive hostility (Smith, 2000). But defensive reactions are probably more likely (e.g., Aronson, 1992; Harmon-Jones, 2000; Miller and Ross, 1975; Montaldi, 2000; Paulhus et al., 1997; Tesser, 2000). People feeling envy will probably find ways to justify their hostility, such as by making downward comparisons (Gibbons and Gerrard, 1991; Wills, 1981), on moral domains, as Montaldi (2000) suggests. In addition, a private, subjective sense of injustice (not self-labeled with the delegitimizing word of "envy") may tend to predominate, fostering a strong sense of being unfairly treated (Scheler, 1915/1972).

Because people feeling malicious envy are likely to sense that open hostility violates social norms, they will probably avoid acting on their hostility in direct ways. In some cases, their actions will suggest the opposite of their feelings, so that others will not attribute these actions to envy (e.g., Foster, 1972; Smith, 2004). Possibly, backbiting and negative gossip directed at the envied coworker will be the typical path (Wert and Salovey, 2004), and secret *schadenfreude* if misfortune befalls the envied person (Smith et al., 1996). As their envy evolves, they might try to convince others of the "unfair" advantage of the envied person, further legitimating their hostility. If so, the attribution of envy will seem remote, transmuted into righteous indignation, perhaps leading to open, unapologetic action designed to undermine the envied person (Hoogland et al., 2016).

CONCLUSION

The shameful nature of envy, its malicious form, in particular, presents special challenges for organizations. As discussed before, the tendency for envy to be unacknowledged can lead to its transmutation into unproductive, malicious actions by the person who feels envy towards the envied other. One way to bring together the various strategies, such as those already noted with regard to the appraisals of deservingness and control, organizations might take to channel envy in the benign direction through attention to the organizational culture. Organizational culture is defined as a complex set of values, beliefs, assumptions, and symbols that define a way a firm conducts itself (Barney, 1986). Prior work has acknowledged the central role organizational culture plays in the emergence of envy (Floyd et al., 2016). While culture is a multifaceted phenomenon with many variables at play, we think organizations can make efforts towards avoiding malicious envy and its negative outcomes, by first consciously addressing the social norms that deny and repress the natural existence of envy in everyday and in organizational life. Prior work looking at how to combat shame around stigmatized groups has found that normalizing seemingly taboo behavior or feelings reduces shame (Adler-Nissen, 2014; Hinshaw, 2009). For instance, if it were made explicit in an organization that envy, in its various forms, is a natural human emotion that is felt frequently, the compounding effects of shame should attenuate. Further, past work has found that merely giving a name to a seemingly negative emotion can create a sense of control in the person experiencing it (Lieberman et al., 2007). Finally, besides normalizing the existence of envy and providing explicit labeling language, organizations could also provide guides on how members can self-manage the envy towards its more beneficial benign form, as well as toward admiration and emulation (e.g., Lockwood and Kunda, 1997), as opposed to its malicious form (van de Ven, 2017).

We do not wish to underestimate the challenges presented by envy. Certain efforts to positively influence organizational culture can have both subtle and unintended effects on the formation of envy. So, we conclude with another sobering example from Thernstrom's book. Harvard was a very selective organization in the mid-1990s (Thernstrom, 1998). At the time of Sinedu and Trang's acceptance, the acceptance rate was the lowest in the world at 14%. Interestingly, some leaders at Harvard were aware of the potential problems that could arise with so many competitive people put alongside each other. To combat this, attempts were made to create a culture in which all members felt "endowed with specialness." At the start of a new class, the Harvard president assured the entering class that Harvard "made no admissions mistakes" and that each student had been deliberately "chosen." This was intended to create a culture in which students felt like they were included within a special set of people. They were the insiders. One might think that this sense of specialness would reduce tendencies to feel envy. Generally, for example, high self-esteem is negatively correlated with state (Smallets et al., 2016; Smith et al., 1999), and dispositional envy (Smith et al., 1999). However, according to Thernstrom, an *unintended* side effect of this endowment of specialness was that there was an assumption that Harvard students did not need help – that they were all, to some extent, "perfect." When Sinedu became painfully aware that she was not measuring up to the image promoted by the university, she began to feel like an outsider within a set of supposed insiders. The desire to create "insider" status is true not just of Harvard, but of many other university and company cultures (e.g., Zappos, Google, etc). It should further be noted though that whenever transitions take place (from one school to another, to university, or into a different company etc.), a new rank order gets established, providing a breeding ground for envy. It is therefore imperative to address these natural occurrences by spreading awareness and conversation about the topic, ideally implemented and facilitated by the organizations themselves.

REFERENCES

Adams, J. S. (1965). Inequity in social exchange. *Advances in Experimental Social Psychology*, 2, 267–299.

Adler-Nissen, R. (2014). Stigma management in international relations: trans- gressive identities, norms, and order in international society. *International Organization*, 68(1), 143–176.

Alicke, M. D., Zell, E., and Bloom, D. L. (2010). Mere categorization and the frog-pond effect. *Psychological Science*, 21(2), 174–177.

Allan, S., and Gilbert, P. (2002). Anger and anger expression in relation to perceptions of social rank, entrapment and depressive symptoms. *Personality and Individual Differences*, 32(3), 551–565.

Aronson, E. (1992). The return of the repressed: dissonance theory makes a comeback. *Psychological Inquiry*, 3(4), 303–311.

Ausubel, D. P. (1955). Relationships between shame and guilt in the socialization process. *Psychological Review*, 62(5), 378–390.

Barclay, L. J., and Kiefer, T. (2014). Approach or avoid? Exploring overall justice and the differential effects of positive and negative emotions. *Journal of Management*, 40(7), 1857–1898.

Barney, J. B. (1986). Organizational culture: can it be a source of sustained competitive advantage? *Academy of Management Review, 11*(3), 656–665.

Barrett, L. F. (2012). Emotions are real. *Emotion, 12*(3), 413–429.

Bedeian, A. G. (1995). Workplace envy. *Organizational Dynamics, 23*(4), 49–56.

Belk, R. (2011). Benign envy. *Academy of Marketing Science Review, 1*(3), 117–134.

Ben-Ze'ev, A. (2000). *The Subtlety of Emotions.* Cambridge, MA, USA: MIT Press.

Berkowitz, L. (1989). Frustration-aggression hypothesis: examination and reformulation. *Psychological Bulletin, 106*(1), 59–73.

Berkowitz, L. (1990). On the formation and regulation of anger and aggression: a cognitive-neoassociationistic analysis. *American Psychologist, 45*(4), 494–503.

Bies, R. J., and Moag, J. S. (1986). Interactional justice: communication criteria of fairness. In R. J. Lewicki, B. H. Sheppard, and M. H. Bazerman (eds), *Research on Negotiation in Organizations* (pp. 289–319). Greenwich, CT, USA: JAI Press.

Blader, S. L., Wiesenfeld, B. M., Fortin, M., and Wheeler-Smith, S. L. (2013). Fairness lies in the heart of the beholder: how the social emotions of third parties influence reactions to injustice. *Organizational Behavior and Human Decision Processes, 121*(1), 62–80.

Brickman, P., and Bulman, R. J. (1977). Pleasure and pain in social comparison. In J. M. Suls and R. L. Miller (eds), *Social Comparison Processes: Theoretical and Empirical Perspectives* (pp. 149–186). Washington, DC, USA: Hemisphere.

Buss, D. M. (1999). *Evolutionary Psychology: The New Science of the Mind.* Boston, MA, USA: Allyn and Bacon.

Campos, J. J., Barrett, K. C., Lamb, M. E., Goldsmith, H. H., and Stenberg, C. (1983). Socioemotional development. In M. M. Haith and J. J. Campos (Vol. eds), *Handbook of Child Psychology: Vol. 2. Infancy and Developmental Psychology* (pp. 783–915). New York, NY, USA: John Wiley.

Cheung, M. P., Gilbert, P., and Irons, C. (2004). An exploration of shame, social rank and rumination in relation to depression. *Personality and Individual Differences, 36*(5), 1143–1153.

Cohen-Charash, Y., and Larson, E. C. (2017). An emotion divided: studying envy is better than studying "benign" and "malicious" envy. *Current Directions in Psychological Science, 26*(2), 174–183.

Combs, D. J. Y, Campbell, G., Jackson, M., and Smith, R. H. (2010). Exploring the consequences of humiliating a moral transgressor. *Basic and Applied Social Psychology, 32*, 128–143.

Crusius, J., and Lange, J. (2014). What catches the envious eye? Attentional biases within malicious and benign envy. *Journal of Experimental Social Psychology, 55*, 1–11.

Dogan, K., and Vecchio, R. P. (2001). Managing envy and jealousy in the workplace. *Compensation and Benefits Review, 33*(2), 57–64.

Dollard, J., Miller, N. E., Doob, L.W., Mowrer, O. H., and Sears, R. R. (1939). *Frustration and Aggression.* New Haven, CT, USA: Yale University Press.

Duffy, M. K., and Shaw, J. D. (2000). The Salieri syndrome: consequences of envy in groups. *Small Group Research, 31*(1), 3–23.

Duffy, M. K., Scott, K. L., Shaw, J. D., Tepper, B. J., and Aquino, K. (2012). A social context model of envy and social undermining. *Academy of Management Journal, 55*(3), 643–666.

Duffy, M. K., Shaw, J. D., and Schaubroeck, J. M. (2008). Envy in organizational life. In R. Smith (ed.), *Envy: Theory and Research* (pp. 167–189). Oxford, UK: Oxford University Press.

Eissa, G., and Wyland, R. (2015). Keeping up with the Joneses: the role of envy, relationship conflict, and job performance in social undermining. *Journal of Leadership and Organizational Studies, 23(1)*, 55–65.

Ellsworth, P. C., and Smith, C. A. (1988). From appraisal to emotion: differences among unpleasant feelings. *Motivation and Emotion, 12*(3), 271–302.

Elster, J. (1998). *Alchemies of the Mind: Rationality and the Emotions.* Cambridge, UK: Cambridge University Press.

envy (2017). In oxforddictionaries.com. Retrieved June 12, 2017, from http://en.oxforddictionaries.com/definitionenvy.

Falcon, R. G. (2015). Is envy categorical or dimensional? An empirical investigation using taxometric analysis. *Emotion, 15*(6), 694–698.

Fein, S., and Spencer, S. J. (1997). Prejudice as self-image maintenance: affirming the self through derogating others. *Journal of Personality and Social Psychology, 73*(1), 31–44.

Festinger, L. (1954). A theory of social comparison processes. *Human Relations, 7*(2), 117–140.

Festinger, L., Schachter, S., and Back, K. (1950). *Social Pressures in Informal Groups: A Study of Human Factors in Housing.* New York, NY, USA: Harper.

Fiske, S. T. (2010). Envy up, scorn down: how comparison divides us. *American Psychologist, 65,* 698–706.

Floyd, T. M., Hoogland, C. E., and Smith, R. H. (2016). The role of leaders in managing envy and its consequences for competition in organizations. In C. Peus, S. Braun, and B. Schyns (eds), *Monographs in Leadership and Management, Vol. 8: Leadership Lessons from Compelling Contexts* (pp. 129–156). Emerald Group Publishing Limited.

Foster, G. M. (1972). The anatomy of envy: a study in symbolic behavior. *Current Anthropology, 13,* 165–202.

Fox, S., and Spector, P. E. (1999). A model of work frustration–aggression. *Journal of Organizational Behavior, 20,* 915–931.

Frank, R. H. (1985). *Choosing the Right Pond: Human Behavior and the Quest for Status.* New York, NY, USA: Oxford University Press.

Frank, R. H. (1999). *Luxury Fever.* New York, NY, USA: The Free Press.

Frijda, N. H., Kuipers, P., and ter Schure, E. (1989). Relations among emotion, appraisal, and emotional action readiness. *Journal of Personality and Social Psychology, 57*(2), 212–228.

Gibbons, F. X., and Gerrard, M. (1991). Downward comparison and coping with threat. In J. M. Suls and T. A. Wills (eds), *Social Comparison: Contemporary Theory and Research* (pp. 317–346). Hillsdale, NJ, USA: Lawrence Erlbaum Associates, Inc.

Gilbert, P. (1992). *Depression: The Evolution of Powerlessness*. New York, NY, USA: Routledge.

Gilbert, P. (1998). What is shame? Some core issues and controversies. In P. Gilbert and B. Andrews (eds), *Shame: Interpersonal Behavior, Psychopathology, and Culture* (pp. 3–38). New York, NY, USA: Oxford University Press.

Goethals, G., and Darley, J. M. (1977). Social comparison theory: an attributional approach. In J. M. Suls and R. L. Miller (eds), *Social Comparison Processes: Theoretical and Empirical Perspectives* (pp. 259–278). Washington, DC, USA: Hemisphere Publishing Co.

Greenberg, J., Ashton-James, C., and Ashkanasy, N. (2007). Social comparison processes in organizations. *Organizational Behavior and Human Decision Processes*, *102*, 22–41.

Harmon-Jones, E. (2000). A cognitive dissonance theory perspective on the role of emotion in the maintenance and change of beliefs and attitudes. In N. H. Frijda, A. S. R. Manstead, and S. Bem (eds), *Emotions and Belief: How Feelings Influence Thoughts* (pp. 185–211). New York, NY, USA: Cambridge University Press.

Heider, F. (1958). *The Psychology of Interpersonal Relations*. New York, NY, USA: John Wiley.

Hill, S. E., and Buss, D. M. (2006). Envy and positional bias in the evolutionary psychology of management. *Managerial and Decision Economics*, *27*(2–3), 131–143.

Hill, S. E., and Buss, D. M. (2008). The evolutionary psychology of envy. In R. H. Smith (ed.), *Series in Affective Science. Envy: Theory and Research* (pp. 60–70). New York, NY, USA: Oxford University Press.

Hinshaw, S. P. (2009). *The Mark of Shame: Stigma of Mental Illness and An Agenda for Change*. New York, NY, USA: Oxford University Press.

Hoogland, C. E., Thielke, S. M., and Smith, R. H. (2016). Envy as an evolving episode. In U. Merlone, M. Duffy, M. Perini, and R.H. Smith (eds) *Envy at Work and in Organizations: Research, Theory, and Applications*. New York, NY, USA: Oxford University Press.

International Symposium (2011). *Envy at Work*. Turin, Italy.

Kelley, H. H. (1967). Attribution theory in social psychology. In D. Levine (ed.), *Nebraska Symposium on Motivation* (pp. 192–238). Lincoln, NE, USA: University of Nebraska Press.

Keltner, D., and Gross, J. J. (1999). Functional accounts of emotions. *Cognition and Emotion*, *13*(5), 467–480.

Khan, A. K., Quratulain, S., and Bell, C. M. (2014). Episodic envy and counterproductive work behaviors: is more justice always good? *Journal of Organizational Behavior*, *35*, 128–144.

Kim, S., O'Neill, J. W., and Cho, H. M. (2010). When does an employee not help coworkers? The effect of leader–member exchange on employee envy and organizational citizenship behavior. *International Journal of Hospitality Management*, *29*(3), 530–537.

Kluger, A. N., and DeNisi, A. (1996). The effects of feedback interventions on performance: a historical review, a meta-analysis, and a preliminary feedback intervention theory. *Psychological Bulletin*, *119*(2), 254–284.

Lange, J., Weidman, A. C., and Crusius, J. (in press). The painful duality of envy: evidence for an integrative theory and a meta-analysis on the relation of envy and schadenfreude. *Journal of Personality and Social Psychology.*

Larsen, J. T., and McGraw, A. P. (2014). The case for mixed emotions. *Social and Personality Psychology Compass, 8*(6), 263–274.

Lazarus, R. S. (1991). *Emotion and Adaptation.* New York, NY, USA: Oxford University Press.

Leventhal, G. S., Karuza, J., and Fry, W. R. (1980). Beyond fairness: a theory of allocation preferences. In G. Mikula (ed.), *Justice and Social Interaction* (pp. 167–218). New York, NY, USA: Springer-Verlag.

Lieberman, M. D., Eisenberger, N. I., Crockett, M. J., Tom, S. M., Pfeifer, J. H., and Way, B. M. (2007). Putting feelings into words: affect labeling disrupts amygdala activity in response to affective stimuli. *Psychological Science, 18*(5), 421–428.

Lindebaum, D. (2017). *Emancipation Through Emotion Regulation at Work.* Cheltenham, UK and Northampton, MA, USA: Edward Elgar Publishing.

Lindebaum, D., and Jordan, P. J. (2012). Positive emotions, negative emotions, or utility of discrete emotions? *Journal of Organizational Behavior, 33*(7), 1027–1030.

Lockwood, P., and Kunda, Z. (1997). Superstars and me: predicting the impact of role models on the self. *Journal of Personality and Social Psychology, 73*(1), 91–103.

Loden, M. (1985). *Feminine Leadership, or, How to Succeed in Business Without Being One of the Boys.* New York, NY, USA: Times Books.

Maier, M. (1999). On the gendered substructure of organization: dimensions and dilemmas of corporate masculinity. In G. N. Powell (ed.), *Handbook of Gender and Work*, (pp. 69–94). Thousand Oaks, CA, USA: Sage.

Michelson, G., van Iterson, A., and Waddington, K. (2010). Gossip in organizations: contexts, consequences, and controversies. *Group and Organization Management, 37*(4), 371–390.

Miller, D. T., and Ross, M. (1975). Self-serving biases in the attribution of causality: fact or fiction? *Psychological Bulletin, 82*(2), 213–225.

Molden, D. C., and Dweck, C. S. (2006). Finding "meaning" in psychology: a lay theories approach to self-regulation, social perception, and social development. *American Psychologist, 61*(3), 192–203.

Montaldi, D. F. (2000). *Dispositional Envy: Envy Types and Schemas.* Unpublished dissertation.

Morse, S., and Gergen, K. J. (1970). Social comparison, self-consistency, and the concept of self. *Journal of Personality and Social Psychology, 16*(1), 148–156.

Neu, J. (1980). Jealous thoughts. In A. O. Rorty (ed.), *Explaining Emotions* (pp. 425–463). Berkeley, CA, USA: University of California Press.

Ng, T. W. (2017). Can idiosyncratic deals promote perceptions of competitive climate, felt ostracism, and turnover? *Journal of Vocational Behavior, 99*, 118–131.

Obloj, T., and Zenger, T. (2017). Organization design, proximity, and productivity responses to upward social comparison. *Organization Science, 28*(1), 1–18.

Ostroff, F., and Smith, D. (1992). The horizontal organization. *The McKinsey Quarterly, 1*, 148–168.

Parrott, W. G. (1991). The emotional experience of envy and jealousy. In P. Salovey (ed.), *The Psychology of Jealousy and Envy* (pp. 3–30). New York, NY, USA: Guilford Press.

Parrott, W. G., and Smith, R. H. (1993). Distinguishing the experiences of envy and jealousy. *Journal of Personality and Social Psychology, 64*(6), 906–920.

Paulhus, D. L., Fridhandler, B., and Hayes, S. (1997). Psychological defense: contemporary theory and research. In J. A. Johnson, R. Hogan, S. Briggs (eds), *Handbook of Personality Psychology* (pp. 543–579). San Diego, CA, USA: Academic Press.

Plutchik, R. (1962). *The Emotions: Facts, Theories, and a New Model.* New York, NY, USA: Random House.

Rawls, J. (1971). *A Theory of Justice.* Cambridge, MA, USA: Harvard University Press.

Russell, B. (1930). *The Conquest of Happiness.* New York, NY, USA: Liveright.

Russell, J. A. (2003). Core affect and the psychological construction of emotion. *Psychological Review, 110*(1), 145–172.

Sabini, J., and Silver, M. (1982). Some senses of subjective. In P. F Secord (ed.), *Explaining Human Behavior* (pp. 71–91). Beverly Hills, CA, USA: Sage.

Salovey, P., and Rodin, J. (1984). Some antecedents and consequences of social-comparison jealousy. *Journal of Personality and Social Psychology, 47*(4), 780–792.

Schaubroeck, J., and Lam, S. S. (2004). Comparing lots before and after: promotion rejectees' invidious reactions to promotees. *Organizational Behavior and Human Decision Processes, 94*(1), 33–47.

Scheff, T. J., and Retzinger, S. M. (1991). *Emotion and Violence: Shame and Rage in Destructive Conflicts.* Lexington, MA, USA: Lexington Books.

Scheler, M. (1972). *Ressentiment* (L. A. Coser, ed., W. W. Holdhein, Trans.). Glencoe, IL, USA: Free Press. (Original work published 1915).

Schoeck, H. (1969). *Envy: A Theory of Social Behavior.* New York, NY, USA: Harcourt, Brace, and World.

Silver, M., and Sabini, J. (1978). The perception of envy. *Social Psychology Quarterly, 41*(2), 105–117.

Smallets, S., Streamer, L., Kondrak, C. L., and Seery, M. D. (2016). Bringing you down versus bringing me up: discrepant versus congruent high explicit self-esteem differentially predict malicious and benign envy. *Personality and Individual Differences, 94*, 173–179.

Smith, R. H. (1991). Envy and the sense of injustice. In P. Salovey (ed.), *The Psychology of Jealousy and Envy* (pp. 79–99). New York, NY, USA: Guilford Press.

Smith, R. H. (2000). Assimilative and contrastive emotional reactions to upward and downward social comparisons. In J. Suls and L. Wheeler (eds), *Handbook of Social Comparison* (pp. 173–200). Boston, MA, USA: Springer.

Smith, R. H. (2004). Envy and its transmutations. In L. Z. Tiedens and C. W. Leach (eds), *The Social Life of Emotions* (pp. 43–63). Cambridge, UK: Cambridge University Press.

Smith, R. H., and Kim, S. H. (2007). Comprehending envy. *Psychological Bulletin, 133*(1), 46–64.

Smith, R. H., Merlone, U., and Duffy, M. (eds) (2016). *Envy at Work and in Organizations*. New York, NY, USA: Oxford University Press.

Smith, R. H., Parrott, W. G., Diener, E. F., Hoyle, R. H., and Kim, S. H. (1999). Dispositional envy. *Personality and Social Psychology Bulletin*, *25*(8), 1007–1020.

Smith, R. H., Parrott, W. G., Ozer, D., and Moniz, A. (1994). Subjective injustice and inferiority as predictors of hostile and depressive feelings in envy. *Personality and Social Psychology Bulletin*, *20*(6), 705–711.

Smith, R. H., Turner, T. J., Garonzik, R., Leach, C. W., Urch-Druskat, V., and Weston, C. M. (1996). Envy and schadenfreude. *Personality and Social Psychology Bulletin*, *22*(2), 158–168.

Smith, R. H., Webster, J. M., Parrott, W. G., and Eyer, H. L. (2002). The role of public exposure in the experience of moral and nonmoral shame and guilt. *Journal of Personality and Social Psychology, 83*(1), 138–159.

Sterling, C. M., and Labianca, G. J. (2015). Costly comparisons: managing envy in the workplace. *Organizational Dynamics*, *4*(44), 296–305.

Sterling, C. M., van de Ven, N., and Smith, R. H. (2016). The two faces of envy: studying benign and malicious envy in the workplace. In U. Merlone, M. K. Duffy, M. Perini, and R. H. Smith (eds), *Envy at Work and in Organizations: Research, Theory, and Applications*. New York, NY, USA: Oxford University Press.

Sullivan, H. S. (1956). *Clinical Studies in Psychiatry*. New York, NY, USA: W. W. Norton, Inc.

Tai, K., Narayanan, J., and McAllister, D. J. (2012). Envy as pain: rethinking the nature of envy and its implications for employees and organizations. *The Academy of Management Review*, *37*(1), 107–129.

Tangney, J. P., and Dearing, R. L. (2002). *Shame and Guilt*. New York, NY, USA: Guilford Press.

Tangney, J. P., and Salovey, P. (1999). Problematic social emotions: shame, guilt, jealousy, and envy. In R. M. Kowalski and M. R. Leary (eds), *The Social Psychology of Emotional and Behavioral Problems: Interfaces of Social and Clinical Psychology* (pp. 167–195). Washington, DC, USA: American Psychological Association.

Tesser, A. (1988). Toward a self-evaluation maintenance model of social behavior. In L. Berkowitz (ed.), *Advances in Experimental Social Psychology: Vol. 21* (pp. 181–227). San Diego, CA, USA: Academic Press.

Tesser, A. (2000). On the confluence of self-esteem maintenance mechanisms. *Personality and Social Psychology Review*, *4*(4), 290–299.

Tesser, A., Millar, M., and Moore, J. (1988). Some affective consequences of social comparison and reflection processes: the pain and pleasure of being close. *Journal of Personality and Social Psychology*, *54*(1), 49–61.

Thernstrom, M. (1998). *Halfway Heaven: Diary of a Harvard Murder*. New York, NY, USA: Plume.

Thibaut, J., and Walker, L. (1975). *Procedural Justice: A Psychological Analysis*. Hillsdale, NJ, USA: Lawrence Erlbaum Associates.

Tyler, T. R., and Blader, S. L. (2003). The group engagement model: procedural justice, social identity, and cooperative behavior. *Personality and Social Psychology Review*, *7*(4), 349–361.

van de Ven, N. (2017). Envy and admiration: emotion and motivation following upward social comparison. *Cognition and Emotion*, *31*(1), 193–200.
van de Ven, N., Hoogland, C. E., Smith, R. H., van Dijk, W. W., Breugelmans, S. M., and Zeelenberg, M. (2015). When envy leads to schadenfreude. *Cognition and Emotion*, *29*(6), 1007–1025.
van de Ven, N., Zeelenberg, M., and Pieters, R. (2009). Leveling up and down: the experiences of benign and malicious envy. *Emotion*, *9*(3), 419–429.
van de Ven, N., Zeelenberg, M., and Pieters, R. (2011). The envy premium in product evaluation. *Journal of Consumer Research*, *37*(6), 984–998.
van Dijk, W. W., Goslinga, S., and Ouwerkerk, J. W. (2008). Impact of responsibility for a misfortune on schadenfreude and sympathy: further evidence. *The Journal of Social Psychology*, *148*(5), 631–636.
van Dijk, W. W., Ouwerkerk, J. W., Goslinga, S., and Nieweg, M. (2005). Deservingness and schadenfreude. *Cognition and Emotion*, *19*(6), 933–939.
Vecchio, R. P. (1997). It's not easy being green: jealousy and envy in the workplace. In R. P. Vecchio (ed.), *Leadership: Understanding the Dynamics of Power and Influence in Organizations* (pp. 542–562). Notre Dame, IN, USA: University of Notre Dame Press.
Vecchio, R. P. (2000). Negative emotion in the workplace: employee jealousy and envy. *International Journal of Stress Management*, *7*(3), 161–179.
Vecchio, R. P. (2005). Explorations in employee envy: feeling envious and feeling envied. *Cognition and Emotion*, *19*(1), 69–81.
Walton, R. E. (1999). From control to commitment in the workplace. In M. Poole (ed.), *Human Resource Management: Critical Perspectives on Business and Management* (pp. 15–29). New York, NY, USA: Routledge.
Webster's New World Dictionary (2nd ed.) (1982). New York: Simon and Schuster.
Wert, S. R., and Salovey, P. (2004). A social comparison account of gossip. *Review of General Psychology*, *8*(2), 122–137.
Wilkin, C. L., and Connelly, C. E. (2015). Green with envy and nerves of steel: moderated mediation between distributive justice and theft. *Personality and Individual Differences*, *72*, 160–164.
Wills, T. A. (1981). Downward comparison principles in social psychology. *Psychological Bulletin*, *90*(2), 245–271.
Zell, E., and Alicke, M. D. (2010). The local dominance effect in self-evaluation: evidence and explanations. *Personality and Social Psychology Review*, *14*(4), 368–384.
Zell, E., Strickhouser, J. E., and Alicke, M. D. (2017). Local dominance effects on self-evaluations and intrinsic motivation. *Self and Identity*, *16*(5), 629–644.

6. Functional and dysfunctional fear at work: dual perspectives

Shane Connelly and Megan R. Turner

Experiencing fear at work is generally not something people strive for. When employees do experience fear, it appears to be an emotion that people do not like to discuss, share with, or show to others. Nevertheless, fear is prevalent in many workplaces for a wide variety of reasons. When organizations downsize, employees may fear losing their jobs (Bommer and Jalajas, 1999). Employees who are untrained, unsupported, or who are otherwise unprepared to succeed may experience fear of failure. Aggression and violence occur in occupations like health care, law-enforcement, public service occupations, and others (Piquero et al., 2013) contributing to a fear of violence (Schat and Kelloway, 2000). Organizations sometimes perpetuate competitive, fear-based cultures (Ashkanasy and Nicholson, 2003) and leaders engage in abusive supervisory behavior, resulting in fear and other negative emotions (Tepper, 2007). These examples imply that fear in the workplace is undesirable, unproductive, and stems from negative actions that should be minimized or eliminated. This may be one reason people do not readily discuss fear or what triggers it. Naming a fear means that one may have to actually deal with it, which could be perceived as worse than just living with the emotion. People may also assume that talking about fear communicates weakness and vulnerability, attributes that are not typically viewed in a positive light.

Despite its negative associations, fear has always been part of basic human experience, ensuring survival and helping humans to adapt, function and even thrive under adversity (Ekman, 1992; Frijda, 1994; Parrott, 2001). Indeed, Lindebaum and Courpasson (2017) write about the role of passions in bureaucracy, offering an insightful discourse on violence in organizations as a transformative force that can, under the right circumstances, provide a driving force for exceptional achievements. It is vital for organizations to explore some of the reasons why employees are or are not talking about their fears. This chapter explores dual perspectives on fear in the workplace as an emotion that can have beneficial as well as detrimental effects at work and as an emotion potentially worth discussing.

Before discussing these perspectives, it is essential to consider the importance of generating a deeper understanding of negative emotions like fear in organizational contexts. First, as highlighted above, fear is undeniably present in day-to-day experiences at work (Lebel, 2017; Leon, 2002). Although some causes of fear in organizations may be fairly obvious, such as abusive supervision, the experiences and outcomes of fear are far more complex and reflect an interplay of individual differences and environmental factors (Lerner et al., 2015). Second, discrete negative emotions tend to be studied noticeably less often than positive emotions in work contexts. There remains a persistent, albeit softening, positivity bias in the literature on emotions in the workplace. Largely, this positivity bias appears to stem from perspectives based heavily in positive psychology. Positive psychology has much to offer organizational research in terms of creating more effective, pleasant workplaces (e.g., Bakker and Schaufeli, 2008; Fredickson, 1998, 2003; Haslam, 2004). However, only recently have researchers begun to address the potentially positive effects of discrete negative emotions such as anger, sadness, and fear in organizations (Forgas, 2013; Lindebaum and Jordan, 2014; Parrott, 2014). As Solomon and Stone (2002) point out, polarizing emotions as "positive" or "negative" oversimplifies the multi-dimensional nature of emotion appraisals and the contextual embeddedness of emotions, requiring a closer look at the complexity of discrete emotional experiences. The positivity bias has led to the erroneous assumption that negative emotions, such as fear, are synonymous with negative outcomes, when that may not necessarily be the case. Lindebaum and Jordan (2014) challenge this idea in a special issue of *Human Relations,* providing evidence that asymmetrical relationships of emotions to outcomes exist. These scholars point out that it can sometimes be "good to feel bad" and "bad to feel good". Parrott's (2014) book *The Positive Side of Negative Emotions* similarly echoes this sentiment and offers research countering the idea that negative emotions should be avoided due to their detrimental outcomes. Although long-standing research on fear in general has highlighted its adaptiveness from an evolutionary perspective (Cosmides and Tooby, 2000; Öhman, 2008) the functional or adaptive nature of fear has not been examined with respect to the workplace. There is a need for a more nuanced and balanced narrative regarding fear at work, one that is informed by theory and data.

This chapter investigates several aspects of the fear literature to generate a more thorough understanding of the causes and consequences of what is considered normal or non-clinical fear at work. Fear is then defined from a functionalist perspective to identify associated appraisals, motives, and behavioral patterns, and it is differentiated from other similar emotions such as anxiety. Next, sources of fear in the workplace are presented in the context of occupational characteristics that heighten the risk for fear-inducing events or episodes. Theoretical and empirical research on fear is then presented with respect to its effects on functional and dysfunctional workplace behavior and outcomes. A discussion of the themes emerging from this research and the multi-level nature of fear is then used to inform some theoretical and practical implications surrounding the concept of workplace fear and organizational dialogue helpful for understanding and managing it.

UNDERSTANDING FEAR

Functionalist Approaches to Fear

Functionalist approaches to emotions suggest that emotions serve important purposes. Emotions typically result in beneficial consequences to humans because they enable us to recognize, solve or otherwise adapt to problems in the environment (Frijda, 1994; Johnson-Laird and Oatley, 1992; Keltner and Gross, 1999; Lazarus, 1991). As an inherent part of many processes or systems (e.g., perceptual-cognitive, physiological, verbal and non-verbal communication) emotions mediate the relationship of environmental stimuli to organism responses (Keltner and Gross, 1999). Appraisal theories suggest that emotions signal the relevance of events to an individual's well-being and goals. When goals are not being met, goal discrepancies are created and negative emotions arise (Frijda et al., 1989; Roseman, 1991; Smith and Ellsworth, 1985). These discrepancies take on different meanings depending on features of the situation and on the individual experiencing the goal discrepancy, resulting in different discrete emotional states. Secondary appraisals associated with the ability to cope with discrete emotions, such as certainty about what will happen, controllability of the situation, and effort required to deal with the situation (Smith and Ellsworth, 1985), shape individuals' motivation, information processing, and behavioral patterns associated with those emotions (Keltner and Gross, 1999). Extending the functionalist view, Baumeister and others (2007) suggest that rather than exerting direct effects on behavior, consciously perceived emotions (especially negative emotions) prompt reflection on the situation, consideration of alternative actions or behavior that will, in the future, result in less negative emotions and outcomes. Thus, emotion provides feedback and stimulates processing of the situation in ways that help people learn lessons and generate different behavioral responses to similar situations in the future.

Frijda (1994) notes that an emotion can be adaptive in general or have reliably beneficial consequences, but that each experience or manifestation of the emotion may not be useful. This certainly seems to be the case with fear when it prevents individuals from pursuing goals (Bagozzi et al., 1998), speaking up (Kish-Gephart et al., 2009) or taking risks that are not in the individual's best interest or that could be harmful to an organization (Lerner and Keltner, 2001; Loewenstein et al., 2001). Although fear is not always productive, it can motivate people to protect themselves or others, to prevent threatening events from occurring in the first place, or to ride out the storm until the threat passes. These types of responses can be considerably useful in some organizational circumstances and contexts.

Fear is often considered from an evolutionary perspective, which suggests that fear helps humans to survive physical and social threats and to adapt over time. For example, primal fear triggers automatic behavioral responses such as flight from imminent danger. However, fear may also operate in the conscious realm where it directs reflection and learning (Baumeister et al., 2007). This dual process approach offers the possibility that processing a fear event after-the-fact creates situation-emotion associations in memory that inform automatic behavioral responses in the future, shaping more adaptive decision and actions. However, Keltner and Gross (1999) point out that there are sometimes "accidental" or less predictable consequences of emotion that are less closely tied to the stimuli, structure, and goals of the emotion responses. Fear can reflect "psychologically distorting" defense mechanisms to help people escape real or perceived threats (Öhman, 2008). It is possible that some of the dysfunctional outcomes linked to fear in work environments exemplify these accidental consequences. In the case of fear, a person who is afraid of public speaking may avoid doing the preparation needed to make a successful presentation at work. While this behavior initially distances the person from the threat, it actually makes the threat worse because now the person has to give an unprepared presentation which will probably go poorly. Additionally, because of its evolutionary basis, fear is difficult to extinguish or unlearn (Kish-Gephart et al., 2009) making it all the more important to understand fear triggers and outcomes in work contexts.

Defining and Differentiating Fear

Fear involves the experience of intense negative feelings in reaction to a specific stimulus. This response includes physiological reactions stemming from the sympathetic nervous system (e.g., increased pulse, sweating, and adrenaline) (Öhman, 2008). Fear is associated with the fight-flight-freeze system (FFFS) within the brain, and it generally helps people prevent, avoid, or escape threat (Perkins et al., 2007). Fear plays a key role in coping responses (e.g., escaping, avoiding, and freezing) because it motivates protection from or prevention of threatening events (Frijda, 1994). Frijda suggests that time, resource availability, and intensity of the fear stimulus affect individuals' ability to cope with and regulate fear. Specifically, high fear intensity and personal resource scarcity make emotion regulation less likely. The appraisal pattern associated with fear involves not only the primary appraisal of unpleasantness, but secondary appraisals such as uncertainty and lack of control (Lerner and Keltner, 2001; Smith and Ellsworth, 1985; Tiedens and Linton, 2001). Even when the trigger or cause of fear is known, how the situation will unfold could still be highly uncertain as well as the amount of control an individual has over the cause or outcome of the fear inducing event. Such appraisal patterns generate a host of action tendencies and behavioral responses, including cautiousness, less risk-taking, systematic information processing, and avoidance, among others (Lerner and Keltner, 2001).

Anxiety shares some of the same features with fear in terms of feelings of dread and heightened physiological activation, but typically has no defined stimulus or trigger (Öhman, 2008). Anxiety reflects anticipation of a future threat which may or may not materialize and because the stimulus is unknown. Because the stimulus is not defined, anxiety is often more difficult to cope with and regulate than fear (Öhman, 2008). Two studies conducted by Perkins, Kemp, and Corr (2007) showed anxiety as only correlated modestly with fear and tended to be more strongly associated with neuroticism than fear. Anxiety was also more negatively correlated with performance on a military performance assessment than fear. Only one of four types of fear (fear of tissue damage) was significantly and negatively related to military performance. These findings in conjunction with a review of other correlational studies of fear and anxiety led Perkins and colleagues (2007) to conclude that these are distinct emotions. In light of such research showing differences in these two emotions (Öhman, 2008), fear is the primary focus of this chapter.

What Causes Fear in the Workplace?

In order to understand fear in the workplace, it may be important to consider different kinds of organizational events and different occupations as sources of fear. Fear at work may stem from characteristics of work tasks, work environments, physical dangers, and risks faced in particular occupations. For example, U.S. military personnel face a range of tasks and environments that are potentially fear inducing (e.g., dangerous combat operations, workplace violence). Such fear inducing threats can be divided into two broad event categories: psychological threat events and physical threat events.

Psychological threats. Psychological threats such as abusive supervision (Martinko et al., 2013; Tepper, 2007) and workplace bullying (Samnani and Singh, 2012) are commonly addressed topics in organizational, management, and occupational health research. These kinds of behaviors intimidate, threaten, and undermine well-being at work, instilling fear in the victims, and often resulting in an unwillingness of victims to speak up (Kish-Gephart et al., 2009; McDonald, 2012). Sexual harassment reflects another workplace behavior that can be both psychologically and physically threatening: "The mental and physical health consequences (of sexual harassment) range from irritation and anxiety to anger, powerlessness, humiliation, depression and post-traumatic stress disorder" (McDonald, 2012, p. 4). More internal and perhaps less consistently useful fears like fear of change, fear of learning, or fear of failure (Appelbaum et al., 1998) often become conditioned in people because these responses were likely adaptive at an earlier point in time. These types of fears served a certain purpose for the individual, who, because of earlier conditioning, still sees fear responses as functional. Negative behaviors like this often come to mind first when thinking about fear at work.

Physical threats. The second broad category of fear inducing threats includes those that present physical danger. Smith (2013) highlighted the 10 most dangerous occupations, based on deaths per year, due to either the tasks or work environment (agriculture – farmers/ranchers, fishing; transportation – truck drivers, pilots, taxi and chauffeur drivers; manufacturing and construction – refuse collectors, roofers, structural iron and steel workers; lumberjacks; and electrical powerline installers/repairers). These jobs involve physically demanding or risky tasks, and often include using heavy machinery or equipment, transportation incidents, or violence on the job. Of the workplace fatalities in 2012, 41% were due to either plane or vehicle crashes, 18% were due to work-related violence, homicides and suicides, and 14% were due to slips, falls and trips (15%)

(Smith, 2013). It is interesting to consider, despite the physical dangers of these jobs, whether employees working in these occupations experience fear and how frequent and intense that fear is. Many of these jobs have strict Occupational Safety and Health Administration (OSHA) regulations involving complex safety policies and procedures which could serve as frequent reminders to employees of the potential threats they face or could be seen as effective measures of protection. Alternatively, procedures intended to keep employees safe could be seen as burdensome or could become routinized to the point where employees take for granted the nature and level of physical threats on the job. Consider the millions of people employed in these occupations in the U.S. alone (Henderson, 2015): 19.2 million mining, construction and manufacturing, 4.7 transportation and warehousing, 0.5 utilities, and 2.1 agricultural and fishing/hunting. Given these numbers, studying the prevalence of fear in these occupations and how it affects perceptions, attitudes, safety and performance on these kinds of jobs seems warranted.

Physical workplace violence is another type of fear-inducing threat that is more prevalent in certain occupations than others according to a recent review of 55 workplace violence studies (Piquero et al., 2013). For general healthcare, coworker, patient and visitor assaults were prevalent in hospitals and outpatient facilities, especially for mental health and security personnel. Rates of physical violence experienced by nurses across six studies described by Piquero et al. (2013) ranged considerably in terms of percentages of each sample reporting being a victim of physical violence (10% Hinchberger, 2009; 12% Gerberich et al., 2004; 19% Campbell et al., 2011; 25% Gacki-Smith et al., 2009; 28% Spector et al., 2007; and 39% Anderson, 2002). Sakellaropoulos and colleagues (2011) even found physical violence rates to be as high as 83% in a sample of 205 nurse anesthetists. Mental health facility employees are at risk for pushing, grabbing, property damage, and other types of violence from patients. Working with children and juveniles and having less work experience in these facilities was associated with higher violence than working with adults and being more experienced. Other occupations included in this review reported somewhat lower levels of violence, including emergency medical services, educators and correctional officers, but there were some important moderators in each of these occupations that increased violence, such as police or gang member presence, low levels of student support and discipline, and working unarmed at night, respectively. Employees in judicial related workplaces experience more verbal threats (52%) than physical violence (1%). With social workers, violence incidents involving clients in rural and urban areas ranged from 3% to 22% (small sample) in the samples studied, with verbal abuse being much higher (49%). Additionally, 7% of taxi-cab drivers reported experiencing physical assault in one study.

Physical workplace violence occurs and is higher for certain occupations and for certain demographics in those occupations (e.g., female nurses) or for those with a prior history of physical violence at work or outside of work. Again, considering the millions of people in the U.S. alone who work in these occupations (Henderson, 2015), understanding the prevalence and effect of fear is important: 5.8 million in wholesale trade, 15.4 retail, 7.9 financial activities, 18 health care and social assistance, 14.7 leisure and hospitality, and 19.1 state and local government (including public school teachers).

As Piquero and colleagues (2013) note, violence is usually purposeful, stress-related, and situationally bound. Rates of violence are also higher for professional and service employees who work with patients and clients who are mentally ill or suffer from drug/alcohol abuse. In line with some of these findings, OSHA identified occupations at greater risk for violence including those that involve exchanging money with the public, working with volatile or unstable people, working alone, working as health care professionals, delivery drivers, customer service employees, or law enforcement personnel (Occupational Safety and Health Administration, 2017). Fear has been identified in models of workplace stress as an important mediator of the relationship between violence events and their harmful effects on attitudes and well-being (Barling, 1996; Leather et al., 1997; Schat and Kelloway, 2000, 2003).

In summary, two broad classes of workplace violence – psychological threat events and physical threat events – have the potential to induce workplace fear. These events can originate from individual sources, such as coworkers, leaders, clients, patients, the general public, or individuals themselves. They might also originate from organizational sources such as a punitive organizational climate, lack of safety climate/policies/procedures, a competitive culture, and unclear or non-existent policies and procedures for managing threatening behavior. Finally, broader environmental factors such as economic volatility, resource scarcity, and industry competitiveness could directly or indirectly contribute to the presence of psychological and physical threats at work. Despite many potential sources of fear in work environments, this emotion may serve some adaptive purposes by directing perceptions, cognitions and behavior in beneficial ways.

OUTCOMES OF FEAR IN THE WORKPLACE

Although some may argue with the idea of functional or healthy fear in the workplace, research suggests that fear influences various cognitive, motivational, and behavioral patterns that could be beneficial in occupational settings. For example, feelings of fear may alert people to goal discrepancies, which could motivate them to work harder (Baumeister et al., 2007). Further, fear may motivate careful information processing and cautious behavior in ways that enable effective or ethical job performance (Leon, 2002). Such careful information processing may highlight the seriousness of consequences for particular tasks leading to greater attention and focus on those tasks. Research findings associated with observing fear in others also shows benefits related to prosocial behavior. Relatedly, extensive research by communication scholars demonstrates the effectiveness of fear appeals (e.g., health messages) under certain conditions (Tannenbaum et al., 2015). Functional outcomes of fear are considered here from two perspectives: (1) outcomes linked to feeling fear and (2) outcomes linked to observing fear in others.

Functional Outcomes of Feeling Fear

Risk assessment and risk-taking are influenced by various emotions including fear (Loewenstein et al., 2001). Since appraisal states associated with fear potentially leads to more careful information processing, fear can result in more critical evaluations of risk and potentially better decisions (Lerner and Keltner, 2001) when risk is costly or needs to be managed. Dispositional and experimentally induced fear has been shown to result in pessimistic judgments of risk, which leads to low-risk decisions (Lerner and Keltner, 2001). Appraisals of uncertainty and lack of control over the situation mediated these effects. The risk-as-feelings hypothesis suggests that specific emotions interact in complex ways with cognitive (rational) evaluation of choices and estimating outcome probabilities to influence decisions (Loewenstein et al., 2001). Additionally, people who have damage to the pre-frontal cortex area of the brain (i.e., deficits to emotional functioning) have difficulty making risky decisions and often make risky choices not in their best interests because they are not experiencing fear (Bechara et al., 1997; Damasio, 1994).

Organizations must continually take and manage a variety of risks in order to sustain a competitive advantage, innovate, or simply stay in business. Being able to accurately evaluate and mitigate unnecessary risks is critical and fear could be instrumental in helping individuals and organizations to do this. Even when organizations make high-risk invest-ments and decisions, the ability to consider and plan for worst-case outcomes is necessary in the event that the risk does not pay off. This requires the kind of pessimistic assessments associated with fear (Lerner and Keltner, 2001). Discussing potential and realized fears when making decisions about organizational strategies and investments may play an important role in preventing organizational losses by preventing hasty decision-making. The conscious processing of fear-inducing events through dialogue could serve as part of the feedback system that informs future automatic and conscious processing of fear (Baumeister et al., 2007).

Grote (2015) proposes that the safety of managing high-risk systems in organizations could be improved by increasing uncertainty in certain ways. Introducing flexible rules to support adaptive decision-making and action is one option. Encouraging employees to voice concerns and doubts about decisions and actions will also increase uncertainty. Both of these may help organizations to avoid rigid adherence to procedures or rules that may not be functional under certain circumstances. These suggestions capitalize on an interesting idea of up-regulating select fear-related appraisals.

Some evidence suggests that ethical decisions are also positively influ-enced by fear, perhaps, in part, because they involve assessing risk and probabilities of good/poor outcomes associated with alternative courses of action (Mumford et al., 2008; Ness and Connelly, 2017). Sensemaking approaches to ethical decision-making emphasize both rational and intuitive aspects of decision-making, acknowledging that emotions play a role in ethical judgments (Mumford et al., 2008; Sonenshein, 2007). Sensemaking processes such as problem recognition, forecasting out-comes, and identifying key causes and restrictions help people to form mental models which then guide further information gathering, solutions generation, and outcome evaluation. Kligyte et al. (2013) conducted an experiment comparing the sensemaking and ethical decisions when fear, anger or no emotion was induced. They found that fear promoted high scores on two sensemaking strategies – recognizing circumstances and considering consequences of actions. Additionally, individuals in the fear condition scored above average in terms of helping others and made better ethical decisions than those in the angry and no-emotion con-ditions. These findings suggest that the appraisals of uncertainty and threat that accompany fear led to more systematic information searching and processing, enabling better sensemaking and better overall decisions.

Another possible explanation for these findings is that fear promotes proactive behavior. Lebel (2017) explores the functionality of fear by exploring how it motivates proactive behavior (i.e., anticipatory goal-directed action aimed at improving a situation or oneself). His theory suggests that certain factors can sway the appraisals and action tendencies of fear away from flight and freeze towards a fight response but that this will only occur with certain types of support in the organization. Fear motivates proactive effort (increased focus on the threat and readiness for defensive action) as well as searching for ways to reduce uncertainty and deal with the threats. Organizational support for this motivation could come from supportive leader communication and efforts to build confidence and efficacy in dealing with difficult situations. In the presence of these supports, employees feeling fearful may feel less uncertainty and a higher sense of control. Emotion regulation knowledge or self-awareness of strategies that have successfully reduced fear in the past is proposed to moderate the relationship between proactive effort and specific proactive behaviors. Individuals experiencing fear may also be more likely to engage in proactive behavior when they feel a sense of responsibility for others. Consistent with this idea, Connelly and colleagues (2004) found positive relationships between distress and feelings of responsibility to interpersonally directed ethical decisions. The functional effects of fear have thus far focused on within- and between-person effects. However, Ashkanasy's (2003) multilevel model of emotions in organizations describes additional levels where emotions exert influence, including interpersonal, group, and organizational. Outcomes of observing fear in others reflect interpersonal and group levels of influence.

Functional Outcomes of Observing Fear in Others

Emotions have a social side. Van Kleef's (2009) Emotions as Social Information (EASI) model sheds light on the informational value of emotional displays in shaping social life, elaborating on the interpersonal rather than intrapersonal dynamics of emotions. Observing another person's emotions provides information about the interaction and offers information through two different routes. Processing emotions through the affective route triggers emotion processes in the observer (e.g., reciprocal emotions, feelings towards the other person), which influences attitudes, behaviors or other responses. Processing emotions through the cognitive or inferential route involves more complex information processing to uncover the meaning the emotional display and it implications. When people are capable and motivated by internal and situational factors to process information in-depth, the inferential route will be the more likely to shape responses in the situation. If the observer thinks the emotions displayed by the other person are appropriate for the situation, an affective route may be more likely. For example, negative emotional displays have the capacity to engender sympathy and social support from others. Displays of sadness and disappointment result in offers of help from others (Clark et al., 1996). Anger displays, however, lead to more concessions from others (van Kleef et al., 2004) and result in the conferral of more social status and salary compared to sadness displays (Tiedens, 2001).

Fear is an emotion that conveys distress to others and has important effects on prosocial behavior when observers accurately recognize expressions of fear (Marsh et al., 2007). In three separate studies, Marsh and colleagues demonstrated that people who more accurately recognized facial expressions of fear pledged more donations of time and money to a person in need expressing fear. The second study used a different task to control for potential confounds influencing money and time donations (e.g., personal finances, busy schedule, and mood). In this study, participants were asked to rate a target person's attractiveness and were either told that the ratings would be used to assess the target's responses to feedback about their attractiveness (prosocial condition) or to validate a set of stimulus photos. Participants in the prosocial condition (i.e., influencing another person's positive affect or preventing negative affect) gave higher attractiveness ratings than those in the control condition behavior. Additionally, accuracy of fear recognition was a stronger predictor of prosocial attractiveness ratings than empathy, the ability to form favorable interpersonal relationships, gender, positive mood, and negative mood. In organizational contexts, expressing fear about a particular assignment or project may foster greater supervisor and coworker prosocial behavior such as offering verbal support, providing resources, or providing opportunities for skill development. Such support will ultimately help the individual face that fear. Relatedly, Gump and Kulik (1997) found that when facing a threat, people affiliate more with others who they presume to be experiencing a similar threat and a similar negative emotion (i.e., fear). These individuals were also more likely to mimic the other person's non-verbal emotional displays.

There are at least two important implications of the research on fear expressions and prosocial behavior at work for talking about fear in the workplace. First, prosocial responses are possible whether a person expresses fear non-verbally through facial expressions or other body language, or expresses them verbally to a coworker or boss. Articulating fears verbally may more clearly identify the issue and may help the individual experiencing fear to cope more effectively. Clear, verbal articulations may also help coworkers or supervisors to provide the type of support that will be most beneficial for the individual experiencing fear. Such emotional expressions and encouragement of discussions about fear could promote social bonding during times of organizational stress or crisis, especially if leaders or coworkers reinforce a "we are all in this together" attitude. Social affiliation stemming from fear could also backfire if the fear is too intense and spreads throughout the organization. Second, organizations that foster the development of emotional abilities such as recognizing emotions (Mayer et al., 2008) may foster more prosocial responses to fear because employees will be better at recognizing it. Emotion recognition is an important first step towards functional conversations about fear.

In addition to its effects on prosocial behavior, fear also appears to benefit specific types of attentional activities such as visual search (Olatunji et al., 2011), which are critically important in occupations like air traffic controllers, baggage screeners, radiologists and police officers. Olatunji and colleagues specifically found that exposure to fearful facial expressions (vs. other emotions) promoted faster target identification. The effects of fear exposure were also different than fear of negative evaluation, trait anxiety, and obsessive-compulsive tendencies. According to these authors, several possible mechanisms could be responsible for this relationship. Fear expressions may prompt observers to look for the stimulus eliciting the fear, increasing vigilance and visual search. Observers could also experience fear themselves through facial mimicry or emotional contagion processes which signals danger or threat in the environment and triggers more efficient visual search. These effects were present when fear exposure lasted 500ms but not when they only lasted 100ms, indicating the presence of temporal boundary conditions (Olatunji et al., 2011).

The somewhat controversial use of fear as a persuasion tactic in strategic and mass communication has also been widely studied. An extensive meta-analysis by Tannenbaum and colleagues (2015) highlights key findings about the success of fear appeals in light of various boundary conditions. Fear appeals generally achieve their desired effects in terms of influencing attitudes, intentions, and behavior with an average Cohen's d of 0.29. Their effectiveness increased when fear messages: (1) targeted the message audience as being highly susceptible to the threatening event and the effects as severe, (2) recommended behavior for reducing the threat (one-time behaviors worked better than ones that had to be repeated over and over), (3) included efficacy statements (reassuring message recipients that they are capable of following the recommendations to reduce/remove the threat), and (4) were directed at female recipients. Possible negative effects of fear messages such as avoidance or rejection of the message were not supported by the data. These findings suggest that fear appeals induce attitudinal and behavioral change under the right conditions – conditions that require more open discussion of threats, fear, and efficacious responses. Organizations facing crisis situations, for example, may benefit from employee responsiveness to fear appeals that make one-time recommendations. However, if fear appeals are continually used, a fear-based organizational climate might emerge. While fear certainly shows potential benefits in work settings, it also has some drawbacks.

Dysfunctional Outcomes of Feeling Fear

One outcome that has been linked to fear in organizations is defensive silence or the "... withholding of ideas, suggestions or concerns about people, products, or processes that might have been communicated verbally to someone inside the organization with the perceived authority to act" (Kish-Gephart et al., 2009, p. 165). There are potentially serious consequences to individuals and organizations when employees experience fear and fail to speak up about problems (e.g., ethical issues, safety concerns, mistakes/errors, harassment) (Kiewitz et al., 2016; Lowy, 2014). As noted earlier, this reluctance to talk about fear inducing events and problems stems from the perceived negative consequences of discussing such events. A climate of fear has pervasive effects in shutting down these kinds of voice behaviors. Additionally, fear climates can also prevent proactive problem solving such as offering new ideas or process improvements, which may result in missed opportunities. Numerous studies cited in the Kish-Gephart et al. (2009) review implicate fear as a driver of employee silence given the possibility of negative outcomes associated with speaking up such as retaliation, loss of social capital or reputation, and job loss. These authors note that socialization processes within and outside of organizations contribute to the conditioning of fears, like the fear of challenging authority, which can exacerbate the problem. Socialization processes and practices like this can lead to unhealthy "fear talk" and "messaging" in the workplace (Kish-Gephart et al., 2009).

Different levels of intensity and immediacy of workplace threats are proposed to drive different types of silence (Kish-Gephart et al., 2009). For example, high intensity threats requiring an immediate response result in fast, automatic, non-conscious threat processing and non-deliberative silence. When threat intensity is high and there is more time for a response, or when threat intensity is low and there is little time for a response, employees rely on existing schemas or knowledge from prior similar situations to guide decisions about remaining silent. Low intensity threats with long timeframes for a response result in deliberative defensive silence. In general, activating fear promotes silence because it is perceived as the safer response. Other research empirically corroborates this idea by demonstrating a positive association of employee fear and employee silence (Kiewitz et al., 2016). Kish-Gephart and colleagues (2009) suggest that overcoming these silences could be possible through activating anger, which is a more approach-based emotion. However, they argue that effective displays of anger that actually minimize repercussions require emotion management capabilities and effective communication skills that not all employees will possess. This implies that effective discussion of fear in the workplace has important boundary conditions.

Other research provides evidence that fear can motivate counterproductive organizational behavior as a remedy for unjust behavior from those in positions of authority (Zoghbi-Manrique-de-Lara, 2006). Interactional organizational justice involves authority figures showing sensitivity, respect, and interpersonal treatment to employees when executing organizational procedures and outcomes (Greenburg, 1993). Zoghbi-Manrique-de-Lara (2006) argues that poor interactional justice, especially when other types of justice are present (e.g., fair outcomes, procedures), make it seem like the rules are unclear and changing in a risky environment. This unjust treatment generates a fear of punishment in employees, who are uncertain about what will happen if they do something wrong. Ironically, fear of punishment unbalances the psychological contract or social exchange relationship, making employees feel more justified in engaging in unproductive work behavior, such as cyberloafing. Finally, organizational exit has also been shown to be a consequence of fear felt in response to involuntary pay reductions and furloughs (Osborne et al., 2012).

Research has also examined the negative psychological and health consequences of fear of violence in the workplace (Schat and Kelloway, 2003, 2005). Schat and Kelloway (2000) validated a model of workplace violence in which fear plays a central role. Workplace violence (direct and vicarious) was highly correlated with fear, while perceived control at work was negatively related to fear. Fear also mediated the effects of these variables on emotional well-being and somatic health (e.g., sleep disturbances, headaches, respiratory infections) showing a negative relationship with both and increasing the perception of future fear of workplace violence. Further, emotional well-being was positively related to somatic health and negatively related to job neglect. Mueller and Tschan (2011) extended this research examining fear of future violence in a sample of civil servants in job centers and social security offices who had experienced violence. Fear of future violence correlated negatively with psychological and physical well-being and positively with irritability. Perceptions of violence prevention and coping ability reduced fears of future violence, suggesting that strategies which address some of the fundamental appraisals associated with fear (i.e., certainty and control) can mitigate the dysfunctional effects of fear. Perceptions and coping ability both have the potential to be positively influenced through explicit discussion of threats and how to address them.

Dysfunctional Outcomes and Fear Climate

Fear may exert influences on work behavior in a more general way than through discrete emotional states triggered by specific threats at work. Ashkanasy (2003) notes the important influence emotions have on organizational climate. Organizational climate reflects shared perceptions of the existence and meaning of organizational policies, practices, and procedures as well as what behavior is expected and rewarded (Schneider et al., 2013). Different types of climates can exist within and across organizations reflecting shared perceptions of different groups of people or units within organizations. Employees communicate with each other about these shared perceptions which often include reactions to organizational policies and practices. Ashkanasy and Nicholson (2003) introduced the concept of emotional climate in organizations and developed a new measure assessing climate of fear. Their measure is comprised of feeling statements (I feel … afraid, fearful, apprehensive, comfortable) about aspects of the work environment which center around fear of repercussion or punishments for mistakes, and feeling that it is not safe to make mistakes or to speak up regarding work issues or sensitive issues. They assessed climate of fear in two organizations, both of which had 12 different geographical sites, finding that the climate of fear differed across the sites in these organizations. They suggest that fear climate is localized and driven by management practices at the different sites.

Fear and punishment have commonly been used as a control strategy in organizations in the hopes of deterring certain undesirable behaviors and encouraging others (Appelbaum et al., 1998). Managers operate under the assumption that reasonable uses of punishment will work if it is directed at the behavior and not a person's character, is paired close in time to the problematic behavior, is consistent, and is a result of an employee's specific actions. This analysis, however, fails to consider that repeatedly punishing mistakes can lead employees to fear failure, which perpetuates the cycle of mistakes and/or results in non-performance (Appelbaum et al., 1998; Vecchio and Appelbaum, 1995).

Fear climate also influences the relationship between fear and employee defensive silence. Kiewitz and colleagues (2016) conducted three studies empirically demonstrating a positive relationship between perceptions of abusive supervision and employee fear. Fear related positively to avoidance behavior in the form of defensive silence, a relationship that was larger for less assertive employees. Higher levels of fear climate also strengthened the positive relationship of fear to silence. Interestingly, while defensive silence was presumably motivated by the desire to avoid further threat or supervisory abuse, this showed positive correlations with abusive supervision evaluated one year later. Silence appears to sustain or passively sanction problematic supervisory behavior.

IMPLICATIONS FOR RESEARCH ON FEAR AT WORK

Fear has been studied by many scholars for decades, resulting in a voluminous literature on the topic. Comparatively speaking, research on fear in the workplace is sparse. It focuses almost exclusively on fear's negative aspects and does not always distinguish between fear and anxiety. Lebel (2017) is a notable exception. There are many unanswered questions about types of fear at work, how fear is experienced and regulated, and the conditions or contexts in which it is motivating and functional versus demotivating and dysfunctional. In considering some of the positive and negative aspects of fear at work, a number of observations are worth noting that have implications for additional research on this topic.

The experience and outcomes of fear at work are complex. Fear can be triggered by psychological and physical threats stemming from a variety of sources internal and external to the organization. It exerts influence whether experienced firsthand or vicariously through others, operating through automatic, direct pathways through primitive brain structures (Öhman, 2008), and through deliberative routes involving cognitive appraisals relating to one's ability to cope with the situation (Frijda et al., 1989; Smith and Ellsworth, 1985). Fear can potentially be experienced in any organization, although it may be more prevalent in some. This could be due to the nature of the organizational climate, destructive leadership behavior, or the nature of the work. The latter has only recently been a topic of study.

Occupational stress research has made some progress in understanding how fear exerts influence in particular occupations at higher risk for dangerous tasks, aggression, and violence (Schat and Kelloway, 2000). However, positive outcomes are rarely the focus in these theories and the characteristics of work tasks in such occupations have not been studied with respect to fear. There are a number of areas for potential future research here. First, it would be useful to examine a wider variety of outcomes, types of fear, and conditions under which fear has positive and negative effects in these types of occupations. For example, is fear capable of reducing accidents, injuries, or errors in some kinds of occupations? Linkages between fear, attention, and vigilance (Olatunji et al., 2011) could be extended to inform this area. Vigilance may benefit performance on certain tasks, but it is unclear whether there are optimal levels of vigilance. Moderating and mediating influences of the effects of fear on important outcomes in risky jobs is also an area ripe for study. Characteristics of the organizational context could promote functional levels or intensities of fear, such as periodic reminders of the dangers on the job to prevent complacency, rigorous safety training, after accident reviews, or rules and procedures that are clear but flexible enough to accommodate deviations from normal operations (Grote, 2015). Finally, it may be important to know the extent to which people in highly dangerous or risky occupations experience fear at work, whether they consciously recognize this emotion, and the coping strategies they use to manage fear. For example, people in police or military organizations may experience fear less intensely and/or may have better coping strategies, enabling them to manage fears in ways that enhance personal and organizational benefits.

Research on negative psychological aspects of the work environment such as abusive supervision, bullying, harassment, and workplace aggression has begun to incorporate fear as a mediating process in the effects of such behaviors on attitudes, well-being, and job performance at the intra-individual level. However, these behaviors are occurring in dyadic exchanges or in groups and unfold in a dynamic way. More of these interpersonal processes need to be examined with fear. What should we know about the emotional contagion of fear? What are some reciprocal emotions others may feel around a fearful person and how do dyadic interactions shape fear over time?

Another interesting observation from this research is that the specific appraisals associated with fear, which shape perceptions of threat and ability to cope, are malleable. Specific fears are difficult to extinguish but could be down regulated by focusing on increasing a sense of control or certainty within the environment. Lebel's (2017) research suggests that proactive versus avoidant responses to fear can be shaped through leaders building task efficacy in employees and communicating clearly. Further, such responses can also be shaped though increasing employees' emotion knowledge and a sense of responsibility to others. This model implies that regulating fear can originate from within the individual employee and through external factors (Gross, 1998; Gross and Thompson, 2007). Employees (or their leaders) can select and modify situations to change the experience or intensity of fear, deploy attention away from the fear stimulus, or reappraise the situation to feel less fear or transform fear into alternative emotions such as righteous anger (Kish-Gephart et al., 2009).

The intensity, frequency and duration of fear at work is also interesting to consider in light of situational requirements and contextual character- istics. Whether or not fear has benefits or drawbacks in work environ- ments seems highly context-dependent. For example, short-lived intense fear could be detrimental if it results in a freezing response during an important proposal presentation to win new business for one's organ- ization. However, that same sort of intense burst of fear may enable an employee to escape injury by quickly moving away from a patient that becomes physically violent. Fear conditioned by exposure to threat stimuli can promote learning and adaptability that contributes to enhanced threat detection and threat neutralization in the future (Baumeister, 2007). Alternatively, threats that are seemingly inescapable such as an abusive supervisor may result in low level frequent fear that degrades motivation, trust, and productivity over time (Tepper, 2007). One potential way forward is to develop models that consider a wider range of organizational criteria and to investigate the extent to which domains of job performance, well-being, or contextual and counter- productive behavior are harmed by or benefit from fear.

Fear can be studied at multiple levels of analysis in the workplace (Ashkanasy and Dorris, 2017; Ashkanasy and Nicholson, 2003). Applying Ashkanasy's (2003) five-level model of emotion in organizations, fear operates in different ways at different levels. At level 1, the within-person level, fear can be examined as an individual's discrete emotional experi- ence, one that fluctuates over time and circumstance. This emotional experience will be activated by particular events for that individual, exerting influences on his or her motivation, cognition, and behavior. Applying experience sampling methodologies in studies of fear in the workplace would be informative for understanding how conscious fear unfolds and resolves over time and how it changes future responding. Level 2 reflects between-person differences in the experience, expression, or regulation of fear. Why do some people have stronger fear responses to workplace threats than others? Similarly, what other personal attributes (e.g., emotional intelligence) drive differences in people's ability to regulate their fears? Level 3 involves understanding how fear is communicated and perceived in dyadic interpersonal exchanges at work. Future research could investigate fear dynamics in interpersonal exchanges between leaders and subordinates, or in other workplace dyads where there is a clear power difference or use of coercive power. Level 4 focuses on how groups are influenced by fear and how leaders may use fear for a variety of purposes (e.g., to motivate or intimidate). Emotional contagion or the spread of fear may be particularly important to understand in workplaces experiencing crises or challenges that threaten the organization's well-being. Finally, at level 5, fear influences organizational climate in ways that may be unhealthy in the short and long term (Kiewitz et al., 2016).

IMPLICATIONS FOR MANAGING FEAR AT WORK

Given the evidence for both functional and dysfunctional outcomes associated with fear in organizations, it is important to understand the ways fear can be recognized and regulated. Knowing that fear operates at multiple levels is important because each level has different implications for how fear might be managed. Organizational discussions about unacceptable behaviors that trigger fear responses (e.g., abusive supervision) may prevent these kinds of avoidable fears from being realized. Alternatively, improving employee's abilities to recognize and regulate fear when causes are occupationally linked and unavoidable could be improved in organizations that accept and encourage discussions of fear.

Individual-Level Strategies

Employees who experience fear at work likely know what causes that fear. However, they may not be aware of the outcomes of this fear. Specifically, employees may not be able to differentiate between fear that serves a useful purpose and fear that is detrimental to their goals and negatively influences their well-being at work. Employees may benefit from personal development approaches to improving emotional self-awareness and coping strategies as opposed to external training in emotional intelligence, which is subject to many barriers (Lindebaum, 2009). Research has shown the benefits of cognitive reappraisal training for developing emotion regulation strategies, including psychological distancing and reinterpretation of the situation (Denny and Ochsner, 2014).

Interpersonal-Level Strategies

Leaders and other employees play a crucial role in the emotional life of organizations (Ashkanasy and Humphrey, 2011). In particular, leaders must be aware of their own emotions as well as those of subordinates, intervening when necessary to help others regulate fear or other emotions that may be having detrimental influences on attitudes or performance. Leaders may need to make an effort to find out what employees are afraid of. Some fears may be well-justified while others may not be. In either case, leaders can often help employees manage fear through effective communication of positive and negative information (Suárez, 1993). Leaders can also work to developing employees' knowledge and skills, and by encouraging them to voice concerns and opinions. This requires leaders to be mindful and intentional rather than reactive in their own emotional displays. Anger is an emotion leaders sometimes display that can trigger other reciprocal emotions, such as anger and fear (Gaddis et al., 2004). Leaders should also be judicious in any intentional use of fear as a motivator. Strategic, skilled and targeted displays of negative emotions are more likely to be effective in exerting influence in ways that are not detrimental in the long run (van Kleef, 2014).

Organizational-Level Strategies

At an organizational level, top management and key figures of influence within organizations must understand that a pervasive climate of fear is likely to lead to poor outcomes such as low satisfaction, high turnover, counterproductive work behavior and even violence. Hiring and promoting leaders who are capable of setting a functional emotional tone and who have emotional awareness will help to prevent a climate of fear. To avoid the negative impacts of fear, organizations should strive to create a climate that has an appropriate tolerance for failure, especially during periods of change or transition where employees are learning new systems, approaches, or other aspects of work that have changed. Organizations can also offer employee assistance programs for managing fear and stress more generally, especially for occupations at higher risk for violence, aggression, danger and fear. It might also be useful to consider what organizational policies or interventions can help people regulate fear in specific ways to reduce specific appraisals (threat level) or heighten others (uncertainty).

CONCLUSION

Taking a functionalist view of fear, this chapter highlights the complexity of this powerful emotion in organizational contexts. Despite assumptions that fear and "talk" about fear should be avoided or prevented in work settings, it appears to serve some useful purposes in helping employees and organizations to function more optimally in some occupations or under some organizational circumstances. Despite the circumstantially specific utility of fear, the darker side of this emotion and its ability to interfere with learning, change, and social functioning should not be underestimated. Continued exploration regarding the boundary conditions (Dubin, 1976; Johns, 2006) surrounding discussions of fear in the workplace will help to reveal when and how to talk about fear in ways that are functional and adaptive as well as when not to talk about fear. Research has only scratched the surface of understanding this emotion's form and function in the workplace and much more research is needed to harness the potentials and pitfalls of fear.

REFERENCES

Anderson, C. (2002). Workplace violence: are some nurses more vulnerable? *Issues in Mental Health Nursing, 23*, 351–366.

Appelbaum, S. H., Bregman, M., and Moroz, P. (1998). Fear as a strategy: effects and impact within the organization. *Journal of European Industrial Training, 22*(3), 113–127.

Ashkanasy, N. M. (2003). Emotions in organizations: a multi-level perspective. In F. Dansereau and F. J. Yammarino (eds), *Research in Multi Level Issues, Vol. 2: Multi-level Issues in Organizational Behavior and Strategy* (pp. 9–54). Bingley, UK: Emerald Group Publishing Limited.

Ashkanasy, N. M., and Dorris, A. D. (2017). Emotions in the workplace. *Annual Review of Organizational Psychology and Organizational Behavior, 4*(1), 67–90.

Ashkanasy, N. M., and Humphrey, R. H. (2011). A multi-level view of leadership and emotions: leading with emotional labour. In A. Bryman, D. Collinson, K. Grint, B. Jackson and M. Uhl-Bien (eds), *Sage Handbook of Leadership* (pp. 363–377). London, UK: Sage Publications.

Ashkanasy, N. M., and Nicholson, G. J. (2003). Climate of fear in organizational settings: construct definition, measurement and a test of theory. *Australian Journal of Psychology, 55*(1), 24–29.

Bagozzi, R. P., Baumgartner, H., and Pieters, R. (1998). Goal-directed emotions. *Cognition and Emotion, 12*(1), 1–26.

Bakker, A. B., and Schaufeli, W. B. (2008). Positive organizational behavior: engaged employees in flourishing organizations. *Journal of Organizational Behavior, 29*(2), 147–154.

Barling, J. (1996). The prediction, experience, and consequences of workplace violence. In G. R. VandenBos, and E. Q. Bulatao (eds), *Violence on the Job: Identifying Risks and Developing Solutions* (pp. 29–49). Washington, DC, USA: American Psychological Association.

Baumeister, R. F., Vohs, K. D., Nathan DeWall, C., and Zhang, L. (2007). How emotion shapes behavior: feedback, anticipation, and reflection, rather than direct causation. *Personality and Social Psychology Review, 11*(2), 167–203.

Bechara, A., Damasio, H., Tranel, D., and Damasio, A. R. (1997). Deciding advantageously before knowing the advantageous strategy. *Science, 275*(5304), 1293–1295.

Bommer, M., and Jalajas, D. (1999). The threat of organizational downsizing on the innovative propensity of R&D professionals. *R&D Management, 29*(1), 27–34.

Campbell, J. C., Messing, J. T., Kub, J., Agnew, J., Fitzgerald, S., Fowler, B., Sheridan, D., Lindauer, C., Deaton, J., and Bolyard, R. (2011). Workplace violence: prevalence and risk factors in the safe at work study. *Journal of Occupational and Environmental Medicine, 53*, 82–89.

Clark, M. S., Pataki, S. P., and Carver, V. H. (1996). Some thoughts and findings on self-presentation of emotions in relationships. In G. J. O Fletcher and J. Fitness (eds) *Knowledge Structures in Close Relationships: A Social Psychological Approach* (pp. 247–274). Hillsdale, NJ, USA: Lawrence Erlbaum Associates.

Connelly, S., Helton-Fauth, W., and Mumford, M. D. (2004). A managerial in-basket study of the impact of trait emotions on ethical choice. *Journal of Business Ethics, 51*(3), 245–267.

Cosmides, L., and Tooby, J. (2000). Evolutionary psychology and the emotions. In M. Lewis and J. M. Haviland-Jones (eds), *Handbook of Emotions* (2nd ed., pp. 91–115). New York, NY, USA: Guilford Press.

Damasio, A. R. (1994). *Descartes' Error: Emotion, Rationality and the Human Brain.* New York, NY, USA: Putnam (Grosset Books).

Denny, B. T., and Ochsner, K. N. (2014). Behavioral effects of longitudinal training in cognitive reappraisal. *Emotion, 14*(2), 425–433.

Dubin, R. (1976). Theory building in applied areas. In M. D. Dunnette, (ed.), *Handbook of Industrial and Organizational Psychology* (pp. 17–39). Chicago, IL, USA: Rand-McNally and Co.

Ekman, P. (1992). An argument for basic emotions. *Cognition and Emotion, 6*(3–4), 169–200.

Forgas, J. P. (2013). Don't worry, be sad! On the cognitive, motivational, and interpersonal benefits of negative mood. *Current Directions in Psychological Science, 22*(3), 225–232.

Fredrickson, B. L. (1998). What good are positive emotions? *Review of General Psychology, 2*(3), 300–319.

Fredrickson, B. L. (2003). Positive emotions and upward spirals in organizations. In K. S. Cameron, J. E. Dutton, and R. E. Quinn (eds), *Positive Organizational Scholarship: Foundations of a New Discipline* (pp. 163–175). San Francisco, CA, USA: Berrett-Kohler.

Frijda, N. H. (1994). Emotions require cognitions, even if simple ones. In P. Ekman and R. J. Davidson (eds), *The Nature of Emotions: Fundamental Questions* (pp. 197–202) New York, NY, USA: Oxford University Press.

Frijda, N. H., Kuipers, P., and ter Schure, E. (1989). Relations among emotion, appraisal, and emotional action readiness. *Journal of Personality and Social Psychology, 57*(2), 212–228.

Gacki-Smith, J., Juarez, A. M., Boyett, L., Homeyer, C., Robinson, L., and MacLean, S. L. (2009). Violence against nurses working in US emergency departments. *Journal of Nursing Administration, 39*(7–8), 340–349.

Gaddis, B., Connelly, S., and Mumford, M. D. (2004). Failure feedback as an affective event: influences of leader affect on subordinate attitudes and performance. *The Leadership Quarterly, 15*(5), 663–686.

Gerberich, S. G., Church, T. R., McGovern, P. M., Hansen, H. E., Nachreiner, N. M., Geisser, M. S., Ryan, A. D., Mongin, S. G., and Watt G. D. (2004). An epidemiological study of the magnitude and consequences of work related violence: the Minnesota nurses' study. *Occupational and Environmental Medicine, 61*(6), 495–503.

Greenburg, J. (1993) The social side of fairness: interpersonal and informational classes of organizational justice. In R. Cropanzano (ed.) *Justice in the Workplace: Approaching Fairness in Human Resource Management* (pp. 79–103) Hillsdale, NJ, USA: Lawrence Erlbaum Associates.

Gross, J. J. (1998). The emerging field of emotion regulation: an integrative review. *Review of General Psychology, 2*(3), 271–299.

Gross, J. J., and Thompson, R. A. (2007). Emotion regulation: conceptual foundations. In J. J. Gross (ed.) *Handbook of Emotion Regulation* (pp. 3–26). New York, NY, USA: Guilford Press.

Grote, G. (2015). Promoting safety by increasing uncertainty–implications for risk management. *Safety Science, 71*(B), 71–79.

Gump, B. B., and Kulik, J. A. (1997). Stress, affiliation, and emotional contagion. *Journal of Personality and Social Psychology, 72*(2), 305–319.

Haslam, S. A. (2004). *Psychology in Organizations: The Social Identity Approach*. London, UK: Sage.

Henderson, R. (December, 2015). Industry employment and output projections to 2024. *Monthly Labor Review*.

Hinchberger, P. A. (2009). Violence against female student nurses in the workplace. *Nursing Forum, 44*(1), 37–46.

Johns, G. (2006). The essential impact of context on organizational behavior. *Academy of Management Review, 31*(2), 386–408.

Johnson-Laird, P. N., and Oatley, K. (1992). Basic emotions, rationality, and folk theory. *Cognition and Emotion, 6*(3–4), 201–223.

Keltner, D., and Gross, J. J. (1999). Functional accounts of emotions. *Cognition and Emotion, 13*(5), 467–480.

Kiewitz, C., Restubog, S. L. D., Shoss, M. K., Garcia, P. R. J. M., and Tang, R. L. (2016). Suffering in silence: investigating the role of fear in the relationship between abusive supervision and defensive silence. *Journal of Applied Psychology, 101*(5), 731–742.

Kish-Gephart, J. J., Detert, J. R., Treviño, L. K., and Edmondson, A. C. (2009) Silenced by fear: the nature, sources and consequences of fear at work. *Research in Organizational Behavior, 29*, 163–193.

Kligyte, V., Connelly, S., Thiel, C., and Devenport, L. (2013). The influence of anger, fear, and emotion regulation on ethical decision making. *Human Performance, 26*(4), 297–326.

Lazarus, R. S. (1991). Progress on a cognitive–motivational–relational theory of emotion. *American Psychologist, 46*(8), 819–834.

Leather, P., Beale, D., Lawrence, C., and Dickson, R. (1997). Effects of exposure to occupational violence and the mediating impact of fear. *Work and Stress, 11*(4), 329–340.

Lebel, R. D. (2017). Moving beyond fight and flight: a contingent model of how the emotional regulation of anger and fear sparks proactivity. *Academy of Management Review, 42*(2), 190–206.

Leon, M. (2002). Work in the trenches: fear and anxiety in the workplace – an exploration. In L. Morrow, I. Verins and E. Willis (eds), *Mental Health and Work: Issues and Perspectives* (pp. 232–249). Adelaide, South Australia: Auseinet.

Lerner, J. S., and Keltner, D. (2001). Fear, anger, and risk. *Journal of Personality and Social Psychology*, *81*(1), 146–159.

Lerner, J. S., Li, Y., Valdesolo, P., and Kassam, K. S. (2015). Emotion and decision making. *Annual Review of Psychology*, *66*, 799–823.

Lindebaum, D. (2009). Rhetoric or remedy? A critique on developing emotional intelligence. *Academy of Management Learning and Education*, *8*(2), 225–237.

Lindebaum, D., and Courpasson, D. (2017). Becoming the next Charlie Parker: rewriting the role of passions in bureaucracies with whiplash. *Academy of Management Review*, amr-2017.

Lindebaum, D., and Jordan, P. J. (2014). When it can be good to feel bad and bad to feel good: exploring asymmetries in workplace emotional outcomes. *Human Relations, 67*(9), 1037–1050.

Loewenstein, G. F., Weber, E. U., Hsee, C. K., and Welch, N. (2001). Risk as feelings. *Psychological Bulletin*, *127*(2), 267–286.

Lowy, J. (2014, May 16). "Silence can kill": GM is fined a record $35 million for not disclosing deadly ignition defect. *Star Tribune*. Retrieved from http://www.startribune.com/business/259520861.html?p._all&prepage_1&c_y-continue.

Marsh, A. A., Kozak, M. N., and Ambady, N. (2007). Accurate identification of fear facial expressions predicts prosocial behavior. *Emotion*, *49*(2), 107–112.

Martinko, M. J., Harvey, P., Brees, J. R., and Mackey, J. (2013). A review of abusive supervision research. *Journal of Organizational Behavior*, *34*(S1), S120–S137.

Mayer, J. D., Salovey, P., and Caruso, D. R. (2008). Emotional intelligence: new ability or eclectic traits? *American Psychologist*, *63*(6), 503–517.

McDonald, P. (2012). Workplace sexual harassment 30 years on: a review of the literature. *International Journal of Management Reviews*, *14*(1), 1–17.

Mueller, S., and Tschan, F. (2011). Consequences of client-initiated workplace violence: the role of fear and perceived prevention. *Journal of Occupational Health Psychology*, *16*(2), 217–229.

Mumford, M. D., Connelly, S., Brown, R. P., Murphy, S. T., Hill, J. H., Antes, A. L., Waples, E. P., and Devenport, L. D. (2008). A sensemaking approach to ethics training for scientists: preliminary evidence of training effectiveness. *Ethics and Behavior*, *18*(4), 315–339.

Ness, A. M., and Connelly, S. (2017). Situational influences on ethical sensemaking: performance pressure, interpersonal conflict, and the recipient of consequences. *Human Performance*, 30, 57–78.

Occupational Safety and Health Administration (2017). Workplace violence. Retrieved from https://www.osha.gov/SLTC/workplaceviolence/.

Öhman, A. (2008) Fear and anxiety: overlaps and dissociations. In M. Lewis, J. M. Haviland-Jones, and L. F. Barrett (eds), *Handbook of Emotions* (3rd ed., pp. 709–729). New York, NY, USA: Guilford Press.

Olatunji, B. O., Ciesielski, B. G., Armstrong, T., and Zald, D. H. (2011). Emotional expressions and visual search efficiency: specificity and effects of anxiety symptoms. *Emotion, 11*(5), 1073–1079.

Osborne, D., Smith, H. J., and Huo, Y. J. (2012). More than a feeling: discrete emotions mediate the relationship between relative deprivation and reactions to workplace furloughs. *Personality and Social Psychology Bulletin, 38*(5), 628–641.

Parrott, W. G. (2001). Implications of dysfunctional emotions for understanding how emotions function. *Review of General Psychology, 5*(3), 180–186.

Parrott, W. G. (ed.) (2014). *The Positive Side of Negative Emotions.* New York, NY, USA: Guilford Press.

Perkins, A. M., Kemp, S. E., and Corr, P. J. (2007). Fear and anxiety as separable emotions: an investigation of the revised reinforcement sensitivity theory of personality. *Emotion, 7*(2), 252–261.

Piquero, N. L., Piquero, A. R., Craig, J. M., and Clipper, S. J. (2013). Assessing research on workplace violence, 2000–2012. *Aggression and Violent Behavior, 18*(3), 383–394.

Roseman, I. J. (1991). Appraisal determinants of discrete emotions. *Cognition and Emotion, 5*(3), 161–200.

Sakellaropoulos, A., Pires, J., Estes, D., and Jasinski, D. (2011). Workplace aggression: assessment of prevalence in the field of nurse anesthesia. *American Association of Nurse Anesthetists Journal, 79*(4 Suppl), S51–57.

Samnani, A. K., and Singh, P. (2012). Twenty years of workplace bullying research: a review of the antecedents and consequences of bullying in the workplace. *Aggression and Violent Behavior, 17*(6), 581–589.

Schat, A. C., and Kelloway, E. K. (2000). Effects of perceived control on the outcomes of workplace aggression and violence. *Journal of Occupational Health Psychology, 5*(3), 386–402.

Schat, A. C., and Kelloway, E. K. (2003). Reducing the adverse consequences of workplace aggression and violence: the buffering effects of organizational support. *Journal of Occupational Health Psychology, 8*(2), 110–122.

Schat, A. C., and Kelloway, E. K. (2005). Workplace aggression. In J. Barling, E. K. Kelloway, and M. R. Frone (eds), *Handbook of Work Stress* (pp.189–218). Thousand Oaks, CA, USA: Sage.

Schneider, B., Ehrhart, M. G., and Macey, W. H. (2013). Organizational climate and culture. *Annual Review of Psychology, 64*, 361–388.

Smith, C. A., and Ellsworth, P. C. (1985). Patterns of cognitive appraisal in emotion. *Journal of Personality and Social Psychology, 48*(4), 813–838.

Smith, J. (August, 2013). America's 10 deadliest jobs. *Forbes.* Retrieved from https://www.forbes.com.

Solomon, R. C., and Stone, L. D. (2002). On "positive" and "negative" emotions. *Journal for the Theory of Social Behaviour, 32*(4), 417–435.

Sonenshein, S. (2007). The role of construction, intuition, and justification in responding to ethical issues at work: the sensemaking-intuition model. *Academy of Management Review, 32*(4), 1022–1040.

Spector, P. E., Coulter, M. L., Stockwell, H. G., and Matz, M. W. (2007). Perceived violence climate: a new construct and its relationship to workplace physical violence and verbal aggression, and their potential consequences. *Work and Stress, 21*(2), 117–130.

Suárez, J. G. (1993). *Managing Fear in the Workplace* (TQLO Publication No. 93-01). Arlington, VA, USA: Department of The Navy, Total Quality Leadership Office.

Tannenbaum, M. B., Hepler, J., Zimmerman, R. S., Saul, L., Jacobs, S., Wilson, K., and Albarracín, D. (2015). Appealing to fear: a meta-analysis of fear appeal effectiveness and theories. *Psychological Bulletin, 141*(6), 1178–1204.

Tepper, B. J. (2007). Abusive supervision in work organizations: review, synthesis, and research agenda. *Journal of Management, 33*(3), 261–289.

Tiedens, L. Z. (2001). Anger and advancement versus sadness and subjugation: the effect of negative emotion expressions on social status conferral. *Journal of Personality and Social Psychology, 80*(1), 86–94.

Tiedens, L. Z., and Linton, S. (2001). Judgment under emotional certainty and uncertainty: the effects of specific emotions on information processing. *Journal of Personality and Social Psychology, 81*(6), 973–988.

van Kleef, G. A. (2008). Emotion in conflict and negotiation: introducing the emotions as social information (EASI) model. In N. M. Ashkanasy and C. L. Cooper (eds), *New Horizons in Management Series: Research Companion to Emotion in Organizations* (pp. 392–404). Cheltenham, UK and Northampton, MA, USA: Edward Elgar Publishing.

van Kleef, G. A. (2009). How emotions regulate social life: the emotions as social information (EASI) model. *Current Directions in Psychological Science, 18*(3), 184–188.

van Kleef, G. A. (2014). Understanding the positive and negative effects of emotional expressions in organizations: EASI does it. *Human Relations, 67*(9), 1145–1164.

van Kleef, G. A., De Dreu, C. K. W., and Manstead, A. S. R. (2004). The interpersonal effects of anger and happiness in negotiations. *Journal of Personality and Social Psychology, 86*(1), 57–76.

Vecchio, R. P., and Appelbaum, S.H. (1995). *Managing Organizational Behavior: A Canadian Perspective*. Toronto, Canada: Harcourt Brace and Company.

Zoghbi-Manrique-de-Lara, P. (2006). Fear in organizations: does intimidation by formal punishment mediate the relationship between interactional justice and workplace internet deviance? *Journal of Managerial Psychology, 21*(6), 580–592.

7. Happiness at work: a tension in contemporary history

Peter N. Stearns

Happiness – often identified as one of the basic emotions – is a prime candidate for an analysis that links the ways emotion is discussed with what we can know of the actual experience in the workplace. Few workplace emotions have been so extensively promoted as happiness, at key points over the past century. To be sure, programs have often focused on satisfaction rather than happiness outright, distinguishing levels of intensity and duration; but both goals highlight a positive work response. Personal predispositions to happiness, tracing the desire to foster more positive reactions, on the part of relevant experts and many of their management sponsors, offers a relatively straightforward topic, though one that also reveals significant rifts in the ways happiness is defined and in the policies aimed at promoting it. Considerable organizational effort, and organizational politics, lie behind the many recommendations and analyses that have graced this subject since the early twentieth century. But the relationship between promotion/discussion on the one hand, and actual emotional experience on the job on the other, is more challenging – partly, of course, because of the divisions in approach as well as some significant changes over time. Indeed, in recent decades many authorities and personnel leaders have pulled back somewhat from happiness claims, unsure of the relationship between personal predisposition to happiness and workplace experience. An approach drawn from emotions history, a new subfield eager to trace and explain changes in emotional standards and link them to current patterns, is well suited to this kind of analysis, as it deliberately seeks relationships between emotional concepts and human experience (Matt and Stearns, 2014).

Existing research on the history of happiness (and its modern companion, cheerfulness) has not usually focused on job conditions, as opposed to family life or consumer expectations – though as we will see the idea of cheerfulness certainly links to a pervasive pressure on service personnel (Kotchemidova, 2005; McMahon, 2006). We do know that, in the Western world, assumptions about the attainability of happiness advanced steadily from the Enlightenment onward, and there is every reason to connect this larger pattern to the experience of work. It was also following the Enlightenment that many employers grew more concerned about the happiness of their charges – as in new efforts to promote smiling among slaves in the United States or the use of a new word, sulky, to describe servants who did not seem cheerful. In what follows, we will first discuss the impact of modern work conditions on worker response. Amid this new if vague interest in more positive responses. Job satisfaction was not at this point an explicit concept, but several approaches developed in the nineteenth century that would strongly condition later policies. Work and happiness were much more widely linked from the late nineteenth century onward, though amid real divisions in emphasis that complicate any assessment of results. A clear tension emerges, between expert inquiry and management policy, on the one hand, and what we know about actual experience on the other. Finally, though the dimensions here are only now emerging, developments around the turn of the twenty-first century suggest a further shift in approach, and an arguable narrowing in management responsibility, as happiness yields to positivity and well-being. Historical analysis suggests both the discrete stages in attention to workplace satisfaction, and the links that connect key aspects of the modern experience.

The idea of identifying happiness at work is surely a modern one, the fruit among other things of an expansion of the whole idea of happiness over the past two centuries. This is not to claim that people were unhappy at work in times past. Pride in skill and achievement or advancement in one's craft; the pleasure of working with family members and neighbors, as in the evening sewing sessions conducted by many peasant women – many traditional settings might combine work with pleasure, despite the nagging concern that somehow the need to work was connected with human sin and a fall from divine grace. Premodern work also commonly mixed labor with what today we would call recreational elements – wandering around, chatting, sometimes singing, grabbing a nap – that could add to the contentment associated with work itself. Indeed, a powerful case can be made that industrial conditions, that accelerated the pace of work, subjected most workers to new forms of supervision, and reduced the play elements, have made happiness on the job harder to achieve than it was in times past. The Marxist idea of worker alienation broadly conveyed some of these changes (Stearns, 2008).

In all probability modern deteriorations in the experience of work help explain why workplace emotion gained new attention in the first place.

This factor operated in combination with the growing interest in happiness, from the Enlightenment, which became a key element in beliefs in social progress. The overall formulation took shape in stages, with a consistent interest in workplace happiness emerging only more recently. But identifying some of the earlier factors is essential in explaining the more contemporary patterns. Indeed, key formulations and their limitations – both worker reactions but especially a new middle-class approach to work – would play a central role in shaping ideas about job happiness that emerged in the twentieth century.

HISTORICAL CONTEXT

Several elements should be highlighted. First, just as industrialization was beginning to disrupt popular work traditions in the late eighteenth/early nineteenth centuries, a new "middle-class" work ethic took shape in elements of the business and professional community (Rodgers, 2014). The ethic extolled hard work – early to bed, early to rise, devotion to the task at all times. Work would produce a reward, in greater wealth and personal advancement. Whether work itself involved happiness, however, was not entirely clear, and this issue continues to bedevil some emotional formulations even today. Work ethic advocates like Samuel Smiles or Horatio Alger were clear that the positive aspects of work surely should prevent anger or grievance; middle-class people professed bafflement when workers did not simply stick to their job and seek to rise in life. And many middle-class people clearly felt a bit adrift when they were not at work, having difficulty for example enjoying a vacation, which indirectly suggested a link between work and satisfaction. But whether work zeal was supposed to generate happiness on the job, as opposed to extrinsic gains, was not entirely clear. Despite this problem, the middle-class ethic assumed that work had a positive valence and that more negative reactions were suspect.

It's worth noting as well that alongside both early industrialization and the middle-class ethic, some utopian thinkers already tried to devise systems that would more explicitly promote happiness on the job (Guarneri, 1991). The ideas of Charles Fourier most clearly generated utopian communities that sought to allocate work according to the interests and capacities of different age groups, both to avoid industrial tedium and to promote job satisfaction and variety. This was a maverick impulse, to be sure, but it suggests the new kinds of thinking that sought alternatives to the factory system in the interest of Enlightenment-derived aspirations for happiness. The utopian impulse also helps explain the first overall surge of interest in happiness at work, both in Britain and the United States, though it proved short-lived in part because most utopian frameworks were so vividly out of keeping with industrial needs.

For their part, in a class-divided industrial society, many workers gradually made some peace with conditions in factories and offices through the bargain commonly labelled as *instrumentalism*. Beginning in the mid-nineteenth century, various urban working groups essentially concluded that they could accept the new work pace and the decline of skill and autonomy in return for greater rewards off the job. Work became an *instrument* of happiness, though not happiness itself, as the bargain suggested that actual jobs were becoming less pleasant (Hobs-bawm, 1965). Workers might nevertheless find some job satisfaction, but much of their focus shifted elsewhere, particularly of course when hours of work also began to decline. And there is no indication that their employers thought much, one way or another, about the happiness of their factory employees, aside from appreciating diligence, trying to generate greater reliability through shop rules and the often harsh supervision of foremen (where negative rather than positive motivations clearly predominated), and possibly rewarding the better workers with higher pay. Finally, instrumentalism was effectively picked up by much of the labor movement, in part because it seemed to reflect worker priorities, but in part because instrumentalist demands, focused on wages and benefits, proved easier to win than protests that called work arrangements themselves into question; employers might resist, but they too understood the instrumentalist equation and were more likely to make concessions in this domain than in other areas.

The decades of active industrialization in the West thus produced two major views of work – apart from the utopians: one, middle-class, emphasized work's positive features and the importance of commitment; the other, more working-class, stressed extrinsic reward. Both these approaches would exercise a powerful influence over more systematic approaches to workplace happiness in the twentieth century and beyond.

Several new elements entered the picture later in the nineteenth century, beginning more directly to set the stage for interactions between ideas of work happiness and actual policies and experiences. The first involved the expansion of white-collar jobs, some of them largely female. Employers made a rather conscious effort to keep the white collar force separate from blue collar, with different standards of dress (obviously) and methods of pay and benefits (Kocka, 1980). And some white-collar workers, in sales jobs, had to be deliberately emotionally trained to present a smiling face to customers (Benson, 1986; Hochschild, 2012). Here was one new reason to reconsider the emotional tone of the workplace. The need to instil certain emotional styles in segments of the labor force – and particularly service personnel and middle management – unquestionably encouraged new types of emotional manipulation, but it also promoted a greater interest in actual job satisfaction as well.

This interest was also encouraged by growing concern about labor unrest, even in blue collar ranks, which a more positive approach to work might address: this was the motivation for a good bit of the early work in industrial psychology. The continued expansion of the labor movement might prompt an openness to innovations in the workplace that, if not directed at happiness per se, would at least seek to moderate discontent and create a more positive atmosphere (Stearns, 1975).

A further development, again in the decades around 1900, involved new recognition that the middle-class personnel themselves could experience strain at work – modifying the earlier simple reliance on the work ethic. The rise of interest in neurasthenia, in the hands of experts like S. Weir Mitchell, focused strongly on how the pressures of work zeal could take a toll on mental and physical health, particularly for middle-class men (Gosling, 1987).

All of this – the growth of the white collar and service sector; the surge of more systematic labor protest; and new concerns about the middle class itself – formed the immediate background for a growing interest in industrial psychology and other workplace studies, that began to create new suggestions about workplace organization and management aimed at greater emotional well-being or (depending on the eye of the beholder) manipulation.

For it was in the late nineteenth century and more clearly the early decades of the twentieth that explicit attention to workplace happiness began to increase rather dramatically, both in Britain and the United States. The expansion of *talk* about happiness on the job is easy to demonstrate, though we need to lay out its dimensions. The clearer challenge is to figure out how talk related, if at all, to emotional experience – the key topic of this volume. The challenge is compounded by the fact that experts and management representatives generated several different and partially conflicting approaches to happiness at work, reflecting some of divergences that had emerged earlier and that complicated resulting policy and impact. This complexity, finally, would yield a somewhat different approach in the final decades of the twentieth century, highlighted by the growing interest in well-being that still today marks so many management initiatives in this domain.

TRACING THE INTEREST IN HAPPINESS AT WORK

There is no question that interest in the links between happiness and work expanded rapidly from the late nineteenth century well into the twentieth century – after the brief surge associated with earlier utopianism and possibly the work-ethic boosters like Horatio Alger and Samuel Smiles. Charts based on Google books data suggest a fairly clear pattern, both in Britain and the United States. The charts trace relevant frequency of a happiness/work combination, relative to all other word use possibilities over the past two centuries. References that linked happiness and work were minimal in the United States until the later nineteenth century, save for the mid-nineteenth-century uptick, but then expanded consistently for several decades. British patterns coincide broadly speaking, with the principal distinction a longer period of high-level interest past the middle of the twentieth century. Google data derive from the millions of English-language books in the database. Word searches – in this case, linked references to work and happiness or vice versa, can be plotted in terms of relative frequency, as against other topics. The measure is a crude one, and at best signals changes in relative overall interest, which in turn invite closer analysis. By the same token, short-term oscillations may be essentially random; the longer-term shifts in frequency form the main point. References for Ngrams here are, to be sure, only suggestive: they provide a framework for further inquiry when frequencies increase or decline, but do not in themselves indicate significance, causation or impact. In this case they clearly confirm the validity of inquiring more deeply into early twentieth-century patterns. And they are complemented by other data, for example the over 2,000 books and articles published, in the United States alone, on job satisfaction from the 1920s until the mid-1970s. The availability of ideas about workplace happiness accelerated rather markedly, and this provides the first target for more extended analysis of the ways happiness on the job has been discussed.

Most of the efforts to define and promote workplace happiness (or the less demanding goal of satisfaction) shared one complexity, which has continued in the relevant literature to the present day: they were mainly looking at the phenomenon less for its own sake than for its role in other aspects of workplace behaviors. A few exceptions stand out, where job satisfaction was part of a larger exploration of how Americans, Britons or others experience contemporary life (Campbell et al., 1976). More commonly, however, satisfaction was seen as a means to another end – workplace stability or productivity – as measured particularly by management. This is one reason that, despite frequent discussion of happiness on

Figure 7.1   Google Ngram chart for "work and happiness" 1800–2008, American English

Figure 7.2   Google Ngram chart for "work and happiness" 1800–2008, British English

the job, satisfaction was the term preferred, presumably because it reflected a higher cognitive, less fully emotional criterion that could be more readily factored into business decisions.

Early studies were thus strongly influenced by concerns about worker protest and the currents of anger or irritability psychologists discovered, to their consternation, on the shop floor (Baritz, 1960). Both Elton Mayo, author of the Hawthorne studies, and Frederick Taylor came to their tasks from middle-class backgrounds in which the positive value of work was taken for granted, which is why they were so easily taken aback by labor dissatisfaction – though their responses moved in somewhat different directions (Roethlisberger and Dickson, 1939). Satisfaction studies and recommendations were not directly measured against strike rates, slacking or absenteeism, but the connections were reasonably clear nevertheless. A second vantage point, though more on the white collar side, stressed the relationship between job satisfaction and sales and customer service: a happy worker could bring a positive outlook to his or her work that would in turn have a favorable impact on the clientele.

Later on, and particularly in more recent decades, job satisfaction studies would seek even more explicit connections between their focus and measurable results such as productivity (happy workers are up to 18% more productive than workers in general), retention and absenteeism (Judge and Watanabe, 1993; Tait et al., 1989). It is vital to note that recent research has muddied the outcomes claims, for example in raising questions about whether effects reflect innate personalities rather than personnel programs (Fisher, 2003; Wright et al., 2002; Zelenski et al., 2008). It remains true that the efforts to assess the results of positive attitudes move away from the emotional experience of the worker him or herself and into a somewhat different basic focus. And they encourage attention to those aspects of job satisfaction that may be most amenable to manipulation or strategic intervention.

THREE DIFFERENT PATHS

This said, the kinds of inquiries into job satisfaction that began to rain down after World War I, mainly though not exclusively in the hands of industrial psychologists and sociologists, took three different and only partially compatible directions, which complicated the impact of the findings at the time and since.

First off the blocks was the efficiency engineering approach associated most clearly with Frederick Taylor, whose *Principles of Scientific Management* appeared in 1909 (Taylor, 1985). Taylor became known primarily for his emphasis on the most efficient organization of work, but he was concerned with job satisfaction, if not happiness, in at least two ways, both premised on the belief that a contented worker would be more productive. First, he urged that worker motivation be more actively considered in hiring and assignment of tasks, as part of the broader efficiency approach. And second, he believed deeply that workers assessed their jobs almost entirely on the basis of wages – hence his insistence, in principle, on "a fair day's work for a fair day's pay", with poor performers meriting less reward. Well-paid workers, called upon to expend only the mental and physical effort required for the job thanks to efficient organization, would perform the best, particularly in the context that Taylor envisaged where management and labor would collaborate more actively than had been true in the more traditional factory setting. Emotions experienced directly on the job counted for little in this scheme that emphasized largely external rewards. The overlap with the kind of instrumentalism that many workers and labor unions had developed made this implicit definition of the basis for worker happiness understandable, but it turned out to be a misleadingly narrow approach to job reactions.

A second approach came less from industrial psychologists than from self-appointed experts particularly interested in influencing white collar and middle-class employees and in linking job reactions to successful sales techniques and constructive interactions within management ranks. Here the emphasis rested on the kind of personality an individual brought into the job: happiness was extremely important, but its sources were largely extrinsic to the work itself. As Dale Carnegie put it, "if we think happy thoughts we will be happy. If we think miserable thoughts we will be miserable." "It isn't what you [the worker] have or who are you or where you are or what you are doing that makes you happy or unhappy. It's what you think about it." Intrinsic personality was part of this formula, but Carnegie and others assumed that, thanks to their stream of advice, many people could remake themselves into the kind of contented, positive workers who would achieve good results. Positive individuals would of course seek out jobs they liked, but the burden was on them and not arrangements intrinsic to the work itself. "Are you bored with life? Then throw yourself into some work you believe in with all your heart, live for it, die for it, and you will find happiness that you thought could never be yours" (Carnegie, 1981).

If the Taylor approach moved out strongly from worker instrumentalism, the self-help approach relied heavily on a modified middle-class work ethic now infused with happiness goals. The approach was additionally appealing because of its focus on worker rather than employer emotional responsibility. For the converse of this happiness formula was an easy dismissal of worker grievances on grounds they did not really derive from the job itself, but from emotional conditions in other aspects of life. By the 1930s personnel literature frequently stressed to disjuncture: "It is known that complaints, very often, have nothing to do with the matter complained about." Angry workers were merely "projecting their own maladjustments upon a conjured monster, the capitalist" (Stearns, 1994). Many workers, it was blithely assumed, had troubled family lives or other personal demons that had far more bearing on their emotional reactions on the job than anything in the work setting itself. And while it is easy enough to see the self-serving qualities in this analysis, the argument would help inspire further inquiries into the impact of intrinsic personality or wider life factors – a crucial component of happiness findings and management strategies even today.

A third general approach, deriving from the work of Mayo, Thurstone and others primarily in the 1920s and 1930s, and then authorities like Frederick Herzberg right after World War II, took a more nuanced and open-ended approach to worker attitudes and the mixture of job components that might affect reactions (Herzberg, 1959, 1966; Mayo, 1933). This group shared with Taylor the belief that contented workers would be less troublesome and more productive, but they saw contentment responding to a mix of factors and not, primarily, to pay and extrinsic reward. Mayo's work is noteworthy for its emphasis on the human factors in workplace reactions. Workers respond favorably when management visibly expresses interest in their activities, and they also depend heavily on the norms and reactions of their colleagues. Improved human relations led to productivity gains almost regardless of other changes in the factory environment. Other researchers, though sharing this general approach, addressed additional aspects of motivation, and particularly the role of challenge and variety in improving satisfaction and reducing tedium. Collectively, these approaches suggested the significance of several workplace components, potentially in combination, while downplaying the role of wage levels and prior personality in shaping worker emotions on the job.

The major efforts to define and explain emotional reactions on the job, and their relationships to actual management policy, raise two challenges in any effort to determine actual emotional experience in modern work history. First, and most obviously, they suggest the need to juxtapose the various factors that bear on workplace happiness, to go farther in exploring what components actually matter the most. Second, they invite an analysis that would move from the emotionally ambiguous notion of satisfaction, to a more active engagement with happiness.

Fortunately, the ideas about workplace emotion generated in the first half of the twentieth century, and particularly the more nuanced approaches of Mayo and others in this broad category, directly stimulated a series of studies that tried to isolate and quantify the various factors relevant to the work experience. A wealth of literature, applying both to Europe and the United States, can be fairly easily summarized as part of the transition from ideas about emotion to actual feelings on the job. The second challenge – moving some satisfaction to happiness – has also been addressed, though with somewhat less precision (Wright, 2006).

FACTORS IN SATISFACTION

Emotional reactions at work vary depending on social category, which is hardly surprising. Satisfaction levels are particularly low among unskilled workers – where eagerness for retirement, funds permitting, is also unusually high. In many studies only 11% express substantial satisfaction. Levels go up among the skilled – to 40% or so; and then soar in managerial and professional ranks, where up to 80% express substantial satisfaction and where interest in early retirement is correspondingly low. Restating this differential from another angle: work expectations rise with education, but college graduates are particularly sensitive to a sense of challenge and "meaningfulness" on the job, factors which have less salience for blue collar workers (Smith et al., 1969).

Gender played a significant role in work satisfaction in earlier periods, but in the United States gender differentials have virtually disappeared as more women commit to substantial involvement with formal employment. But in Britain, at least until recently, female job satisfaction, other factors held constant, surpasses that of men; the same is currently true in South Korea. Age is a factor, with older workers expressing greater contentment than younger – partly, of course, because skill, challenge and reward often correlate with age (Smith et al., 1969).

National distinctions merit attention, finally: European workers seem more sensitive to job arrangements than their American counterparts, and also possibly more responsive to collegial feelings among their workmates. Americans, by contrast, are more responsive to pay – a point to which we must return (Judge and Watanabe, 1993).

Going beyond the differentials, however, some other common findings emerge, in studies ranging from the 1930s until quite recently. First: most studies until recently have consistently suggested that about a third of the emotional reactions at work were a function of genetics, independent of the job itself (estimates ranged from 30–35%, based among other things on studies of twins). This specific finding was often amplified, more vaguely, by statements that overall life satisfaction had more to do with work reactions than the other way around, implying both that work played a lesser role in overall emotional experience than might be imagined (a 1976 study pegged this at 20%) and that life off the job might impinge on work even beyond the genetic component. The impulses of earlier enthusiasts like Dale Carnegie were not fully confirmed, in stressing the importance of attitudes brought to the job, but they won some support (Argyle, 2002; Smith et al., 1969; Veroff et al., 1981; Wanous et al., 1997).

Second: pay and promotion play a relatively modest role in job satisfaction (one study suggested that wages accounted for about 15% of overall reactions), but with some caveats. The generalization assumes pay above the most minimal levels (the finding does not apply, for example, to many part-time workers where low pay combines with job insecurity). A sense of fairness in pay can also impinge: knowledge that comparable categories are paid better can color emotional reactions more than pay levels in themselves. Promotion opportunities count for something, but again at a more modest level (Wanous et al., 1997).

This leaves, as primary factors, the components that Mayo and others had emphasized: level of challenge (so long as this was not outweighed by feeling overburdened – the stress/challenge relationship was a delicate one); sense of meaningfulness; relations with supervisors and colleagues. While this final factor has historically been studied less than its high priority might suggested, recent research, for example on the positive role of "companionate love" among work colleagues, is beginning to redress the balance (Barsade and O'Neill, 2016).

Finally, when all components were in, most studies (at least applying to the United States and Britain) have suggested that about 30% of all workers/all categories were very satisfied with work; another 30–40% fairly satisfied but would in principle be eager to change jobs; and the final quarter to a third unhappy to some degree (Campbell et al., 1976; Wanous et al., 1997). The cumulative factor analysis, in other words, also began to generate probable answers concerning the relationship between satisfaction, a broader category, and the more positive emotions reasonably associated with happiness. Various measurements included distinctions between "high" satisfaction (27% in a 1981 U.S. study) versus the somewhat larger category that was merely satisfied (47%, in the same analysis). Or questions might zero in on what a person would do if no longer compelled to work: 30% responding that they would remain at their present job; another 35% pledging to work but only if they could change jobs; the rest too alienated to seek work at all. Or in another common strategy: individuals were asked if, were they able to do things all over again, they would make the same job decision: again, the end result identified about a third or slightly less, who responded affirmatively.

A similar mixed to negative impression emerges from analysis of Studs Terkel's intriguing interview data, from the 1970s. A few workers claimed happiness simply because they earned enough to have an adequate life off the job; one noted happiness because of meaningful work as a publicist. Far more, however, either ignored the emotion (happiness was mentioned infrequently) or highlighted ways that management tactics reduced any possibility of happiness. While Terkel's interviews showed an impressive capacity on the part of a wide array of workers in creating some attachment to the job, it rarely went as far as happiness (Terkel, 1985).

These various data were discouraging in many ways. If for example, about 30% of job satisfaction depended on larger life satisfaction, and not the job itself – two common findings – positive aspects of work, rather than predisposition, might be generating little strong satisfaction. Distinctions among job categories were also daunting: since about 80% of professional people normally responded positively to questions about choosing the same job again, levels for other job categories were far from affirmative.

Finally, beyond the specific job surveys, other data pointed to some further challenges, at least in the United States. The protest mood of the 1960s generated important initiatives to improve workplace conditions, aimed at expanding interest and "meaningfulness," and this focus has persisted as a key element in more recent studies of effective worker motivation (Pink, 2011). In Sweden and elsewhere, management and labor crafted agreements to redesign jobs in order to promote greater challenge and variety at work – putting into practice some of the findings derived from component analysis. And the result did improve reported emotional response. But in the United States, similar efforts – as in the Lordstown automobile plant – ran aground when workers discovered that these improvements had a negative impact on pay levels. The demanding requirements of American consumerism, in other words, outweighed potential emotional benefits on the job, whatever the formal studies about the lower priority of pay levels might suggest (Stearns, 2008; Weller, 1973).

Pervasive findings about emotional reactions on the job suggest that consistent workplace happiness – as opposed to more fleeting pleasures in job mastery or camaradarie – is a minority experience in advanced industrial societies. Concern about pay levels affect these findings to some degree, but pay raises – elusive in any event since the 1980s – have only modest impact on emotional experience. Claims that job emotions reflect a strong personality or genetic component, rather than direct features of the work itself, are partially justified by the data. The significance of factors such as challenge, a sense of meaningfulness, or relations among colleagues and with managers, does show through, but for most workers not at levels that would move into an active happiness category outside top management and professional ranks.

TRENDS: A QUESTION MARK

As the previous section suggested, most examinations of worker satisfaction reveal considerable stability over time, with the clearest variations reflecting blips in job security associated with recessions – as was true for two years after 2008, in the United States. Changes in expectations, however, might generate more complex results. As women developed fuller work identities, and as consciousness of gender pay gaps increased, women's work satisfaction shifted downward in the United States early in the twenty-first century, and this had some impact on overall reported levels (Tait et al., 1989). One study suggested a similar expectations-based downturn from the mid to late 1970s (though contentment with colleagues remained constant, as seems quite generally to be the case) (Chelte et al., 1982).

More recent trend analysis is simply inconclusive. On the one hand, Conference Board studies suggest a significant slide in worker reactions from the late 1980s to 2014. In 1987, 61% of workers were reporting satisfaction – a figure similar to levels reported by the various one-time studies cited above; but by 2010 the figure had dropped to 43.6%, reflecting among other things the lingering effects of the recession and the marked increase in unstable part-time jobs, but also definably negative judgments about benefits and promotions. Interest in work and collegiality still won the highest ratings (around 60% satisfaction) but even these dropped slightly and did not in any event compensate for other factors. In 2014, 52% said they were unhappy at work. Some complementary studies, suggesting for example a generational shift in work goals, with "millennials" more interested than their predecessors in "meaningfulness" at work suggest some additional reasons for the drift (Adams, 2014).

But against these findings the Gallup organization reported absolutely the reverse: a pronounced increase in the "completely satisfied" category (28% in 1989; 35% in 1997, but a whopping 44% in 2015, with virtually no recession impact even earlier) and 54% in 2016. Most of these gains reflected movement from the "somewhat satisfied" category, but there was a modest overall drop in the "somewhat or completely dissatisfied" group as well (11% 1989; 13% 1997; 18% 2011, presumably marking the recession's greatest impact; 13% 2015 and 9% 2016). Collegiality, job security, recognition were the most important overall positives in 2016, benefits and stress the leading problems (but serious only for a minority) (Gallup, 2016).

Disparities of this sort, in the findings of fully reputable polling organizations, clearly reflect the difficulty of measuring job reactions and the role of different weighting systems among the components that make up these reactions. The data are far less conclusive than one might wish. At the same time, and particularly for the Gallup group, a final shift in criteria during the past two decades – from the admittedly amorphous category of satisfaction to a new emphasis on well-being – may be affecting trend analysis as well, in another case where ideas about work reactions interact with assessments in complex fashion. A very recent shift in personnel vocabulary and policy requires assessment, picking up also potentially modifying earlier findings about the complex interaction between employer goals and workplace results.

FROM HAPPINESS TO WELL-BEING

For one final development in the ideas about workplace emotion, emerging strongly from the late twentieth century onward though particularly in the United States, adds an intriguing new twist. Concern about workplace happiness persisted, though according to Google data with a measurable decline in frequency, but it was increasingly replaced, or modified, by the surge of attention to well-being (Bailyn, 2006). Even before the famous manifesto of positive psychology – the Martin Seligman presentation to the American Psychological Association in 1998 – happiness interests were beginning to morph into the newer focus on well-being, with a great deal of attendant discussion about the relationship between the two concepts. Applied to the workplace, the result maintained some earlier emphases – for example, on the importance of meaning and purpose – but also modified the structure of expectations in several revealing ways; and the transition had significant impact on a new set of workplace experiments. Several organizations, including the Gallup group, became heavily invested in the well-being movement and, one might argue, in generating evidence of positive results.

For the most obvious shift implicit in the well-being movement was to highlight the emphasis on individual responsibility over other aspects of the work environment – and older themes that now gained new salience (Horowitz, in press; Gillham et al., 2001). Revealingly, many well-being experts began to argue that as much as 50% of the emotional experience on the job was genetic – a huge, if largely unexamined, shift from the common expert wisdom earlier in the twentieth century. Correspondingly, both managers and individual workers were urged to probe preexisting

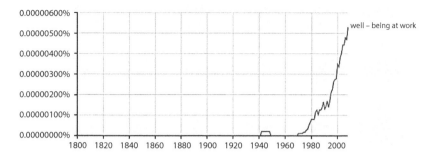

Figure 7.3   Google Ngram chart for "well-being at work" 1800–2008, American English

"strengths" in making or seeking workplace assignments. Testing agencies now went beyond earlier efforts to screen job applicants, trying to identify personality features that could be utilized and enhanced by appropriate tasks, to generate greater productivity and smoother individual responses alike. Happiness was partially redefined, accordingly, to embrace momentary pleasures; sense of purpose; but also the deployment of pre-existing strengths.

The shift to well-being also responded, though quietly, to the increasing stagnation of wages, along with growing income inequalities. Attention to personal growth and opportunities to explore self-help advice – not a new element in workplace approaches, but now expanding in significance – might compensate for these constraints, generating other sources of positive experience. Preparatory moves in positive psychology, accelerating particularly during the 1980s, coincided clearly with the setbacks in the instrumental component of workplace reactions.

Moving forward, certainly by the early twenty-first century, the shift from satisfaction/happiness to well-being in arranging and evaluating work experiences created additional ramifications, though with important overlaps with earlier concepts as well. Though outcome results were still disputed, researchers in the positivity vein offered a number of claims about how employees with "high well-being" will thus be more productive (as happy or satisfied employees were in earlier formulations). High well-being, translated into workers who enjoyed and were engaged with their jobs, involved a sense that the employing organization was supportive – another continuity, though with new vocabulary, from the older findings of Mayo and others that anything management did to create an impression of involvement would have a salutary effect. Well-being exercises also might allow workers a greater sense of control over pace, if for example they were authorized to take breaks to engage in yoga exercises or meditation (Achor, 2012; Kohner, 2016; Warr, 1999).

But the strong emphasis well-being advocates placed on physical and mental health did shift attention away from other aspects of the job – even beyond pay levels – toward personal responsibility for a positive outlook. Human relations offices increased their discussions of what was called work–life balance, with the strong implication that jobs could and should be only a minor component of overall life satisfaction, with the main management responsibility focused on supporting flexible schedules and e-work that would allow adequate time for the "life" part of the personal equation. In return, workers were urged to develop habits that would directly promote a more positive outlook on the job. Along with taking advantage of management-promoted exercises – physical and meditative – "well-being" workers should learn to improve their happiness by savoring daily experiences and promoting their own optimism and gratitude; this directly recalled that earlier strain in the middle-class work ethic that had stressed individual responsibility for a positive work environment, among other things tending to make "meaningfulness" primarily a matter of personal adjustment. It remained unclear, in the new positive psychology as in earlier formulations, what could be done with the minority of workers whose productivity continued to suffer because they were "unhappy with life." It was vital to remember that, in the well-being approach, happiness caused success, not the other way around – again, not an entirely new formula but one that moved away from detailed attention to the emotional implications of the job itself, in the well-being.

Happiness and work have a complex modern history, whether the focus is on the emotional experience on the job, management efforts to adjust work conditions or manipulate worker reactions, or larger ideas about what work satisfaction is all about. Assessments in term of emotions history are obviously qualified by a lack of clear baseline data, about work reactions before the advent of industrialization. Class-specific definitions of modern work, from labor instrumentalism to the middle-class ethic, color actual emotional experiences and expert formulations alike; even the current well-being enthusiasm largely picks up on earlier middle-class concerns and expectations. Assumptions that work reaction is shaped by external personality, whatever their degree of accuracy, have consistently affected – or more properly, deflected – policy responses on the part of management.

The recurrent tension between insistence on factors extrinsic to the job itself – whether prior personality or pay – and intrinsic qualities most obviously bedevils both analysis and management policy. It has proved so tempting to turn the focus away from work conditions themselves – and workers, as in Lordstown, have sometimes contributed to this diversion through their own instrumentalism. Current fascination with well-being maintains the tension, though redefining it in the direction of more personal responsibility. With due recognition of class and individual differences, however, it seems clear that workplace happiness depends above all on a balance among several components, with a sense of meaning and collegial relationships front and center in guiding actual emotional experience. Management can address this complexity, but it requires effort and, often, a willingness to modify some standard features of contemporary work arrangements.

This study, though clearly reflecting the complexity of assessing workplace happiness either in the past or present, has suggested three broad periods in the modern experience since industrialization began. For many decades in the nineteenth century, despite growing emphasis on happiness in other aspects of life, job satisfaction did not generate wide interest – some interesting flurries from utopian socialists and work ethic enthusiasts aside. The pressures of industrialization almost certainly reduced levels of contentment, though they did ultimately generate the instrumentalist response. Then through the mid-twentieth century a surge of attention reflected the rise of industrial psychology and new management concerns about worker response. The tantalizing question at this point centers on what impact the interest had, complicated of course by the divisions in approach among the experts themselves. Most data suggest fairly limited results, as the multitude of studies highlighted considerable sluggishness in satisfaction rates. Finally, though most obviously in the United States, a third period may have opened up by the end of the twentieth century, marked by the shift toward well-being and the marked reduction in direct links between happiness references and work. This decline of overt interest in workplace happiness thus coincides with huge new instabilities in workplace arrangements, stagnations in income, the rise of part-time employment, the reduction of labor unions – all suggesting deteriorations in job satisfaction in the recent past and for the foreseeable future, outside the professional ranks. Rather than confront these factors directly, many relevant experts are heightening the emphasis on workers' own input into their happiness with a bit of human resources guidance from management, leaving the larger issues aside or taking comfort in the few anomalous studies that claim to find massive improvements in worker well-being and placed greater emphasis on the individual worker and his/her attitude.

REFERENCES

Achor, S. (2012). Positive intelligence. *Harvard Business Review, 90*(1), 100–102. Retrieved December 13, 2016, from https://hbr.org/2012/01/positive-intelligence.

Adams, S. (2014). Most Americans are unhappy at work. *Forbes Leadership.* Retrieved December 8, 2016, from http://www.forbes.com/sites/susanadams/2014/06/20/most-americans-are-unhappy-at-work/#598e26c35862.

Argyle, M. (2002). *The Psychology of Happiness.* New York, NY: Routledge.

Bailyn, L. (2006). *Breaking the Mold: Redesigning Work for Productive and Satisfying Lives* (2nd ed.) Ithaca, NY: Cornell University Press.

Baritz, L. (1960). *The Servants of Power: A History of the Use of Social Science in American Industry.* Middletown, CT: Wesleyan University Press.

Barsade, S., and O'Neill, O. A. (2016). Manage your emotional culture. *Harvard Business Review, 94*(1), 14.

Benson, S. P. (1986). *Counter Cultures: Saleswomen, Managers, and Customers in American Department Stores, 1890–1940.* Urbana, IL: University of Illinois Press.

Campbell, A. Converse, P. E., and Rodgers, W. L. (1976). *The Quality of American Life: Perceptions, Evaluations and Satisfactions.* New York, NY: Russell Sage Foundation.

Carnegie, D. (1981). *How to Win Friends and Influence People.* New York, NY: Pocket Books.

Chelte, A. F., Wright, J., and Tausky, C. (1982). Did job satisfaction really drop during the 1970's? *Monthly Labor Review, 105*(11), 33–36. Retrieved December 8, 2016, from http://www.bls.gov/opub/mlr/1982/11/rpt1full.pdf.

Fisher, C. D. (2003). Why do lay people believe that satisfaction and performance are correlated? Possible sources of a commonsense theory. *Journal of Organizational Behavior, 24*(6), 753–777.

Gallup (2016). The relationship between engagement at work and organizational outcomes. Retrieved from www.gallup.com.

Gillham, J. E., Shatté, A. J., Reivich, K. J., and Seligman, M. E. (2001). Optimism, pessimism, and explanatory style. In E. Chang (ed.), *Optimism and Pessimism: Implications for Theory, Research, and Practice* (p 53–75). Washington, DC: APA Press.

Gosling, F. G. (1987). *Before Freud: Neurasthenia and the American Medical Community, 1870–1910.* Urbana, IL: University of Illinois Press.

Guarneri, C. J. (1991). *The Utopian Alternative: Fourierism in Nineteenth-Century America.* Ithaca, NY: Cornell University Press.

Herzberg, F. (1959). *The Motivation to Work.* New York, NY: Wiley.

Herzberg, F. (1966). *Work and the Nature of Man.* New York, NY: World Publishing Co.

Hobsbawm, E. J. (1965). *Labouring Men: Studies in the History of Labour.* New York, NY: Basic Books.

Hobsbawm, E. J. (1967). *Labouring Men: Studies in the History of Labour.* London: Weidenfeld and Nicolson.

Hochschild, A. R. (2012). *The Managed Heart: Commercialization of Human Feeling*. Berkeley, CA: University of California Press.

Horowitz, D. (in press). *Positively Happy: A History of Happiness Studies and Positive Psychology, 1945–2015*. New York, NY: Oxford University Press.

Judge, T. A., and Watanabe, S. (1993). Another look at the job satisfaction–life satisfaction relationship. *Journal of Applied Psychology, 78*(6), 939–948.

Kocka, J. (1980). *White Collar Workers in America, 1890–1940: A Social-Political History in International Perspective*. London and Beverly Hills: Sage Publications.

Kohner, J. (2016). How to achieve wellbeing in the workplace – it's possible! *Salesforce Blog: Careers, Cloud, Leadership*. Retrieved from https://www.salesforce.com/blog/2016/09/achieve-wellbeing-in-the-workplace.html.

Kotchemidova, C. (2005) From good cheer to "drive-by smiling": a social history of cheerfulness. *Journal of Social History 39*(1), 5–38.

Matt, S. J., and Stearns, P. N. (eds) (2014). *Doing Emotions History*. Urbana, Chicago, and Springfield, IL: University of Illinois Press.

Mayo, E. (1933). *The Human Problems of an Industrial Civilization*. New York, NY: The Macmillan Company.

McMahon, D. M. (2006). *Happiness: A History*. New York, NY: Atlantic Monthly Press.

Pink, D. H. (2011). *Drive: The Surprising Truth About What Motivates Us*. New York, NY: Penguin.

Rodgers, D. T. (2014). *The Work Ethic in Industrial America, 1850–1920* (2nd ed.). Chicago, IL: University of Chicago Press.

Roethlisberger, F. J., and Dickson, W. J. (1939). *Management and the Worker: An Account of a Research Program Conducted by the Western Electric Company, Hawthorne Works, Chicago*. Cambridge: Harvard University Press.

Smith, P. C., Kendall, L. M. and Hulin, C. L. (1969). *The Measurement of Satisfaction in Work and Retirement: A Strategy for the Study of Attitudes*. Chicago, IL: Rand McNally and Co.

Stearns, P. N. (1975). *Lives of Labor: Work in a Maturing Industrial Society*. New York, NY: Holmes and Meier.

Stearns, P. N. (1994). *American Cool: Constructing a Twentieth-Century Emotional Style*. New York, NY: New York University Press.

Stearns, P. N. (2008). *From Alienation to Addiction: Modern American Work in Global Historical Perspective*. Boulder, CO: Paradigm Publishers.

Tait, M., Padgett, M. Y., and Baldwin, T. T. (1989). Job and life satisfaction: A reevaluation of the strength of the relationship and gender effects as a function of the date of the study. *Journal of Applied Psychology, 74*(3), 502–507.

Taylor, F. W. (1985). *The Principles of Scientific Management*. Easton, PA: Hive Pub. Co.

Terkel, S. (1985). *Working: People Talk About What They Do All Day and How They Feel About What They Do*. New York, NY: The New Press.

Veroff, J., Douvan, E., and Kulka, R. A. (1981). *The Inner American: A Self-Portrait from 1957 to 1976*. New York, NY: Basic Books.

Wanous, J. P., Reichers, A. E., and Hudy, M. J. (1997). Overall job satisfaction: how good are single-item measures? *Journal of Applied Psychology, 82*(2), 247–252.

Warr, P. (1999). Well-being and the workplace. In D. Kahneman, E. Diener, and N. Schwarz (eds), *Well-Being: The Foundations of Hedonic Psychology* (pp. 392–412). New York, NY: Russell Sage Foundation.

Weller, K. (1973). The Lordstown struggle and the real crisis in production. *Solidarity, 45*, 1.

Wright, T. A. (2006). The emergence of job satisfaction in organizational behavior: a historical overview of the dawn of job attitude research. *Journal of Management History, 12*(3), 262–277.

Wright, T. A., Cropanzano, R., Denney, P. J., and Moline, G. L. (2002). When a happy worker is a productive worker: a preliminary examination of three models. *Canadian Journal of Behavioural Science 34*(3), 146–150.

Zelenski, J. M., Murphy, S. A., and Jenkins, D. A. (2008). The happy-productive worker thesis revisited. *Journal of Happiness Studies, 9*(4), 521–537.

8. Employee pride and hubris

Mathew L. A. Hayward, Neal M. Ashkanasy and Robert A. Baron

Richard Branson (CEO, Branson Holdings): "Above all, you want to create something you are proud of. That's always been my philosophy of business. I can honestly say that I have never gone into any business purely to make money."

(Hubbard, 2014, p. 6)

Tom Chappell (CEO/co-founder, Tom's of Maine): "Sure I am a religious man … but I am also a CEO, with all the bad habits and attitudes that are natural to the species. I am still naturally self-interested, overconfident, full of pride, and eager to control a meeting as any CEO in America. Every day, I struggle with my ego."

(Ardi, 2014, p. 161)

The Oxford English Dictionary[1] defines pride as "a feeling of deep pleasure or satisfaction derived from one's own achievements, the achievements of one's close associates, or from qualities or possessions that are widely admired." Tracy and Robins (2007a) argue further that "Pride is a cornerstone emotion that fuels several fundamental human pursuits: the desire to achieve, to attain power and status, to feel good about one's self …" (p. 127). In effect, understanding the nature and impact of pride on organizational members is critical to understanding their responses to successful achievements. Yet, to date, organizational behavior scholars have largely failed to develop this topic to its full potential. Our aim in this chapter is to offer a brief introduction to the nation of pride and to propose a preliminary model (Figure 8.1) as to how pride can impact employee performance outcomes.

What makes pride especially interesting is that it can take two forms as can be seen in the two quotes from well-known CEOs that we present at the beginning of this chapter. In the first, Richard Branson states on the one hand that pride in his companies' achievements is his primary source of motivation. In the second, on the other hand, Tom Chappell relates that

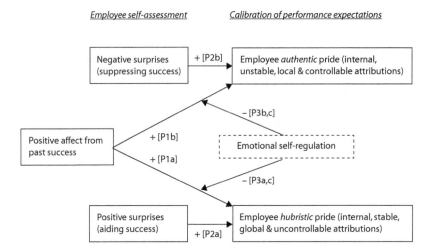

Figure 8.1   Linking employee pride and performance

his pride is an essential component of his ego. In this regard, based in a semantic and factor analysis of pride-related concepts and subjective experiences, Tracy and Robins (2004, 2007a, 2007b) concluded that actors' perceptions of favorable outcomes can be experienced as either *authentic pride* (attributed to effort) or as *hubristic pride* (attributed to own disposition and capabilities).

In view of this distinction, the role of pride in affecting employee performance and productivity remains a matter of contention. Traditionally, pride has been viewed as linked to, if not actually generating, beneficial effects including those cited by the prominent CEOs above (Katazenbach, 2003). Tracy and Robins (2007a, 2007b, 2007c) found in their research that pride is also related to persistence, goal accomplishment, and even generosity. Nonetheless, as Tom Chappell comments (in the opening vignette), pride can also be linked to important negative outcomes, including arrogance, overconfidence, aggression, and hostility, each of which can be powerfully socially dysfunctional and self-destructive (e.g., Hiller and Hambrick, 2005; Tracy et al., 2009; Tracy and Robins, 2004a, 2004b). Some commentators even argue that pride is one of the "seven deadly sins", leading prideful people to treat others in a haughty and dismissive manner (Schimmel, 1997; Williams and DeSteno, 2009).

These contrasting observations concerning the nature and effects of pride raise an intriguing organizational behavior question upon which we will focus: How can it generate both beneficial and detrimental effects in an organizational setting? In this chapter, we will take up this question, answering it by pointing to research suggesting that pride is not one emotion but two – authentic pride in accomplishments and hubristic pride in the self (Tracy and Robins 2004, 2007a, 2007b). The first, *authentic pride*, is rooted firmly in concrete performance achievements. Such pride represents a positive reaction to actual accomplishment. As such, it tends to be associated with beneficial work behaviors and attitudes. The second, *hubristic pride*, is a very different matter. Employees experiencing hubristic pride attribute their success largely, if not entirely, to stable, internal causes such as their own talent, intelligence, and good judgment. Thus, in their view, they, and little else, account for the positive outcomes they experience. Such pride promotes arrogance, conceit, self-aggrandizement, or over-confidence. Workers who display it can evoke fiercely negative, even resentful reactions (e.g., Tracy and Robins, 2007a, 2007b, 2007c). In this chapter, we first define pride and then review evidence pertaining to each of these types, referring in particular to attribution theory (Weiner, 1985, 1986, 2014) and emotional self-regulation theory (Gross, 1998). Our essay addresses the theme of this volume insofar as pride is a powerful emotion directly related to the social functions of emotions and how we talk about them.

WHAT IS PRIDE?

As is true for other emotions, pride is precipitated by a class of events. In the case of pride, these follow success in an achievement-relevant activity (Tracy et al., 2012). Pride also contains both positive affect about the event, as well as attributions that make the event meaningful to the individual. Moreover, this affect and cognition may be experienced consciously or unconsciously (Leary and Tangney, 2003). To illustrate this idea, consider a builder who completes a house on time. S/he may attribute his/her pleasure to completing work modules to schedule. On the other hand, if a surgeon is named "best medical practitioner in California," s/he may attribute her or his delight to the capability of operating with careful procedures. Employees who enjoy their work outcomes and attribute them to such capabilities would also experience pride.

Common themes in these examples help to distinguish an individual's personal feelings of pride from related emotions and cognition. In the first instance, unlike other emotions (e.g., anger, fear, and shame) a person's pride involves two potentially competing components: (a) positive affect from at least meeting goals, and (b) an attribution of such affect to the employees' own effort, disposition, or contribution, rather than to other sources and interpretations of positive affect including sensory arousal and mood swings. In addition, and this time like other emotions, pride can have lasting effects insofar as employees can continue to feel good about their contributions in anticipated and ensuing events (Weiss and Cropanzano, 1996). Thus, by generating positive affect, it is possible for the employee to build and to broaden her or his cognitive repertoire, which in turn paves the way to other resources, including social capital (Fredrickson, 2001).

Stemming from the foregoing discussion, it is clear that, while pride is a psychologically robust and distinctive construct, it involves two distinct and potentially conflicting facets that may cause employees to behave functionally or dysfunctionally in their organizations (e.g., Hayward and Hambrick, 1997; Louro et al., 2005; Ruys and Stapel, 2008; Weiner, 1985). Some psychologists even go so far as to assert that pride is one of the most frequently reported and impactful positive emotions at work (Basch and Fisher, 2000; see also Lazarus and Cohen-Charash, 2001). More relevant here is evidence that employees attribute success either to their own efforts or to their stable abilities. Such individuals are therefore likely to experience positive affect in the process (Weiner, 1985, 1986, 2014).

In this way, pride represents a direct emotional response to goal achievement. This is in contrast to self-efficacy, which is a cognitive appraisal of ability (Bandura, 1997). Accordingly, scholars empirically delineate pride from other constructs (Williams and DeSteno, 2008). Table 8.1 further elaborates major points of contrast between pride and related constructs: self-efficacy, self-esteem, core self-evaluation, and confidence. As can be seen in the table, distinctions relate to antecedent events, the nature of affect, cognition or trait associated with each construct, selective implications for organizational leadership, and their respective theoretical foundations.

Overall, evidence of pride in the workplace is consistent with research that employees gain pleasure from at least meeting expectations because they can attribute this to their ability, effort, and even control (e.g., Heider, 1958; Staw et al., 1983; Weiner, 1985, 1986, 2014). All of this begins to beg the question, however, as to what the functional and dysfunctional aspects of pride look like in social settings such as organizations.

Table 8.1 Distinguishing pride from related constructs

Distinguishing Dimensions	Pride	Self-efficacy	Self-esteem/Generalized Positive Affect	Core Self-evaluation	Confidence
Definition	Positive affect that arises from attributing outcomes	Level of belief in one's ability to succeed on certain tasks (Bandura, 1997)	Level of positive/negative towards oneself (Banaji and Prentice, 1994; Baumeister, 1998)	Broad, higher order latent trait indicated by: self-esteem, global self-efficacy, neuroticism and locus of control (Judge et al., 1997)	Level of belief in one's knowledge; certainty of future state; and ability to produce outcomes (Griffin and Varey, 1996)
Antecedent Trigger	After at least meeting expectations/goals	When evaluating goals and tasks, separate from affect states	Globally experienced trait	Globally experienced	When judging
Basis in Cognition/ Affect/Trait	Cognition: from attribution achievement theory Affect: from outcome interpretation	Cognitive: appraisal of ability on tasks	Affective: positive or negative valence	Generalized trait	Cognitive: from calibration paradigm
Implications for Leaders	Hubristic or authentic leadership	Leaders high in self-efficacy	Leaders high in self-esteem	Linked to hubris: Hiller and Hambrick (2005)	Linked to hubris: Hayward and colleagues (2006)
Theoretical Foundations	Attribution theory Affective events theory	Social cognitive theory	Motivation theory	Dispositional theory	Behavioral decision theory

AUTHENTIC AND HUBRISTIC ARE DIFFERENT FACETS OF PRIDE ARISING FROM SUCCESS

Turning now to discuss in particular the relationship between successful achievement and personal pride, we return to the Tracy and Robins' (2004, 2007a, 2007b) distinction between authentic and hubristic pride. In fact, and as Skowronski and Carlston (1989) point out (see also Tracy and Robins, 2004a, 2004b), successful outcomes elicit both forms of pride. Moreover, pride is inherently ego-invoking. In one case, people tend insufficiently to distinguish their successful work and activity from their successful self at any time (i.e., hubristic pride). Alternatively, people can choose to connect successful outcomes to successful efforts as they occur in time and place (i.e., authentic pride). Pride may thus represent a natural outgrowth of success. Moreover, successful achievement has potential to result in either authentic or hubristic pride. Thus, as their firms achieve more success, organizational members should experience both greater authentic and greater hubristic pride. This leads to our first propositions:

Proposition 1a: *Greater employee success leads to greater hubristic pride.*

Proposition 1b: *Greater employee success leads to greater authentic pride.*

But how exactly do these types of pride differ? And what determines which type of pride employees might experience? Tracy and Robins (2004a, 2004b, 2007a) found that the two types of pride exhibit a positive, but modest correlation. That is, they do not feature at opposite ends of a pride spectrum, and intense authentic pride is not tantamount to low pride. Overall, authentic pride is associated with achievement orientation, accomplishment, and confidence. Hubristic pride, conversely, is associated with arrogance, conceit, antisocial behavior, and a tendency to overestimate social consensus with one's beliefs (Picone et al., 2014). These differences, which are generalizable across employees, are summarized in Table 8.2.

Table 8.2 Differences between authentic and hubristic pride

	Authentic Pride	Hubristic Pride
General associations with:	Achievement orientation Accomplishment Confidence	Arrogance Conceit, antisocial behavior Overestimate social consensus
Positive correlations with:	Genuine self-esteem Authenticity	Narcissistic personality
Negative correlations with:	Machiavellianism Narcissistic personality disorder	Genuine self-esteem Authenticity

Sources: Tracy and Robins, 2007a; Tracy et al., 2009.

THE NATURE OF HUBRISTIC AND AUTHENTIC PRIDE

We now examine each type of pride in more detail before considering how organizational employees may potentially self-regulate to experience more functional forms of pride. As we shall see, the most fundamental difference between the two types of pride is how individuals make sense of their success. That is, the two types of pride show different attributional patterns. In this regard, we refer to Weiner's (1985, 1986, 2014) theory of attribution, which recognizes four key dimensions: (1) internal versus external; (2) stable versus unstable; (3) controllable versus uncontrollable; and (4) global versus local.

Hubristic pride. Hubristic pride arises when employees attribute organizational success to internal, global, stable, and uncontrollable determinants (Tracy and Robins, 2007b). Success from this point of view relates to *internal* determinants – when employees attribute it to their own capabilities rather than the environment. Attributions are *global* when employees perceive that causes are efficacious beyond a focal context (e.g., that can be leveraged across the development and sale of products, services, and potentially, industries). They are *stable* insofar as the employees perceive that the causes will remain the same in the future. Finally, they are *uncontrollable* when they are caused by unchanging capabilities that do not require effort or difficult development over time. This resonates with Dweck's (2006) notion of a "fixed mindset". Put differently, employees can express positive affect from their performance. They can attribute their attainment to their own (internal) characteristics that are also global, stable, and uncontrollable. Such attributes might include intelligence, creativity, charisma, or justice. Hubristic pride is also associated with less consultation with colleagues and a tendency toward antisocial behaviors (Cheng et al., 2010).

For hubristic pride to arise, it is necessary for employees to attribute success to themselves as opposed to their efforts, and this state becomes heightened as their attributions become more global, stable, and uncontrollable (cf. Weiner, 1986). Some people are more prone to these types of attributions than are others. In general, self-aggrandizing, shame-prone and disagreeable employees tend to experience hubristic pride in response to a pride-eliciting event (Tracy and Robins, 2007a, 2007b). Situational factors may also encourage this attributional configuration. In this instance, employees experiencing hubristic pride are prone to discount situational factors underlying their successful outcome. Instead, employees often attribute their personal success to their ability because they are motivated to explain, to predict, and to control performance. In particular, they tend to over-attribute successful behaviors and outcomes to their dispositions relation to situations in order to project themselves favorably (Bettman and Weitz, 1983; Clapham and Schwenk, 1991; Martinko et al., 2007; Staw et al., 1983; Weiner, 1985, 1986, 2014).

Another situational factor that might spur hubristic pride has to do with situational "surprises" – material and unanticipated changes in the employee's environment – which may be positive or negative. Consider a scenario in which productivity improvements owing to technology have been increasing organization-wide for some years, where expected future productivity increases are incorporated into performance expectations. Afterwards, an unexpected technological innovation contributes to a strong performance improvement. Employees with a tendency to over-attribute successful behaviors and outcomes to their dispositions (relative to situations) could attribute this salutary outcome to some stable, generalized capability like superior relationships with superiors and co-workers.

Situations where successful performances are attributable to positive environmental surprises, therefore, tend to spur employees' hubristic pride, relative to situations with no surprises. Put differently, a defining characteristic of hubristic pride is that employees (who experience high hubristic pride) attribute success to their capabilities in the presence of positive environmental surprises. Thus:

Proposition 2a: The greater the presence of positive environmental surprises, the greater the tendency for success to increase employees' hubristic pride.

Authentic pride. Similar to hubristic pride, authentic pride also contains an internal attribution for success. That is where the attributional similarity ends, however. Authentic pride includes a constellation of local, unstable, and controllable attributions (Tracy et al., 2009). An internal attribution, of course, arises when employees perceive that they, rather than their situation, shape outcomes. Local (as opposed to global) attributions infer that efforts and abilities are efficacious in a domain marked by success but are not necessarily useful more broadly. Unstable attributions reflect expectations that determinants and outcomes are changeable because they reflect effort and circumstance rather than ability. Further, such performance is controllable insofar as managerial influence derives from effort instead of relatively uncontrollable backgrounds, dispositions, and genetic endowments (e.g., "my initiatives X, Y, Z helped us win customer A" versus "outstanding customer service is part of my DNA").

Earlier, we suggested that success is a necessary condition for employees to experience authentic pride. When these positive expectations are realized, especially when the successful outcome was achieved in the face of a negative environmental surprise, the employee is likely to more keenly appreciate effort-based achievements and thereby to experience greater authentic pride. Contrary to hubristic pride, authentic pride seems to be more prevalent among employees high in genuine self-esteem and with more socially desirable traits like extraversion, agreeableness, and conscientiousness (Tracy and Robins, 2007a). In this case:

Proposition 2b: *The greater the need to overcome negative environmental surprises, the greater the tendency for success to increase employees' authentic pride.*

Having elaborated on the nature of authentic and hubristic pride, we turn to look at how employees can self-regulate to moderate the relationship between success and pride.

EMOTIONAL SELF-REGULATION MODERATES EMPLOYEE'S EXPERIENCE OF PRIDE OR HUBRIS

Emotional self-regulation processes allow employees to manage their affective responses to events (Weiss and Cropanzano, 1996). These, in turn, influence their attributions of internal and/or stable causality (Weiner, 1985, 1986, 2014) and are likely to be communicated to external or internal stakeholders (Dweck, 1999; Higgins, 1997; see also

Heath et al., 1998, for a partial review). Emotional self-regulation helps employees to control and to direct their cognition and behavior, including but not limited to attributions (see Markus and Wurf, 1987; Ochsner and Gross, 2005). This process operates to accomplish goals, to delay gratification, as well as to promote more adaptive social interactions (Damasio, 1994; Karoly, 1993).

Gross (1998) suggests, in particular, that emotional regulation serves to attenuate the effects of affective stimuli on subsequent affective experiences. Taylor et al. (2008, p. 197) also help to identify the neurophysiological basis of this process, noting that "dispositional reactivity" of neural structures serve to reduce neurological responses to affective events (stressors). In the context of organizational and strategy scholarship, employees and executives experience events affectively, including the way they regard organizational performance and environmental performance (see Ashton-James and Ashkanasy, 2008, for a review).

A central tenet of this evidence is that employees and others with greater emotional self-regulation should be able to buffer the effects of positive and negative emotions elicited from external events. As a result, their attributions and other cognitive responses to events are likely to be less influenced by affective reactions (Weiss and Cropanzano, 1996). The implication for the arguments we present in this chapter is that emotional self-regulation serves as a moderator or brake on the relationship between organizational success and employee pride.

Proposition 3a/b: *Employees' ability to self-regulate their emotions negatively moderates the effect of perceived success on their experience of pride, such that the relationship between perceived success (and associated attributions) and (a) hubristic or (b) authentic pride will be weaker for employees who are higher in emotional self-regulation ability.*

We argue further that social- and self-regulation processes favor the development of authentic over hubristic pride if employees can talk about emotion and recognize the virtues of the former and seek to prevent the latter (Higgins, 1997). Three core mechanisms underlie emotional self-regulation (Karoly, 1993): (a) commitment to clear standards, goals, or expectations; (b) self-awareness of performance relative to standards; and (c) the capacity to adopt corrective initiatives. Employees may therefore experience authentic pride through emotion regulation because more accurate attributions foster better grounded and potentially superior learning about the causes of performance, thereby enhancing the scope for corrective actions (Ashton-James and Ashkanasy, 2008).

Employees may also be aware of their performance relative to standards, which can be highlighted by their espoused interpretations of unstable attributions. Other interpretations reflect local attributions, such as specific reference to the products and geographic markets where progress is expected. Yet other reminders concern whether employees believe that controllable attributions can be made for uncontrollable outcomes. Some employees, for instance, may regard a supervisor's urging for ever-higher performance as uncontrollable factors, whereas others may perceive that their effects are controllable through upward management techniques.

We highlighted in the foregoing sections how employees can emotionally self-regulate in order to adopt the attributions associated with authentic pride. Baumeister et al. (2007) successfully operationalized the strength of self-regulation by tapping employees' commitment to standards, self-awareness of performance relative to standards, and the capacity to adopt corrective initiatives. If employees can recognize the merits of authentic pride and the costs of hubris, then at least normatively they will be motivated to direct emotional self-regulation towards attenuating the latter. This is reinforced insofar as authentic pride is associated with internal, unstable, local, and controllable attributions, while hubristic pride is associated with internal, stable, global, and uncontrollable attributions. In other words:

Proposition 3c: *The moderating effect of emotional self-regulation on pride and attributions will be stronger for hubristic than for authentic pride.*

DISCUSSION

Based on the aforementioned arguments, we suggest there are both functional and dysfunctional properties, depending upon the type of pride in question. Authentic pride has positive, functional connotations. For example, it tends to boost effort and to lead to future positive performance gains. It is also likely to be contagious, initiating the spread of waves of authentic pride in productive behavior through the organization. Hubristic pride has more negative, dysfunctional connotations, however. This is because it is associated with less consultation with colleagues and a tendency toward antisocial behaviors.

We argue that a fresh conceptualization of workplace pride arises from the framework we present in this chapter. Pride may be a good or bad thing in organizations, depending upon which type of pride we are discussing. In presenting this framework, we note there are many seemingly innocuous events that are likely to invoke the wrong kind of pride. For instance, employee awards and performance appraisals could tend to harden the view that a worker's talents are due to general and global traits. As such, this sort of positive feedback could actually derail the considerable effort required to accomplish success.

IDEAS FOR FUTURE RESEARCH

Intriguing questions remain for an ongoing research agenda, nonetheless. One concerns the extent to which employees' pride has ripple effects throughout the organization. For example, pride in her or his organization's achievements and expressed by a senior manager is likely to be reflected in similar pride expressed by employees at all levels of the organization. Another is whether employees can experience a shift from one type of pride to another. For example, a celebrated employee may gradually become more hubristic over time. This could result from the adulation that follows success, perhaps from the business media but also from the possibility that subordinates could become reticent about expressing their genuine concerns (Hayward, 2007). Much work also remains to be done to answer such questions and to identify interventions effective in preventing the development of hubristic pride – which, we suggest, may be one important reason why some see their own initial effectiveness vanish in a cloud of exaggerated and inaccurate beliefs about their talents and capacities (Kramer, 2003).

In particular, questions for an ongoing research agenda would include: Can authentic pride morph into hubristic pride and vice versa? Does the positive affect associated with hubristic pride create more scope for workers to experience authentic pride subsequently? Can more hubristic pride help firms become better prepared to take advantage of unexpected, positive surprises from the environment than authentic pride, hence mitigating some of its deleterious impact on firm performance? How does an array of personality and contextual factors impinge on the arguments presented above? We have also been notably silent here about unconscious expressions of pride, instead presenting the empirical evidence that pride as a self-conscious emotion (Williams and DeSteno, 2008; Tracy and Robins, 2007b). Yet, there is a burgeoning literature on unconscious intuition (e.g., Dane and Pratt, 2007) and implicit emotions.

This work is significant here because the manner in which pride is experienced may well affect subsequent judgments. Finally, we acknowledge that employee differences, with respect to a wide range of traits and skills, may play a role. For example, Ashkanasy and Jordan (2008) suggest that emotionally intelligent leaders are likely to be better at regulating emotions than their less emotionally intelligent counterparts, resulting in more authentic leadership, less prone to hubris.

Warnings about the dangers of excessive pride date from ancient times, and are reelected in today's ethical training. For example, pride (Latin: *superbia*) is one of the "seven deadly sins" and talked about every day as in, "Don't be so puffed up!" Despite the frequency of such cautions, the nature and impact of employee pride on organizational processes and performance has not, to date, been extensively examined. We seek to address this gap in the existing literature by distinguishing between authentic and hubristic pride. This transition, we suggest, is facilitated by the operation of basic affective and cognitive processes. To the extent that the former occurs, then employees are likely to work effectively with teammates and follow their initial successes with even greater achievements. Nonetheless, to the extent that employees experience hubristic pride, they may well see their initial success vanish in a dense and enveloping cloud of inaccurate attributions, inappropriate emotion, and counterproductive behaviors.

NOTE

1. English Oxford Living Dictionaries. https://en.oxforddictionaries.com/definition/pride. Accessed November 21, 2017.

REFERENCES

Ardi, D. (2014). *The Fall of the Alphas: The New Beta Way to Connect, Collaborate, Influence – and Lead.* New York, NY: St. Martin's Press.

Ashkanasy, N. M., and Jordan, P. J. (2008). A multi-level view of leadership and emotion. In R. H. Humphrey (ed.), *Affect and Emotion: New Directions in Management Theory and Research* (pp. 19–42). Charlotte, NC: Information Age Publishing.

Ashton-James, C. E., and Ashkanasy, N. M. (2008). Affective events theory: a strategic perspective. In W. J. Zerbe, C. E. J. Härtel, and N. M. Ashkanasy (eds) *Research on Emotion in Organizations* (Vol. 4, pp. 1–34). Bingley, UK: Emerald Group Publishing/JAI Press.

Banaji, M. R., and Prentice, D. A. (1994). The self in social contexts. *Annual Review of Psychology, 45*, 297–332.

Bandura, A. (1997). *Self-efficacy: The Exercise of Control.* New York, NY: Freeman.

Basch, J., and Fisher, C. D. (2000). Affective events-emotions matrix: a classification of work events and associated emotions. In N. M. Ashkanasy, C. E. J. Härtel, and W. J. Zerbe (eds) *Emotions in the Workplace: Research, Theory, and Practice* (pp. 36–49). Westport, CT: Quorum Press.

Baumeister, R. F. (1998). The self. In D. T. Gilbert, S. T. Fiske, and G. Lindzey (eds), *Handbook of Social Psychology* (4th ed., Vol. 1, pp. 680–740). New York, NY: McGraw-Hill.

Baumeister, R. F., Vohs, K. D., and Tice, D. M. (2007). The strength model of self-control. *Current Directions in Psychological Science, 16*, 351–355.

Bettman, J., and Weitz, B. (1983). Attributions in the boardroom: causal reasoning in corporate annual reports. *Administrative Science Quarterly, 28*, 165–183.

Cheng, J. T., Tracy, J. L., and Henrich, J. (2010). Pride, personality, and the evolutionary foundations of human social status. *Evolution and Human Behavior, 31*, 334–347.

Clapham, S., and Schwenk, C. (1991). Self-serving attributions, managerial cognition, and company performance. *Strategic Management Journal, 12*, 219–229.

Damasio, A. (1994). *Descartes' Error: Emotion, Reason, and the Human Brain.* New York, NY: Putnam.

Dane, E., and Pratt, M. G. (2007). Exploring intuition and its role in managerial decision making. *Academy of Management Review, 32*, 33–54.

Dweck, C. S. (1999). *Self-theories: Their Role in Motivation, Personality and Development.* Philadelphia, PA: Psychology Press.

Dweck, C. S. (2006). *Mindset: The New Psychology of Success.* New York, NY: Random House.

Fredrickson, B. L. (2001). The role of positive emotions in positive psychology: the broaden-and-build theory of positive emotions. *American Psychologist, 56*, 218–226.

Griffin, D. W., and Varey, C. A. (1996). Towards a consensus on over-confidence. *Organizational Behavior and Human Decision Processes, 65*, 227–231.

Gross, J. J. (1998). The emerging field of emotion regulation: an integrative review. *Review of General Psychology, 2*, 271–299.

Hayward, M. L. A. (2007). *Ego Check: Why Executive Hubris is Wrecking Companies and Careers and How to Avoid the Trap.* Chicago, IL: Kaplan.

Hayward, M. L. A., and Hambrick, D. C. (1997). Explaining the premiums paid for large acquisitions: evidence of CEO hubris. *Administrative Science Quarterly, 42*, 103–127.

Hayward, M. L. A., Shepherd, D. A., and Griffin, D. (2006). A hubris theory of entrepreneurship. *Management Science, 52*, 160–172.

Heath, C., Larrick, R. P., and Klayman, J. (1998). Cognitive repairs: how organizational practices can compensate for individual shortcomings. *Review of Organizational Behavior, 20*, 1–37.

Heider, F. (1958). *The Psychology of Interpersonal Relations.* Hillsdale, NJ: Lawrence Erlbaum Associates, Inc.

Higgins, E. T. (1997). Beyond pleasure and pain. *American Psychologist, 52*, 1280–1300.

Hiller, N. J., and Hambrick, D. C. (2005). Conceptualizing executive hubris: the role of (hyper-)core self-evaluations in strategic decision-making. *Strategic Management Journal, 26*, 297–319.

Hubbard, M. (2014). *Reversing the Senses: Increasing Your Internal Capacity to Lead and Achieve*. Austin, TX: River Grove Books.

Judge, T. A., Locke, E. A., and Durham, C. C. (1997). The dispositional causes of job satisfaction: a core evaluations approach. In B. Staw (ed.), *Research in Organizational Behavior* (vol. 19, pp. 151–188). Oxford, UK: Elsevier Science.

Karoly, P. (1993). Mechanisms of self-regulation: a systems view. *Annual Review of Psychology, 44*, 23–52.

Katzenbach, J. R. (2003). Pride: a strategic asset. *Strategy and Leadership, 31*, 34–38.

Kramer, R. M. (2003). The harder they fall. *Harvard Business Review, 81*(10), 58–68.

Lazarus, R., and Cohen-Charash, Y. (2001). Discrete emotions in organizational life. In R. Payne and C. Cooper (eds), *Emotions at Work: Theory, Research, and Applications for Management* (pp. 45–84). Chichester, UK: Wiley.

Leary, M. R., and Tangney, J. P. (2003). The self as an organizing construct in the behavioral and social sciences. In M. R. Leary and J. P. Tangney (eds), *Handbook of Self and Identity* (pp. 1–18). New York, NY: Guildford Press.

Louro, M. J., Pieters, R., and Zeelenberg, M. (2005). Negative returns on positive emotions: the influence of pride and self-regulatory goals on repurchase decisions. *Journal of Consumer Research, 31*, 833–840.

Markus, H., and Wurf, E. (1987). The dynamic self-concept: a social psychological perspective. *Annual Review of Psychology, 38*, 299–337.

Martinko, M. J., Harvey, P., and Douglas, S. C. (2007). The role, function, and contributions of attribution theory to leadership: a review. *The Leadership Quarterly, 18*, 561–585.

Ochsner, K. N., and Gross, J. J. (2005). The cognitive control of emotion. *Trends in Cognitive Sciences, 9*, 242–249.

Picone, P. M., Dagnino, G. B., and Minà, A. (2014). The origin of failure: a multidisciplinary appraisal of the hubris hypothesis and proposed research agenda. *Academy of Management Perspectives, 28*, 447–468.

Ruys, K. I., and Stapel, D. A. (2008). How to heat up from the cold: examining the preconditions for (unconscious) mood effects. *Journal of Personality and Social Psychology, 94*, 777–791.

Schimmel, S. (1997). *The Seven Deadly Sins: Jewish, Christian, and Classical Reflections on Human Psychology*. New York, NY: Oxford University Press.

Skowronski, J. J., and Carlston, D. E. (1989). Negativity and extremity biases in impression formation: a review of explanations. *Psychological Bulletin, 105*, 131–142.

Staw, B. M., McKechnie P. I., and Puffer, S. M. (1983). The justification of organizational performance. *Administrative Science Quarterly, 28*, 582–600.

Taylor, S. E., Burklund, L. J., Eisenberger, N. I., Lehman, B. J., Hilmert, C. J., and Lieberman, M. D. (2008). Neural bases of moderation of cortisol stress responses by psychosocial resources. *Journal of Personality and Social Psychology, 95*, 197–211.

Tracy, J. L., and Robins, R. W. (2004). Putting the self into self-consciousness emotions: a theoretical model. *Psychological Inquiry, 14*, 103–125.

Tracy, J. L., and Robins, R. W. (2007a). Emerging insights into the nature and function of pride. *Current Directions in Psychological Science, 16*, 147–150.

Tracy, J. L., and Robins, R. W. (2007b). The psychological structure of pride: a tale of two facets. *Journal of Personality and Social Psychology, 92*, 506–525.

Tracy, J. L., and Robins, R. W. (2007c). The prototypical pride expression: development of a nonverbal behavioral coding system. *Emotion, 7*, 789–801.

Tracy, J. L., Cheng, J. T., Robins, R. W., and Trzesniewski K. H. (2009). Authentic and hubristic pride: the affective core of self-esteem and narcissism. *Self and Identity, 8*, 196–213.

Tracy, J. L., Shariff, A. F., and Cheng, J. T. (2012). A naturalist's view of pride. *Emotion Review, 2*, 163–177.

Weiner, B. (1985). An attributional theory of achievement motivation and emotion. *Psychological Review, 92*, 548–573.

Weiner, B. (1986). *An Attributional Theory of Motivation and Emotion.* New York, NY: Springer-Verlag.

Weiner, B. (2014). The attribution approach to emotion and motivation: history, hypotheses, home runs, headaches/heartaches. *Emotion Review, 6*, 353–361.

Weiss, H., and Cropanzano, R. (1996). Affective events theory: a theoretical discussion of the structure, causes and consequences of affective experiences at work. In B. M. Staw and L. L. Cummings (eds), *Research in Organization Behavior* (Vol. 18, pp. 1–74). Greenwich, CT: JAI Press.

Williams, L., and DeSteno, D. (2008). Pride and perseverance: the motivational role of pride. *Journal of Personality and Social Psychology, 94*, 1007–1017.

Williams, L., and DeSteno, D. (2009). Pride: adaptive social emotion or seventh sin? *Psychological Science, 20*, 284–288.

9. The deeper side of sadness at work: why being sad is not always bad

Kristi Lewis Tyran

INTRODUCTION

In the movie "Inside Out," an 11-year old girl's emotions are portrayed as animated characters living in a control room in her brain. Happiness is the leader, and keeping this young girl experiencing happiness and forming happy memories is the goal. But as the parent of any budding adolescent knows, moodiness becomes the norm and the negative emotions of sadness and anger start to play a larger role in her life. Sad memories form more and more often and her personality starts to change. As time goes on, the characters of happiness and sadness must work together as new aspects of her personality develop. In the end, sadness plays a vital role in forming the core of who she is. The message of the movie is that all emotions, both negative and positive, play important roles in the growth and development of people in childhood through adulthood.

Experiencing and expressing sadness – defined as a negative emotional response to loss – is an essential part of life (Barrett, 2017). Because people spend so much time at work, sadness is an essential part of work life as well. The question of whether or not sadness has solely a negative impact at work is an important one. In this chapter, I argue that a deeper understanding of the emotion of sadness can help to facilitate more positive outcomes from experiences of sadness, and other negative emotions as well. In discussing sadness, however, the complexity of emotional experience must be acknowledged. Emotional complexity means it is rare for one emotion to be experienced, expressed or observed in isolation. Sadness is often highly interrelated with anger, as will be explained in more depth later. It is not uncommon for people experiencing sadness to oscillate between sadness and other emotions, including anger, fear, anxiety, and happiness (Bonanno, 2009). In addition, personal power is often associated with stronger negative emotions like anger as opposed to sadness. How people respond to expression of a negative emotion can vary based on interpretation of the emotion's power. Sadness is often associated with weakness, while anger indicates strength (Lewis, 2000). In this chapter, I address the complexity of how expression of sadness is interpreted and responded to by others.

While there is much research on the basic emotions, including sadness, and extensive research into the role of emotion in the workplace, the majority of existing research focuses on happiness (consistent with rising interest in positive psychology) and anger, with little research on sadness in organizations. Indeed, this situation led Porath and Pearson to state that "The organizational literature is nearly devoid of studies of sadness" (2012, p. E330). Gooty et al. (2009) urge emotion scholars in organizational behavior to, among other things, focus on discrete emotions in context, and further research on sadness at work would do just that. Ashkanasy and Humphrey (2011) argue there is "untapped potential" in emotion research in organizational behavior, and I agree that in the case of sadness there is great potential for expanding our understanding of how sadness affects organizations.

This chapter seeks to address both the lack of organizational literature on sadness and the need to focus on discrete emotions in context by integrating the literature on sadness with what we know about emotion in organizations. From this integration, I seek to summarize conclusions we can draw about the antecedents and consequences of both the experience of sadness and the expression of sadness in the workplace and connect what people talk about and experience of sadness at work with theoretical models related to sadness and other negative emotions. The chapter starts with a discussion of what we currently know from the research about sadness in general, and sadness at work more specifically. Then, I outline the specific antecedents and consequences of sadness as studied by organizational researchers. I also talk about how better understanding sadness at work can help managers be more effective. Finally, I discuss future research opportunities relating to the topic of sadness at work.

WHAT WE KNOW ABOUT SADNESS

Sadness is considered one of the basic emotions (Johnston and Olson, 2015; Lord et al., 2002). These basic emotions are considered "universal" in part because they are identified easily across human cultures and because they are thought to have evolved "as a specific adaptive response to an environmentally salient stimulus" (Johnston and Olson, 2015, p. 48). Scholars differ in how they categorize basic and universal emotions, but overall there is consensus that the four basic emotions include fear, anger, happiness, and sadness, with the two additional emotions of disgust and surprise sometimes added to this list (Johnston and Olson, 2015).

There are clear physiological differentiators for these basic emotions, including sadness. Sadness is considered to be one of the most easily recognized emotions (Johnston and Olson, 2015). The facial expression of sadness is difficult to mask. A sad person's face sags, the eyebrows pinch together and rise up toward the hairline, while the jaw goes slack and the lower lip goes down (Bonanno, 2009). Often sadness is associated with tears welling in the eyes accompanying the general facial expression.

A key signal of sadness can be crying. Crying appears to elicit supportive behavior, but how the helping person judges the crying person is dependent on how they interpret the situation and appropriateness of crying. When a person cries, it may be a sign of sadness or anger (or joy). Recent research indicates that crying signals a need for empathy and support from others (and a need for attackers to back off), however, crying is not always interpreted as a sign of sadness (Hendriks et al., 2008). The actual situation is critical in how adult crying is interpreted. Interestingly, people judge a crying person less positively than a non-crying person, and feel more negative emotions in the presence of a crying person, but still want to engage in efforts to support the crying person (Hendriks, et al., 2008).

Sadness results from a perception that a loss has occurred without the possibility of recovery given the current situation and the person's current abilities (Carver, 2004; Lench et al., 2016). The loss is generally defined in one of two ways: a relationship loss, in the context of social situations, or perception of failure, often defined as goal loss, in a non-social context (Lench et al., 2011, 2016). A key to differentiating sadness from other negative emotions is the sense of irrevocability of the loss. When a person sees the loss as not reversible and acknowledges that any action on their part will not be effective, a sense of hopelessness regarding the specific event that caused the sadness sets in, such as when someone perceives an important project will never be completed.

When individuals perceive that a loss has occurred, the analysis of such a loss can result in a multitude of emotional responses related to grieving the loss. Elisabeth Kübler-Ross (1973) proposed a stage model of grief that was quite popular for a time. Recently, however, this model has been questioned as an oversimplification of a very complex – and individual – experience (Bonanno, 2009). Sadness can often be accompanied by anger, joy, disgust, frustration, and fear. An individual may experience these emotions in sequence, or sometimes all at once, and thus each individual's experience of grief is unique, frequently not fitting the linear stage model proposed by Kübler-Ross. This is an example of how the complexity of actual emotional experience of a specific emotion – such as sadness – often contradicts theoretical and popular models.

It is important to differentiate the emotion of sadness from other negative experiences often associated with sadness such as grief, depression, and melancholy. The emotional granularity of the experience leads individuals to describe their own emotion based on the intensity of feeling, thus melancholy is similar to sadness but less intense, while depression is often used to describe deep sadness that lasts a long time (Barrett, 2017). How people characterize and differentiate their own emotional experiences can vary widely, but scientifically, we know that while depression may be associated with emotional experiences of sadness, depression is a psychiatric diagnosis that is associated with not only behavior, but physiological issues that can be treated chemically and with individual therapy (Bonanno, 2009). Thus, we often talk about being or feeling "depressed" in an inaccurate way, while we are truly only experiencing the emotion of sadness due to an experience of loss.

Research shows that experiencing and expressing sadness is useful in individual growth and progress (Bonanno, 2009; Keltner and Gross, 1999; Lord et al., 2002). Sadness can be both positive and negative in terms of outcomes depending on how one copes with the loss itself. Individuals who experience sadness may lose hope and become despondent, at least temporarily, as in grieving the loss of a loved one (Bonanno, 2009). The expression of sadness causes others to respond to the sad individual. How others respond to individuals who express sadness depends on a number of factors, including the social congruency of the expression of sadness, or the "match" between the sadness expressed and others' perception of the social context (Celik et al., 2016). There has been a great deal of research recently into the consequences of both the experience and expression of sadness in life that can be extrapolated to the organizational context. Later in this chapter, I explore this research in more depth.

As suggested earlier, sadness, as one of the basic negative emotions, is experienced in all cultures by all people. In the organizational context, understanding the causes of experiencing sadness is helpful in further exploring the role of sadness at work. Because this has been relatively neglected in organizational research, and the experience of sadness so common, expanding this understanding is a clear contribution to the study of emotion in organizations. In the following sections I explore the role of sadness in organizations both from the perspective of the individual and the manager to expand our understanding of the implications of sadness in the workplace.

WHY DO PEOPLE FEEL SAD AT WORK?

There are two broad categories of organizational situations that can cause sadness: (a) personal loss, such as that experienced after a tragedy (Miller, 2002), and (b) personal failure, such as failing to achieve a goal, getting fired or demoted, or failing to get a promotion or some other desired recognition for one's work (Celik et al., 2016; Kreamer, 2011).

In terms of personal loss, the workplace is rife with events and situations that can cause sadness, and experiencing sadness at work is more common than may be generally thought. Workplace relationships can change and become negative, such as when a person perceives incivility from coworkers (Porath and Pearson, 2012). For example, in response to incivility, a person might feel hurt, angry, fearful, or sad, all at once or in succession (Porath and Pearson, 2012). Similarly when grieving (for example in the face of change), a person may oscillate between sadness, anger, frustration, and happiness as they react to the stress of extreme personal loss (Bonnano, 2009). At a group level, events that are experienced simultaneously by everyone in an organization – or subgroup in an organization – can cause sadness. Examples of such events include workplace violence or mass layoffs (Miller, 2002; Lanctôt and Guay, 2014).

In terms of personal failure, a person's perception of why a goal is not met is critical in differentiating the emotional response to personal failure. If a person perceives that the goal was not met due to something (or someone) blocking their ability to succeed, then anger is often the response because goal attainment is thought possible only if the person could remove the obstacle to success (Carver, 2004; Lench, et al., 2016). However, if a person perceives that the failure is irrevocable and beyond their ability to repair, no matter the cause, then sadness is felt in response to this failure (Keltner et al., 1993).

Goal failure can occur when a project does not end successfully or some career goal is not achieved and one perceives that they have no control over addressing this failure. Negative performance evaluations can cause sadness if a person perceives that the cause (e.g., poor economic conditions impacting on sales) cannot be addressed successfully given their current situation (Celik et al., 2016). Perceptions of failure in general can cause an individual to feel sad about their job, depending on their individual personality and whether they see the failure as a step toward success (which can be motivating) or evidence of permanent failure.

Because emotions are complex and often interrelated, sometimes people have multiple reactions to failure, and feel both angry and sad, or often may oscillate between the two emotions as they cognitively process the event surrounding the emotional experience (Bonanno, 2009). Emotions are defined as temporary mood states, and as discussed previously, sadness itself must be differentiated from long-term depression or depressed mood (Bonnano, 2009). As such, the experience of sadness may be brief and interconnected with other emotions. The complexity of when and how sadness is experienced is further understood when exploring the importance of past personal history and how this affects a person's perception of loss in both the social and non-social context.

SADNESS AND PERSONAL HISTORY

The perception of a specific case of failure as irrevocable and unchangeable leads to the experience of sadness, and as such this perception may be associated with individual characteristics such as previous life and work experiences. Very little research has been done on predispositions toward sadness, anger, or other emotions in response to events. The limited research that has been done has explored the causes of sadness as they relate to racism and sexism. This research found that non-white and female employees sometimes experience and express sadness in response to situations where white men may not. For example, in response to disrespect from others, men were more likely to respond with anger, while women were more likely to respond with sadness (Blincoe and Harris, 2011). These differences may be related to previous experiences with disrespect at work, such that previous experiences may be perceived as specific to an individual or related to a person's identity.

The differences between men and women in terms of emotion – and specifically sadness – are due to both biology and socialization (McRae et al., 2008). Across cultures, women report feeling more powerless emotions – including sadness – while men report feeling more powerful emotions such as anger (Fischer et al., 2004). However, experiences at work may sometimes vary between men and women due to sexism in the workplace. When men and women experience conscious or unconscious bias at work, this can cause an emotional reaction of anger or sadness, depending on how they perceive the extent to which the cause of bias is personal, institutional, or changeable. This interpretation and perception is likely to be heavily influenced by prior experience with racism or sexism (Johnson et al., 2011).

In addition to how sadness is experienced, we perceive sadness in other people based on context and assumptions related to gender, race, age, and other stereotypes. For example, women are often judged to be sad when they express other emotions based on gender stereotyping of emotional display (Johnson et al., 2011). In other words, if a woman cries when angry, she is often not seen as angry, but instead, is viewed as sad. Perceptions of men and women who express emotion at work are often based on gender role expectations and work role expectations, or a combination of the two (Eagly and Karau, 2002). For example, there is evidence that women who express anger are perceived to be less effective leaders than men who express anger, but both men and women who express sadness are perceived to be less effective (Lewis, 2000). Crying is often perceived as an expression of sadness, despite the fact that tears may result from other emotions as well, including joy, anger, and frustration (Ellsbach and Bechky, 2017). However, when men cry in the workplace, they are often perceived as compassionate, while tears in women are seen as a sign of weakness (Kreamer, 2011). Ellsbach and Bechky (2017) found that men are perceived more positively than women when they cry, and the consequences for women who cry are almost always negative (Ellsbach and Bechky, 2017).

Culture can also impact on when sadness is felt and how it is perceived. Researchers have found that cultural dimensions are related to emotional experience and expression (Fernández et al., 2008). Yan, Ashkanasy, and Mehmood (2017) found that experiences of sadness (and anger) differed across cultures, depending on gender. Culture also impacts our response to situational cues that may cause sadness. For example, Kimel and others (2017) found that in response to social rejection, Westerners respond with more anger than sadness, possibly seeing the rejection as something they may be able to address and thus not irrevocable. In contrast, they found that Easterners report feeling anger and sadness in equal measure, and depending on the situation they may see the rejection as irrevocable and inevitable, leading to sadness (Kimel, et al., 2017). These findings demonstrate that past experience – whether associated with culture, gender, or race – impact how we experience sadness and how we perceive it in others.

One positive aspect of the experience of sadness is that it may reduce the reliance on heuristics as expressed in stereotypes when compared with happiness (Park and Banaji, 2000). Sadness may lead to more objective moral reasoning that relies less on stereotypes and more on the analysis of the situation as it is (Bodenhausen et al., 1994). Sadness appears to cause people to slow down, be more reflective, and see things from multiple perspectives, all good things when objective observation and judgment is needed. More research on this phenomenon in organizational settings is needed to provide managers with a better understanding of how sadness and stereotypes are related in the workplace.

WHEN SADNESS IS EXPERIENCED COLLECTIVELY AT WORK

Collective experience of emotion occurs when an event is perceived by all involved in a consistent manner. As with other emotions, it is possible for sadness to be experienced collectively in organizations (Collins et al., 2013). For example, collective feelings of sadness can be caused by any type of crisis that is perceived as irrevocable – such as the death of a cherished colleague, a natural disaster, a man-made tragedy such as a mass shooting, large-scale layoffs, or an organizational level failure (Doré et al., 2015). Some people work in jobs where they are more likely to experience events that cause sadness, such as nurses in an Oncology unit or Emergency Medical Technicians (Kendall, 2007). Man-made tragedies that have affected organizations include the terrorist attacks in the U.S. on September 11, 2001, when many organizations in New York City and Washington, D.C. had wide-scale losses of life and property. An example of organizational failure that generated sadness occurred when Lehman Brothers abruptly closed and ended business during the global financial crisis in the late 2000s.

In terms of positive emotions, collective experiences of sadness can lead to more cohesion and solidarity after a tragedy, as people are drawn to each other for comfort and a chance to process the experience (Miller, 2002). Anecdotally, we know that as people experience crisis, they draw together in collective response. For example, in World War II, after the invasion of France by Nazi Germany, the Resistance was a powerful collective force that ultimately contributed to and supported the invasion and ultimate defeat of the Nazi forces there. This collective optimism and defiance are, in part, a response to the collective sadness experienced by those who suffer under such a tragedy.

There are many examples of tragedies experienced collectively in organizations and the widespread shared sadness they caused and the positive outcomes that sadness generated. Miller (2002) writes about a tragedy experienced when she was teaching at Texas A&M – the collapse of a traditional bonfire where several students died. In this situation, caring was important, but many professors felt a need to engage in "emotional labor" to help others heal from the collective sadness experienced at the university as an organization (Hochschild, 1983). Engaging in healing efforts in the aftermath of workplace violence can be very important in promoting positive outcomes, in part because collective sadness can occur in combination with other emotions as part of generalized emotional distress (Lanctôt and Guay, 2014). In the case of collective sadness, relationships are frequently strengthened, leading to persistence and resilience in the face of tragedy (Graham et al., 2008). As a result, sadness may lead to positive change after the tragedy, leading to more cohesion, commitment, and higher general morale among employees.

Over time, sadness can change as a tragic event is processed. Doré and his colleagues (2015) found that people's emotional response to the Sandy Hook Elementary School shooting evolved from sadness to anxiety over time as details of the event faded. How the sadness is processed collectively varies, depending on perceptions of the event and how it impacts the organization. A leader can greatly influence how collective sadness is processed in an organization through her or his actions in supporting positive healing and bonding. In a crisis where sadness is experienced collectively, leaders can empathize and express sadness themselves. By recognizing others' sadness and providing support to them as whole people, followers are more likely to feel valued and important. This has the potential to increase cohesion among those experiencing the sadness and increase engagement in the healing after the tragedy is over (Baggett et al., 2016). Later in this chapter, I provide recommendations for how managers can respond to sadness – both individually and collectively – so that the chances for positive outcomes are maximized.

CONSEQUENCES OF SADNESS IN ORGANIZATIONS

Because the research shows that experiencing emotions is useful in life and also at work, we want to know: What is useful about sadness? There are many social benefits of experiencing and expressing negative emotions, including sadness (Lindebaum and Jordan, 2014). Other people often respond to sadness by providing comfort when the loss is irrevocable or assistance in strategizing goal achievement after a personal failure to achieve a goal (Burgoon et al., 2011; Lench and Levine, 2008). In the workplace, this means that coworkers are inclined to want to help someone who is experiencing sadness. Most people respond to someone expressing sadness with empathy and approach that person in a helpful way, especially if that person is a friend (Clark and Taraban, 1991). If the sad person is a stranger, the response is more likely to be avoidance and dislike (Clark and Taraban, 1991). Really, a key to determining the response is perception of the appropriateness of the emotional expression of sadness (Graham et al., 2008). If sadness is viewed as appropriate to the situation, then others move toward helping, nurturing, and supporting the sad person. If the sadness seems inappropriate, sad people may be judged as less likeable and may be avoided (Sommers, 1984).

There are many other social benefits to experiencing and expressing sadness. For example, sad people may distribute resources using criteria of fairness more than non-sad people (Tan and Forgas, 2010). People respond to expressions of sadness by assisting the sad person in reflecting on and attempting new efforts towards goal achievement (Graham et al., 2008). People experiencing sadness may be more generous in negotiation (Polman and Kim, 2013). In addition, expressing sadness can have positive relationship outcomes. Others respond to sadness with comfort, and this can result in the building of new close relationships and heightened closeness in existing close relationships (Graham et al., 2008).

Sadness motivates individuals to act differently depending on whether a person perceives the cause of sadness to be social or non-social. If the cause is a non-social one, such as personal failure, a person may withdraw and become reflective. If the cause is more social, such as a loss through death or tragedy, then a person is more likely to be motivated to engage in social behaviors to share their feelings and gain support (Gray et al., 2011). In organizations, this may lead to better processing of the loss and more cohesion in the organization. For example, as discussed previously, Miller (2002) found that professors who empathized and helped students process their sadness after the tragic bonfire collapse at Texas A&M were able to support others in their experience of sadness toward a positive social outcome.

There are many individual benefits to experiencing sadness that can also lead to organizational benefits. Experiencing sadness can increase judgmental accuracy, reduce gullibility, and increase skepticism, in part because it causes individuals to slow down physiologically and pay attention to details by using a more adaptive processing approach (Forgas, 2007). This is beneficial for organizations when a more analytical approach leads to better decisions and outcomes. In addition, people who are sad are better at detecting deception (Forgas and East, 2008), have better eyewitness memory (Forgas et al., 2009), and are less likely to commit the fundamental attribution error when explaining the behavior of others (Forgas, 1998).

Because of this increased attention to detail and more analytical approach, sadness has the potential to have positive impacts on teamwork and creativity. As previously mentioned, sadness in one individual, or even in the team as a whole, can lead to closer relationships and higher cohesion, leading to more effective teams. Recent research on creativity in organizations demonstrates that negative emotions in general can either enhance or inhibit creativity in individuals (To et al., 2015). While the few research studies on negative emotions and creativity do not focus specifically on sadness, there is some indication that sadness, by slowing down the process of analyzing a situation, may increase creative thought and idea generation (To et al., 2012). For example, the company Pixar routinely engages in "post-mortems" after various stages in developing a new movie (Catmull and Wallace, 2014). These post-mortem discussions involve deeply and critically analyzing a project's failures and successes in hopes of learning new ways of enhancing creative collaboration. A sad individual may contribute more to that analysis through their efforts to slow down the process and help avoid groupthink.

Another benefit of experiencing sadness is that it can signal that change is needed (Celik et al., 2016). People who are sad are sometimes guided by "emotivations" related to wanting to change one's situation (Polman and Kim, 2013). Such change has the potential to be positive for organizations. Sometimes it can lead to a desire to change that is not actualized in a positive way, perhaps due to a sense of hopelessness (Polman and Kim, 2013). However, because expressing sadness may lead to others offering social support in goal achievement, positive change is more likely when sad people rely on others for help and support. For example, if someone is sad because they have failed to succeed in a work project, such as a new product launch, others may be motivated to provide support in analyzing the failure, why it happened, and how another new product launch may be redesigned so as to succeed in the future.

There are potential negative consequences to sadness as well. Sadness can lead to lethargy, a lack of focus and/or attention, and decreased motivation (Johnston and Olson, 2015). Experiencing sadness can cause people to be judged as less likable, less social, and less popular (Sommers, 1984). Sad individuals may be more evasive in a negotiation context (Forgas and Cromer, 2004). Emotional contagion means that sadness in one person may lead to others "catching" another person's sadness. When tragedy is experienced and sadness is more collective, this may also involve emotionally complex responses that include and/or oscillate between fear, anxiety, anger, and happiness (Lanctôt and Guay, 2014). As discussed previously, sadness is not the same as depression, although expression of sadness can often be mistaken for depression.

Among other individual negative consequences, sad individuals tend to be impatient for financial gain (Lerner et al., 2013) and spend more for a commodity than non-sad individuals (Cryder et al., 2008; Lerner et al., 2004). Sadness increases self-focus and reflection, which may result in a desire to have immediate gratification rather than defer gratification for a greater financial gain. This can have negative consequences for organizations when individuals make poor financial decisions in their organizational roles. For example, a sad person may decide to invest in a long-term project that has higher failure risk for the organization, perhaps because they perceive there will be significant personal gain for themselves in the short-run, perhaps through notoriety or promotion potential. However, if the sad person experiences support from coworkers, and sharing occurs, it can lead to increased motivation and patience, counteracting this desire for immediate gratification.

Often, in response to a negative experience of hurt feelings in the workplace, people may struggle when deciding whether to express sadness or anger. In reality, they may *feel* both as they vacillate between interpreting the hurt feelings as something either within or outside of their own control. When the goal of wanting to be treated with respect is not attained, the response of anger acknowledges that the disrespect comes from outside of the self. However, individuals may perceive that the disrespect is due to who they are inside, and if they are unwilling to change themselves (particularly if the incivility is seen as unwarranted), they may feel sad as they acknowledge that the person who is the source of the incivility is not likely to change their behavior or experience any negative consequence for their actions (Porath and Pearson, 2012). For example, in a performance appraisal, a person may experience sadness at their inability to achieve high performance (if self-esteem is low), or anger at others for not recognizing their excellence (if self-esteem is high). This may also be the case in incidents of sexual harassment, when a person may perceive that complaining about the harassment will only result in negative consequences to the victim, with no consequences at all for the perpetrator.

In a study of personnel evaluations, the expression of sadness was seen as a positive response to a negative evaluation of someone's "warmth" in the workplace (Celik et al., 2016). This was because sadness indicated an attempt to change their lack of warmth in a positive way. This is consistent with other research that indicates a person's response to or interpretation of a person's expression of sadness is dependent on their perception of the social congruency of the sadness to the event – it is difficult to "fake" sadness to elicit responses of social sympathy if the situation does not warrant it (Celik et al., 2016). For instance, as individuals decide how to respond to negative performance evaluations, it is important they understand how their response will be interpreted in light of what they hope to achieve post-evaluation (i.e., continued employment, positive reference for the future, maintenance of positive work relationships). As the research discussed in this section indicates, the expression of sadness or anger has potential positive or negative consequences, and deciding how or when to express these emotions has important implications for their work situation.

Given these potential positive and negative consequences of sadness in the workplace, managers are urged to increase their awareness and understanding of how to best support sad individuals they work with. Having a workplace environment where employees feel cared for has many positive benefits beyond just addressing employees who feel sad (Baggett et al., 2016). While there is little research on leadership and sadness, in the next section, advice is given to managers based on the research available.

ADVICE FOR MANAGERS

Managers have much to gain from both expressing genuine sadness and responding appropriately to others who are experiencing sadness. When individual employees are experiencing and expressing sadness, managers can use talk to support them through empathy and providing resources that can promote healing and hope. Especially when employees are experiencing sadness due to a failure at work, managers can help employees reflect on the cause of their failure and find ideas in their reflection for positive change in their lives. In cases when sadness is experienced collectively, managers have a vital role in facilitating healing and renewal following trauma. When tragedy occurs and sadness is experienced collectively, a leader's expression of emotion as it is perceived to be consistent with the situation matters (Kim and Cameron, 2011).

Managers themselves should not avoid expressing emotion, especially multiple emotions demonstrating the complexity of emotions in response to organizational events. Rothman and Melwani (2017) argue that expression of emotion by leaders can increase cognitive flexibility, helping followers be more accepting and understanding of changes the leader proposes. In addition, expressing sadness may produce higher quality persuasive messages that are more effective in influencing others (Forgas, 2007). If a leader truly wants to influence others to buy into and engage in successful organizational change, acknowledging the sadness in response to the loss involved in the change may be an effective persuasive technique. Visser et al. (2013) found that leader displays of happiness enhanced follower creative performance, while a leader's expression of sadness increased analytical performance. As mentioned earlier, however, the expression of sadness must be authentic and consistent with the situation as perceived by others.

As discussed earlier, managers need to be aware of how gender impacts the ways in which expressions of sadness are perceived. A woman's status, her work role, and others' gender bias may influence the perceptions of her emotional expression (Brescoll and Uhlmann, 2008). Men who express sadness may or may not be viewed more negatively as leaders. However, given that emotional complexity means that emotions are rarely expressed in isolation, the context of the sadness is important in understanding how expressing sadness will be interpreted by others. When leaders express sadness they are demonstrating a willingness to express negative emotions, and this may lead to more positive relationship outcomes (Graham et al., 2008).

Demonstrating that managers care for others is a key component of authentic leadership, and has been shown to lead to positive outcomes in the health-care setting (Baggett et al., 2016). When employees express sadness, managers can show they care by providing support and empathy. Particularly when an employee is sad after a personal failure, managers can listen with empathy and engage in dialogue regarding future plans and changes that the employee can make to take a positive post-failure direction. When managers have established a caring attitude in the past, employees are more likely to feel cared for when a tragedy occurs and collective sadness is experienced. Caring expressed toward sad colleagues provides needed support, but also models behaviors for others in the organization. By responding to workplace incivility with compassion and actions to reduce negative interactions, managers demonstrate that they care about their employees' experience and corresponding emotional response of sadness (Porath and Pearson, 2012).

Managers can be more effective in managing change by increasing their awareness of the implications of sadness experienced and expressed in the workplace. Responding to both individual and collective perceptions of loss, and providing a caring and nurturing environment in their workplace can lead to more successful change. They can also provide a platform for better performance through increased use of the adaptive processing approach to problem solving, leading to a more analytical and unbiased approach in decision making as well. All in all, there are tremendous benefits to managers of understanding the causes and consequences of sadness in the workplace.

FUTURE RESEARCH OPPORTUNITIES RELATED TO SADNESS AT WORK

There is a great deal of research on negative emotions – and to some degree, sadness in life – but more needs to be done to connect this research to the organizational setting. In this chapter, there is an implicit assumption that the causes and consequences of experiencing and expressing emotion generalize to the organizational setting. More work is needed to see if this is the case. Even the research that has been conducted in an organizational setting to date has limited generalizability to organizations. Much more needs to be done, and here I propose some specific opportunities that have emerged from my chapter for future research:

- Understanding the consequences of specific managerial behaviors, actions, and comments in response to expression of sadness by employees.
- Increased focus on sadness as a discrete emotion in specific contexts within organizations. For example, sadness in response to layoffs or tragedy (Gooty et al., 2009; Ashkanasy et al., 2017).
- Research on the impact of sadness oscillating with other emotions on social relationships and individual performance in organizations.
- A better understanding of how experiencing and expressing sadness impacts individual performance on specific types of tasks at work.
- More understanding of how incivility and other negative treatment (such as sexual harassment or bias due to stereotyping) impacts the experience of sadness in the workplace.
- Understanding how social functional theoretical views of sadness relate to actual work behavior.
- Research on how sadness resulting from non-work experiences (such as grieving the loss of a loved one) impacts work-related behaviors.
- Research on impacts of personal characteristics and past personal experience – including culture, race, and gender – on the experience and expression of sadness in the workplace.

There are many other avenues for research into workplace experiences of sadness. The research on sadness in life in psychology and sociology provides a broad and solid platform for exploring the role of sadness in the organizational context.

CONCLUSION

Throughout this chapter, I have presented evidence showing that the experience and expression of sadness in the workplace involves dynamic and complex processes. We know that sadness, while classified as a negative emotion, is not always negative in practice or experience. There are often positive consequences from the experience and expression of sadness, particularly in how feeling sad can motivate more social support, better and closer relationships, more analytical exploration of situations, and less use of stereotypes. Managers and leaders in particular can benefit from understanding how to respond to sadness experienced and expressed by their employees. However, future research is needed to clarify exactly how sadness at work may influence organizations. In particular, understanding sadness in the context of overall emotional complexity will improve our general understanding of the impact of emotion in organizations.

Organizations are expected to deal with the causes and consequences of sadness on both an individual and collective level every day. In addition, sadness generated by individual experiences outside of the workplace can still have significant consequences for organizations, both positive and negative. As with many negative emotions, many employees avoid acknowledging or thinking about sadness and considering the implications for individuals and the organization in terms of organizational outcomes, like performance, engagement and individual well-being. Based on the evidence in this chapter, organizational and individual sadness have implications for organizations. A greater understanding of sadness can assist in creating a workplace where the organizational experience of emotion as a whole more will be more positive. As managers respond to individual and collective sadness appropriately, with empathy and support, the organizational environment overall can become more supportive. As a result, employees' attention to emotional experiences in general increase, resulting in more emotional intelligence expressed throughout the organization. This can only have positive outcomes for organizations, regardless of the extent to which sadness is observed in the workplace.

REFERENCES

Ashkanasy, N. M., and Humphrey, R. H. (2011) Current emotion research in organizational behavior. *Emotion Review.* 3(2): 214–224.

Ashkanasy, N. M., Humphrey, R. H., and Huy, Q. N. (2017) Integrating emotions and affect in theories of management. *Academy of Management Review.* 42(2): 175–189.

Baggett, M., Giambattista, L., Lobbestael, L., Pfeiffer, J., Madani, C., Modir, R., Zamora-Flyr, M. M., and Davidson, J. E. (2016) Exploring the human emotion of feeling cared for in the workplace. *Journal of Nursing Management.* 24(6): 816–824.

Barrett, L. F. (2017) *How Emotions are Made: The Secret Life of the Brain.* New York, NY: Houghton Mifflin.

Blincoe, S., and Harris, M. (2011) Status and inclusion, anger and sadness: gendered responses to disrespect. *European Journal of Social Psychology.* 41(4): 508–517.

Bodenhausen, G. V., Sheppard, L. A., and Kramer, G. P. (1994) Negative affect and social judgment: the differential impact of anger and sadness. *European Journal of Social Psychology.* 24: 45–62.

Bonanno, G. A. (2009) *The Other Side of Sadness: What the New Science of Bereavement Tells Us About Life After Loss.* New York, NY: Perseus Books Group.

Brescoll, V. L., and Uhlmann, E. L. (2008) Can an angry woman get ahead?: Status conferral, gender, and expression of emotion in the workplace. *Psychological Science.* 19(3): 268–275.

Burgoon, J. K., Guerrero, L. K., and Manusov, V. (2011) Nonverbal signals. In M. L. Knapp and J. A. Daly (eds), *The Sage Handbook of Interpersonal Communication* (4th ed., pp. 239–282). Thousand Oaks, CA: Sage.

Carver, C. S. (2004) Negative affects deriving from the behavioral approach system. *Emotion.* 4(1): 3–22.

Catmull, E., and Wallace, A. (2014) *Creativity, Inc.: Overcoming the Unseen Forces That Stand in the Way of True Inspiration.* New York, NY: Random House.

Celik, P., Storme, M., and Myszkowski, N. (2016) Anger and sadness as adaptive emotion expression strategies in response to negative competence and warmth evaluations. *British Journal of Social Psychology.* 55(4): 792–810.

Clark, M. S., and Taraban, C. (1991) Reactions to and willingness to express emotion in communal and exchange relationships. *Journal of Experimental Social Psychology.* 27(4): 324–336.

Collins, A. L., Lawrence, S. A., Troth, A. C., and Jordan, P. J. (2013) Group affective tone: a review and future research directions. *Journal of Organizational Behavior.* 34(S1): S43–S62.

Cryder, C. E., Lerner, J. S., Gross, J. J., and Dahl, R. E. (2008) Misery is not miserly: sad and self-focused individuals spend more. *Psychological Science.* 19(6): 525–530.

Doré, B., Ort, L., Braverman, O., and Ochsner, K. N. (2015) Sadness shifts to anxiety over time and distance from the national tragedy in Newtown, Connecticut. *Psychological Science.* 26(4): 363–373.

Eagly, A. H., and Karau, S. J. (2002) Role congruity theory of prejudice toward female leaders. *Psychological Review.* 109(3): 573–598.

Ellsbach, K. D., and Bechky, B. A. (2017) How observers assess women who cry in professional work contexts. *Academy of Management Discoveries.* Published online before print July 20, 2017, doi: 10.5465/amd.2016.0025 ĀCAD MANAGE DISCOVER.

Fernández, I., Carrera, P., Páez, D., and Sánchez, F. (2008) Interdependent self-construal, competitive attitudes, culture and emotional reactions on sadness. *Psychologia.* 51(3): 214–234.

Fischer, A. H., Mosquera, P. M. R., van Vianen, A. E. M., and Manstead, A. S. R. (2004) Gender and culture differences in emotion. *Emotion.* 4(1): 87–94.

Forgas, J. P. (1998) On being happy and mistaken: mood effects on the fundamental attribution error. *Journal of Personality and Social Psychology.* 75(2): 318–331.

Forgas, J. P. (2007) When sad is better than happy: negative affect can improve the quality of effectiveness of persuasive messages and social influence strategies. *Journal of Experimental Social Psychology.* 43(4): 513–528.

Forgas, J. P., and Cromer, M. (2004) On being sad and evasive: affective influences on verbal communication strategies in conflict situations. *Journal of Experimental Social Psychology.* 40(4): 511–518.

Forgas, J. P., and East, R. (2008) On being happy and gullible: mood effects on skepticism and the detection of deception. *Journal of Experimental Social Psychology.* 44(5): 1362–1367.

Forgas, J. P., Goldenberg, L., and Unkelbach, C. (2009) Can bad weather improve your memory? An unobtrusive field study of mood effects on memory in a real-life setting. *Journal of Experimental Social Psychology.* 45(1): 254–257.

Gooty, J., Gavin, M., and Ashkanasy, N. M. (2009) Emotions research in OB: the challenges that lie ahead. *Journal of Organizational Behavior.* 30(6): 833–838.

Graham, S. M., Huang, J. Y., Clark, M. S., and Helgeson, V. S. (2008) The positives of negative emotions: willingness to express negative emotions promotes relationship. *Personality and Social Psychology Bulletin.* 34(3): 394–406.

Gray, H. M., Ishii, K., and Ambady, N. (2011) Misery loves company: when sadness increases the desire for social connectedness. *Personality and Social Psychology Bulletin.* 37(11): 1438–1448.

Hendriks, M. C. P., Croon, M. A., and Vingerhoets, J. J. M. (2008) Social reactions to adult crying: the help-soliciting function of tears. *The Journal of Social Psychology.* 148(1): 22–41.

Hochschild, A. (1983) *The Managed Heart: Commercialization of Human Feeling.* Berkeley, CA: University of California Press.

Johnson, K. L., McKay, L. S., and Pollick, F. E. (2011) He throws like a girl (but only when he's sad): emotion affects sex-decoding of biological motion displays. *Cognition.* 119(2): 265–280.

Johnston, E., and Olson, L. (2015) *The Feeling Brain: The Biology and Psychology of Emotions*. New York, NY: W. W. Norton and Company.

Keltner, D., and Gross, J. J. (1999) Functional accounts of emotions. *Cognition and Emotion.* 13(5): 467–480.

Keltner, D., Ellsworth, P. C., and Edwards, K. (1993) Beyond simple pessimism: effects of sadness and anger on social perception. *Journal of Personality and Social Psychology.* 64(5): 740–752.

Kendall, S. (2007) Witnessing tragedy: nurses' perceptions of caring for patients with cancer. *International Journal of Nursing Practice.* 13(2): 111–120.

Kim, H. J., and Cameron, G. T. (2011) Emotions matter in crisis: the role of anger and sadness in the publics' response to crisis news framing and corporate crisis response. *Communication Research.* 38(6): 826–855.

Kimel, S. Y., Mischkowski, D., Kitayama, S., and Uchida, Y. (2017) Culture, emotions, and the cold shoulder: cultural differences in the anger and sadness response to ostracism. *Journal of Cross-Cultural Psychology.* 48(9): 1307–1319.

Kreamer, A. (2011) *It's Always Personal: Navigating Emotion in the New Workplace.* New York, NY: Random House.

Kübler-Ross, E. (1973) *On Death and Dying: What the Dying Have to Teach Doctors, Nurses, Clergy and Their Own Families*. Abingdon, UK: Taylor and Francis.

Lanctôt, N., and Guay, S. (2014) The aftermath of workplace violence among healthcare workers: a systematic literature review of the consequences. *Aggression and Violent Behavior.* 19(5): 492–501.

Lench, H. C., and Levine, L. J. (2008) Goals and responses to failure: knowing when to hold them and when to fold them. *Motivation and Emotion.* 32(2): 127–140.

Lench, H. C., Flores, S. A., and Bench, S. W. (2011) Discrete emotions predict changes in cognition, judgment, experience, behavior, and physiology: a meta-analysis of experimental emotion elicitations. *Psychological Bulletin.* 137(5): 834–855.

Lench, H. C., Tibbett, T. P., and Bench, S. W. (2016) Exploring the toolkit of emotion: what do sadness and anger do for us? *Social and Personality Psychology Compass.* 10(1): 11–25.

Lerner, J. S., Li, Y., and Weber, E. U. (2013) The financial costs of sadness. *Psychological Science.* 24(1): 72–79.

Lerner, J. S., Small, D. A., and Loewenstein, G. (2004) Heart strings and purse strings: carryover effects of emotions on economic decisions. *Psychological Science.* 15(5): 337–341.

Lewis, K. M. (2000) When leaders display emotion: how followers respond to negative emotional expression of male and female leaders. *Journal of Organizational Behavior.* 21(2): 221–234.

Lindebaum, D., and Jordan, P. J. (2014) When it can be good to feel bad and bad to feel good: exploring asymmetries in workplace emotional outcomes. *Human Relations.* 67(9): 1037–1050.

Lord, R. G., Klimoski, R. J., and Kanfer, R. (eds) (2002) *Emotions in the Workplace: Understanding the Structure and Role of Emotions in Organizational Behavior.* San Francisco, CA: Jossey-Bass.

McRae, K., Ochsner, K. N., Mauss, I. B., Gabrieli, J. J. D., and Gross, J. J. (2008) Gender differences in emotion regulation: an fMRI study of cognitive reappraisal. *Group Processes and Intergroup Relations.* 11(2): 143–162.

Miller, K. (2002) The experience of emotion in the workplace: professing in the midst of tragedy. *Management Communication Quarterly.* 15(4): 571–600.

Park, J., and Banaji, M. R. (2000) Mood and heuristics: the influence of happy and sad states on sensitivity and bias in stereotyping. *Journal of Personality and Social Psychology.* 78(6): 1005–1023.

Polman, E., and Kim, S. H. (2013) Effects of anger, disgust, and sadness on sharing with others. *Personality and Social Psychology Bulletin.* 39(12): 1683–1692.

Porath, C. L., and Pearson, C. M. (2012) Emotional and behavioral responses to workplace incivility and the impact of hierarchical status. *Journal of Applied Social Psychology.* 42(S1): E326-E357.

Rothman, N.B., and Melwani, S. (2017) Feeling mixed, ambivalent, and in flux: the social functions of emotional complexity for leaders. *Academy of Management Review.* 42(2): 259–282.

Sommers, S. (1984) Reported emotions and conventions of emotionality among college students. *Journal of Personality and Social Psychology.* 46(1): 207–215.

Tan, H. B., and Forgas, J. P. (2010) When happiness makes us selfish, but sadness makes us fair: affective influences on interpersonal strategies in the dictator game. *Journal of Experimental Social Psychology.* 46(3): 571–576.

To, M. L., Fisher, C. D., and Ashkanasy, N. M. (2015) Unleashing angst: negative mood, learning goal orientation, psychological empowerment and creative behavior. *Human Relations.* 68(10): 1601–1622.

To, M. L., Fisher, C. D., Ashkanasy, N. M., and Rowe, P. A. (2012) Within-person relationships between mood and creativity. *Journal of Applied Psychology.* 97(3): 599–612.

Visser, V.A., van Knippenberg, D., van Kleef, G. A., and Wisse, B. (2013) How leader displays of happiness and sadness influence follower performance: emotional contagion and creative versus analytical performance. *The Leadership Quarterly.* 24(1): 172–188.

Yan, L., Ashkanasy, N. M., and Mehmood, K. (2017) The experience of anger and sadness in response to hurtful behavior: effects of gender-pairing and national culture. *Asia Pacific Journal of Management.* 34(2): 423–441.

10. Talking about schadenfreude: sharing versus the social function

Paul Harvey and Marie T. Dasborough

Since the affective revolution in the organizational sciences (Barsade et al., 2003), there has been great interest in emotions and how they impact organizational life. More recently, as the field has further matured, we are seeing a new focus on discrete emotions, and on moral emotions in particular (see Lindebaum et al., 2017). Moral emotions are defined as those which function as a type of moral barometer; they provide immediate and salient feedback on social and moral acceptability (Tangney et al., 2007). We agree that the study of moral emotions is critical to promote ethical behavior in organizations, yet we have concerns about how they are sometimes represented as being purely positive or negative in nature.

We aim to add new insights to the current debates in the literature on the oversimplification of emotions (Lindebaum and Jordan, 2012, 2014). To illustrate our concerns about simplified views of emotions, we focus specifically on the moral emotion of schadenfreude. Our motivation for this chapter is to highlight the complexities of this specific moral emotion, especially in the case of talking about it with others. Talking about schadenfreude (e.g., verbalizing, sharing) can have reputational effects, for both the target and the source, that are distinct from its intended social functions (Dasborough and Harvey, 2017). As we will discuss in the following sections, there are pros and cons to sharing schadenfreude with others. Rather than viewing it as a purely positive or negative moral emotion, we urge scholars to consider the various ways in which it may be perceived by others.

Our chapter is structured as follows. First, we define schadenfreude and explain how it is an emotion that is commonly kept private. Next, we outline why it may be shared with others and we highlight a variety of benefits that can stem from this. We then move on to explain how there can be a negative side for the person expressing the schadenfreude, as observers may perceive them in a negative light. However, this is positive for the observers, as the sharing of schadenfreude tells us a lot of information about the person expressing it. We end the chapter with some practical guidelines for individuals and offer some directions for future scholarly work in the area of talking about schadenfreude.

WHAT IS SCHADENFREUDE?

Schadenfreude refers to feelings of pleasure in response to the misfortune of others (Heider, 1958; Feather, 2008). The word is somewhat unique in the English language in that it is not, in fact, a word in the English language. This fact often becomes apparent when native English-speakers first try to say it, or (worse) try to spell it. It has even been speculated that the word was in danger of falling out of the English lexicon toward the end of the twentieth century until a noticeable uptick in usage was observed following its use in a 1991 episode of *The Simpsons* (Cohen, 2015). Because the emotion has no English equivalent, however, Anglo-philes of the world have borrowed the term from the German language. The closest English equivalent we are aware of, epicaricacy, has, perhaps unsurprisingly, failed to enter the common vernacular.

As prefaced in our introduction, schadenfreude is a complex emotion that individuals are often reluctant to acknowledge – sometimes even to themselves. Although the frequency with which people experience schadenfreude can vary based on factors such as personality traits and situational norms (as we discuss below), research suggests that nearly all of us indulge in this "malicious joy" from time to time (e.g., Hoogland et al., 2015). Individuals are less likely to express schadenfreude when the target of the schadenfreude is personally known to the person expressing it. This is because expressing schadenfreude sends a different social message in this context, as we will discuss later in the chapter.

People can feel schadenfreude in response to any misfortune affecting anyone else. This includes complete strangers with no status; for example, witnessing a person across the street stepping in dog droppings (see Szameitat et al., 2009). The frequency of this type of schadenfreude is evidenced by the popularity of YouTube videos and TV shows which highlight regular people experiencing a misfortune, that others find highly amusing (Pozner, 2010). While this type of schadenfreude is commonly experienced, it is relatively short-lived when the misfortune is viewed as being underserved by the victim and the observer may experience guilt as a result (Li et al., 2018). In such cases, Li et al. (2018) argue that the initial schadenfreude emotion is reappraised and, due to the lack of social legitimacy, it manifests as *ambivalent schadenfreude* which is frequently suppressed instead of being expressed to others.

It is also common for individuals to experience schadenfreude in response to the misfortune of individuals with higher social status than themselves. This can be seen in the pleasure observers feel in response to failures or public embarrassment of professional athletes, famous sport teams, political figures, and celebrities, and the eagerness of media outlets to capitalize on these misfortunes. Although these individuals are not closely connected to the person feeling the schadenfreude, due to the elevated social status of such targets, the schadenfreude feelings are more intense than in the case of strangers and lower status individuals (Watanabe, 2016). This feeling is further amplified when the misfortune is perceived as being deserved, and the initial emotion is re-appraised by the observer as *righteous schadenfreude* (Li et al., 2018). For the purposes of this chapter on "talking about schadenfreude", we focus our discussion only on *righteous schadenfreude*, because in contrast to ambivalent schadenfreude, righteous schadenfreude is more likely to be outwardly expressed and shared with others.

Individuals tend to report higher levels of schadenfreude and a greater willingness to share the emotion with others when the misfortune befalls highly successful people who are perceived to deserve it (e.g., Dasborough and Harvey, 2017; Feather and Nairn, 2005; Li et al., 2018). It is argued by some that this is due to envy, yet there are mixed results in studies testing this claim (see van Dijk et al., 2006). Discussions of schadenfreude often venture into issues of envy, so much so that scholars have taken pains to clarify that the two are different emotions. Feather and Sherman (2002), for example, challenged the argument that schadenfreude is an extension of envy toward an individual experiencing misfortune. They argued that schadenfreude occurs when observers experience resentment toward the target individual rather than envy. Empirically, they found that envy toward the target of misfortune was unrelated to schadenfreude, while resentment was positively related and impossible to fully separate from schadenfreude, from a measurement perspective. Similarly, scholars have recently found evidence of neurological separation between schadenfreude and envy in brain-imaging analyses (Santamaría-García et al., 2017).

Relatedly, there has been some discussion of a form of "reverse-schadenfreude" in which individuals experience emotional pain in response to the success of others – particularly disliked and/or highly successful others. In this regard, it briefly appeared as though the Germans had come to the aid of English-speakers once again as authors began using the ostensibly German word "glückschmerz" to describe this emotion (Cikara et al., 2014; Hoogland et al., 2015). While the origins of glückschmerz are a bit unclear, its status as an imposter of the German language was allegedly exposed when an audience member questioned a presenter's failure to place an umlaut over the "u" at an academic conference (Cohen, 2015). In place of glückschmerz, the Australian term "Tall Poppy Syndrome" has become increasingly popular for describing the tendency to feel either negatively in response to individuals' continued success, or positively in response to their failures (Dasborough, 2018; Feather, 1989). In both cases, the emotion of envy appears to play some role.

Schadenfreude has also been viewed as the reverse of sympathy, although researchers have generally concluded that the two emotions are not polar opposites (Feather and Sherman, 2002; van Dijk et al., 2008). Unlike the "concordant" reaction of sympathy, schadenfreude establishes an antagonistic relationship to the unfortunate other. For this reason, Heider (1958) saw schadenfreude as harmful to social relations, a point we will expand upon later in the chapter.

HOW DOES SCHADENFREUDE FEEL?

Before we expand on the social benefits and consequences of schadenfreude, it is helpful to understand the internal experience of the emotion. Research from psychological and neurological perspectives suggests that schadenfreude is generally experienced as a pleasurable emotion. In their 2017 study, Dasborough and Harvey included a quotation to this effect:

> Unlike most things that light up your ventral striatum [a region in the brain], schadenfreude is free, it's not fattening, and you don't have to take your clothes off. It can't hurt, and it just might make you feel a little better (Zweig, 2009).

As the definition above suggests, schadenfreude is associated with feelings of joy (Boecker et al., 2015; Dasborough and Harvey, 2017; Schumpe and Lafrenière, 2016). Indeed, joy is part of the word itself ("Freude" is a German word for "joy" whereas "schaden" denotes "harm"). Joy and schadenfreude represent distinct cognitive appraisals, however, to the point that electromyography analysis can detect the different facial expressions associated with each type of emotion (Boecker et al., 2015).

The distinction between schadenfreude and joy, as well as other positive emotions such as happiness (Jung, 2017), stems from the dissonance inherent in deriving a positive affective state from a negative outcome (see also Li et al., 2018). The experience of schadenfreude can be accompanied by feelings of guilt or shame for this reason (e.g., Kramer et al., 2011; Vanman, 2015). Based on this observation, it is not surprising that individuals with guilt-inhibiting personality traits, such as the "Dark Triad" traits (i.e., narcissism, psychopathy, Machiavellianism), report higher levels of schadenfreude enjoyment (James et al., 2014; Porter et al., 2014). We reiterate, however, that the enjoyment of schadenfreude does not always indicate a psychopathic personality. Although we are not always comfortable admitting it, it is a feeling that most of us enjoy regardless of our personality types (Dasborough and Harvey, 2017).

Given the connection of schadenfreude to the experience of guilt and shame, people are often reluctant to share this emotion with others. This occasional reluctance to confide our schadenfreude is another unique aspect of the emotion (Li et al., 2018). But, when and why do we keep it private? We now turn our focus to the individual and situational dynamics that influence the decision to share or hide schadenfreude feelings, and the potential consequences of both alternatives.

PRIVATE VERSUS SHARED SCHADENFREUDE

Beneficial social outcomes are often amplified when positive emotions are expressed to others, rather than hidden. Cropanzano, Dasborough and Weiss (2017) recently theorized on how the sharing of positive emotions over time between a leader and a follower is required in order to develop high quality leader–member relationships in the workplace. Similarly, a recent meta-analysis (Chervonsky and Hunt, 2017) indicates that emotional suppression, including both negative and positive emotions, is negatively associated with social well-being. This includes outcomes such as negative first impressions, lower social support, lower social satisfaction and quality, and poorer relationship quality. Hence, it seems important socially to share emotions with other people.

At first glance, this appears to be especially true for positively-valenced emotions. However, in the case of schadenfreude (a positive emotion because it is pleasurable for the person experiencing it), individuals may refrain from sharing their feelings with others. Individuals who are cognizant that their emotional response of schadenfreude is not socially acceptable often elect to report low amounts of schadenfreude, if any at all (Porter et al., 2014). Individuals may even actively mask their schadenfreude by suppressing their emotional expressions (Li et al.,

2018), and by displaying mock concern for the target, known as "hidden schadenfreude" (Combs et al., 2009).

We note that although individuals may attempt to reduce their expression of schadenfreude pleasure, it is difficult to conceal such felt emotions (see Porter and ten Brinke, 2008). For example, individuals frequently leak their true feelings of socially taboo emotions such as schadenfreude by unconsciously smiling (Baker et al., 2016). Whether or not this can be considered a "personal failing" is debatable. Indeed, facial expressions such as smiling communicate our emotions, transmit valuable information to others, and thus serve various social functions (e.g., Ekman, 1993).

This brings us to the social functional account of emotions, which proposes that emotions are a means of coordinating social interactions and maintaining relationships (Keltner and Haidt, 1999). Emotions are social, in that they are shared between people in order to communicate information about feelings, beliefs, and intentions (Dasborough and Harvey, 2017). We do tend to share emotions, and this sharing of emotions – even the emotion of schadenfreude – serves a social purpose! We outline the positive social outcomes of sharing schadenfreude with others in the following section.

POSITIVE OUTCOMES OF SHARING

Group Bonding

A noted, but controversial, outcome of sharing schadenfreude is group bonding (Cikara, 2015; Fischer, 2014). The "controversy" about this outcome centers on if – and under what circumstances – it qualifies as a desirable form of bonding. In contexts characterized by healthy competition, (e.g., friendly rivalries between organizational departments, fans of opposing sports teams), the social bonding caused by shared schadenfreude is generally thought to be beneficial (Fischer, 2014; Ouwerkerk and van Dijk, 2014). In this regard, both contemporary and seminal work (Buckley, 2014; Nietzsche, 1954) has noted the role of humor, laughter, and positivity associated with shared feelings of schadenfreude on the strengthening of social bonds.

Perhaps unsurprisingly, given the nature of the emotion, schadenfreude has also been linked to potentially counterproductive forms of social bonding. A key determinant appears to be the extent to which the schadenfreude being shared stems from perceived inferiority, as opposed to healthy competition. Here too, Nietzsche (1967) weighed in on the issue, noting that perceptions of in-group inferiority often fuel schaden-freude reactions to the failures of out-groups. Building on this premise, Leach and Spears (2008) observed that feelings of in-group inferiority were stronger predictors of out-group schadenfreude than were feelings toward the outgroup. In other words, schadenfreude may reflect, and solidify, group members' sense of inferiority relative to other groups. Taken to an extreme, schadenfreude-driven group bonding has even been linked to collective violence toward out-groups that are viewed as a threat to the in-group (Cikara, 2015).

This research suggests that pre-existing perceptions regarding in-group and out-group members (e.g., social inferiority) appear to play a key role in determining the constructiveness of schadenfreude-driven group bonding. We revisit these perceptual mechanisms in greater detail in the section on attributional contingencies below.

Behavioral Norms

In their 2017 study, Dasborough and Harvey adopted a social functional perspective on schadenfreude, noting that it can serve as a socializing element. They argued that the social sharing of schadenfreude can teach and reinforce organizational norms to members. More specifically, they argued and observed that individuals were more likely to share their schadenfreude feelings in response to violations of ethical norms. For example, subjects were more likely to share schadenfreude regarding a fellow employee who was punished for violating ethical guidelines (e.g., unauthorized use of organizational funds) than an employee who was terminated for poor performance.

This research suggests that schadenfreude can signal the presence of ethical norms, such that a newcomer might quickly deduce that employ-ees are taking pleasure in a peer's downfall because the behavior in question violated their shared views on acceptable behavior. Similarly, Dasborough and Harvey (2017) noted that schadenfreude can act as a deterrent against violating these norms if employees understand that such violations will make them the target of schadenfreude rather than sympathy.

From the perspective of ethical relativism, however, it should be noted that this socializing aspect of schadenfreude can communicate and reinforce organizational norms that are not shared by society at large. Li and colleagues (2018) discuss the role of schadenfreude within the context of binding values, individualizing values, and organizational civility climate. While this is true of most socialization tactics, the avoidance of schadenfreude at one's own expense can be a particularly powerful motivator to conform to both ethical and unethical norms.

Self-image

It can be deduced from existing research that schadenfreude can have both positive and negative effects on one's self-image. Consistent with some of the group-level dynamics noted above, schadenfreude stemming from the failures of out-group members can boost the self-esteem of in-group members. To explain this effect, Bénabou and Tirole (2002) invoke both attributional and social comparison processes. The authors explained that individuals' attributions regarding their own ability correlate positively with the perceived ability of in-group members and negatively with out-group members. Poor performance or failures by out-group members, and the resulting schadenfreude, may therefore increase self-esteem or efficacy.

The aforementioned group research also suggests that schadenfreude may reinforce an existing sense of inferiority (e.g., Leach and Spears, 2008). Consistent with this perspective, a number of studies have shown that low self-esteem is a strong predictor of schadenfreude (Feather et al., 2013; van Dijk et al., 2011). Van Dijk and colleagues (2011) argued that this effect stems from a desire for self-protection and a desire for self-affirmation. In other words, schadenfreude may be used as a means for protecting a fragile self-image from further harm rather than, or in addition to, improving a strong self-image.

A recurring theme of the preceding discussion is that schadenfreude can have beneficial outcomes, but its use toward such ends is fraught with peril. It can facilitate social bonding, but may do so in a destructive way that reinforces feelings of group inferiority. It can raise employees' awareness of organizational norms, but may pressure them into compliance even when the norms themselves are ethically dubious. It can improve one's self-image, but can also be used to prop up a fragile ego, and does so at the expense of others.

NEGATIVE OUTCOMES OF SHARING ... TOO MUCH AND TOO OFTEN

In this section of our chapter, we examine the types of perceptions that individuals form about others who socially share their schadenfreude feelings with others too much and too often. When individuals express they are feeling schadenfreude, either by verbally telling someone else, or by smiling (even just a hint of a smile) in the moment, they are being perceived by others. In cases where the observer does not share the same feelings toward the schadenfreude target, and where there is an ongoing pattern of schadenfreude, there is more likely to be a negative perception formed about the person expressing schadenfreude.

Leach, Spears, Branscombe, and Doosje (2003) note that schadenfreude can present "a particularly insidious threat to social relations" (p. 932) because the experience of this positive emotion requires the suffering of another. Hence, there can be a perception by observers that people expressing schadenfreude lack empathy for others. James and colleagues (2014) state that enjoying pleasure at another's misfortune suggests a "dark" individual. Following a similar line of thought, within the context of sports, McNamee (2003) argued that individuals feeling schadenfreude towards other athletes reflects poor character.

The continuous expression of schadenfreude may be viewed as behavior that violates social norms. Many scholars assume that the "Dark Triad" is a prominent antecedent of such behaviors (Muris et al., 2017). There is empirical research on these traits as predictors of schadenfreude, which we will draw on. In this chapter, however, we take a slightly different view. Instead of viewing the traits as antecedents to schadenfreude feelings, we look at schadenfreude expressions as being the antecedent to observers' perceptions of these personality traits in the person expressing the schadenfreude. These perceptions, based on internal attributions, may or may not be completely accurate. Regardless, observers' perceptions of personality traits will impact how social relationships develop.

The Dark Triad and Beyond

The Dark Triad of personality includes narcissism, machiavellianism, and psychopathy. Recently, researchers have proposed that "everyday sadism" should be included with the Dark Triad constructs to form the "Dark Tetrad", given its similar impact on malicious social behaviors (Buckels, 2012; Meðedović and Petrović, 2015; Paulhus and Williams, 2002). Of particular relevance to schadenfreude, Buckels (2012) found one key difference in this regard, concluding that "only sadists were willing to work to aggress against an innocent person" (p. 1).

In line with Porter et al. (2014) and Wai and Tiliopoulos (2012), we feel that it is the emotional coldness, or lack of empathy, aspects of these traits that connect them with expressions of schadenfreude (Jonason et al., 2014). Next, we outline each of the dark traits in the Dark Tetrad, and examine why they may be used to label an individual who is known for their schadenfreude expressions. Some of these traits are more likely than others to emerge in such scenarios.

Narcissism

Narcissism is a term introduced by Freud in reference to the mythical Greek character Narcissus, who fell in love with his own image reflected in water (Bushman and Baumeister, 1998). It refers to individuals who display excessive self-love. Facets of narcissism include grandiosity, entitlement, dominance, and superiority (Paulhus and Williams, 2002). This is a subclinical individual difference which has important everyday consequences, such as self-enhancement in perceptions of one's self and one's own behaviors (Ames et al., 2006).

There have been mixed findings on the relationship between narcissism and schadenfreude. In Porter et al.'s (2014) experimental study, assessing schadenfreude tendencies by asking if individuals seek out to watch videos of people in pain, they found that narcissists did not engage in such behaviors – unlike other individuals characterized by machiavellianism and psychopathy. The explanation provided was that these individuals are able to empathize with the suffering of others, and do not derive pleasure from more serious misfortunes of others. As Wai and Tiliopoulos (2012) explain, narcissists possess the ability to recognize the emotional expressions of others; they have the highest degree of emotional intelligence of the dark traits. Hence, they can be empathic.

However, the story is a little more complicated when taking into account the different types of narcissists that exist. As evidenced by Dickinson and Pincus (2003), important distinctions can be drawn between grandiose and vulnerable narcissism. While grandiose narcissists are unrealistically self-enhancing, vulnerable narcissists rely on defensive ego-protection to mask weak self-perceptions (Gabbard, 1998). Vulnerable narcissists seek constant feedback from other people to maintain their sense of self-worth (Miller et al., 2010). Given this distinction, vulnerable narcissists are more likely to use schadenfreude as a strategy to enhance their self-esteem (James et al., 2014). Vulnerable narcissists use schadenfreude as a downward social comparison to feel better about themselves (e.g., Krizan and Johar, 2012; James et al., 2014). However, grandiose narcissism does not appear to influence schadenfreude levels (Krizan and Johar, 2012).

The connection between the other dark traits and schadenfreude is a lot more clear-cut. We discuss these next – in less detail – due to the simplified nature of the relationships.

Psychopathy

Psychopaths are individuals who exhibit high levels of impulsivity and thrill-seeking, and demonstrate low empathy and anxiety (Paulhus and Williams, 2002). These individuals often appear normal to external observers, and may even seem charming. These characteristics, however, enable psychopaths to be manipulative and volatile (see also Walker and Jackson, 2017).

A study by James and colleagues (2014) found that high levels of psychopathy were associated with greater levels of schadenfreude in all of the experimental scenarios they tested. Psychopathy was also a predictor in the study by Porter and colleagues (2014), who utilized an interesting indicator of schadenfreude in the real-world setting – a question asking about watching YouTube videos of others experiencing pain. On a related note, there is evidence that psychopaths exhibit negative (e.g., maladaptive, aggressive) humor styles (Veselka et al., 2010). Such humor has been related to schadenfreude. Hence, there was a clear link between psychopathy and schadenfreude, largely enabled by their lack of empathy for others.

Machiavellianism

Machiavellianism, synonymous with manipulative personality, emerged from Richard Christie's selection of statements from Machiavelli's original books (see Christie and Geis, 1970). Individuals high on machiavellianism are characterized by a focus on self-interest and personal gain (Dasborough and Ashkanasy, 2002), a duplicitous inter-personal style and cynical disregard for morality (Jones and Paulhus, 2009). Hence, they are likely to behave in a cold and manipulative fashion. Machiavellians are focused on manipulating others to gain and maintain power, and are likely to use hard management tactics in order to do so (Kessler et al., 2010). As explained by Christie, Machiavellian individuals are successful manipulators because they are not concerned with conventional morality (Christie and Geis, 1970); instead, they have low ideological commitment, and they lack interpersonal affect in social relationships. Therefore, similar to psychopaths, Machiavellian individuals are more likely to experience schadenfreude, as evidenced in Porter and colleagues' (2014) experimental study. Again, the lack of concern for others makes it easy for the Machiavellian to feel schadenfreude.

Sadism

As indicated earlier, sadism has recently been added to the Dark Triad to form the Dark Tetrad (Buckels, 2012). Everyday sadism can be conceptualized as a nonclinical form of sadism, differing from clinical sadism in that the individual does not harm others out of the need for cruelty, but rather for the pleasure derived from the act (Buckels, 2012). This makes everyday sadism even more closely related to the concept of schadenfreude. In a series of empirical studies, Buckels and colleagues found that sadism was associated with the enjoyment of cruelty in mundane situations, among ordinary people in everyday life. For example, sadism predicted cyber-trolling (Buckels et al., 2014), and also predicted readiness to kill bugs among a population of undergraduate students in a laboratory experiment (Buckels et al., 2013). In a recent study, Schumpe and Lafrenière (2016) found that sadism moderated the relationship between misfortune and schadenfreude, such that sadists expressed comparatively high levels of schadenfreude for severe misfortunes.

Looking at these four traits together and the supporting scholarly empirical evidence – we conclude that dark personalities often actively seek out stimuli that induce feelings of schadenfreude. While we agree that these dark personality traits will lead to individuals desiring to feel schadenfreude, we also take the view that the expression of schadenfreude in the presence of others will lead observers to perceive these dark personality traits in the person expressing it. These parts of an individual's personality could remain hidden if the individuals do not express their schadenfreude feelings to others too much or too often.

TALKING ABOUT SCHADENFREUDE

We now shift our focus to the topic that this book seeks to explore: the differences and similarities between the social functional roles of schadenfreude and the ways in which we "talk" about the emotion. As discussed elsewhere in this text (see also Lindebaum, 2017), a disconnect between these two treatments of emotions can impede interpersonal communication and decision making in significant ways. More specifically, the manner in which individuals treat emotions in their general discourse can potentially negate the useful social functions of these emotions.

As the other chapters in this book show, this disconnect can impact a wide range of emotions. At the risk of sounding biased, we argue that schadenfreude is uniquely relevant in this regard. When it comes to how we talk about the emotion, recall that the English language does not even have a word for it! It is naturally difficult to talk about an emotion when one does not know what it is called (or how to pronounce it) – as is likely the case for a sizeable portion of English-speakers.

Thus, unlike other discrete emotions, such as anger, guilt, and shame, where social function and discourse sometimes diverge, schadenfreude struggles to even enter the discourse of the English-speaking world. Other emotions such as gloating and malice are often used as imperfect proxies, but these words do not fully capture the essence of schaden-freude (Dasborough and Harvey, 2017; Meier, 2000). That said, most humans are familiar with the feeling of schadenfreude, even if they do not know what to call it. We can therefore assume that imprecise descriptors such as these are reasonably effective in communicating the true emotion when the situational context allows them to do so.

In spite of these challenges, it is clear that humans generally find a way to discuss and share their thoughts on schadenfreude (Dasborough and Harvey, 2017). Like some of the other "negative" emotions discussed in this book, this discourse does not often paint schadenfreude in a positive light. Given the fact that its very existence requires others to suffer, it is not surprising that schadenfreude is often classified as a "socially undesirable" emotion (McNamee, 2003, 2007). This negative discourse about schadenfreude undermines its important social functions.

Several of these social functions were discussed above, including bonding, socialization and self-image protection. While an admittedly imperfect path to any of these outcomes, we suggest that schadenfreude's role in normative socialization is particularly important. Despite having many of the same shortcomings shared by other socialization tactics, as described above, schadenfreude is an undeniably powerful tool for teaching and reinforcing behavioral norms (Dasborough and Harvey, 2017). Fostering a climate where the feeling and sharing of schaden-freude is frowned upon (i.e., a civility climate; Li et al., 2018), can therefore deprive organizations of an effective socialization (and control) tactic.

Although slightly more speculative in nature, we also argue that schadenfreude can serve a valuable signaling function by which indi-viduals communicate aspects of their personality. As described in detail above, schadenfreude is felt more commonly and intensely by those who possess generally undesirable personality traits (e.g., the Dark Tetrad traits). An organizational climate where schadenfreude is artificially suppressed might prevent such individuals from revealing their true nature.

The argument that schadenfreude can serve social functions in organizations cannot be made without recognizing the aforementioned dark sides of the emotion. Sharing schadenfreude feelings has the potential to damage one's reputation, solidify perceptions of inferiority, motivate counterproductive behaviors, among other consequences. Each of these outcomes suggests an important conclusion: there is a time and place (and personality type) for schadenfreude. More specifically, there appears to be situational and individual-level limits to schadenfreude's social functionality. Although we see this as an area where additional research is needed, we discuss some practical guidelines that can be deduced from existing research.

Practical Advice on Schadenfreude

Since schadenfreude is a human emotion that most individuals will experience at some point, this advice is targeted to a broad audience, and not just to those individuals who experience schadenfreude on a regular basis. The sharing of schadenfreude with others can be damaging, even if only done so on rare occasions. This is especially the case where schadenfreude is viewed as violating the norms of an organization's civility climate (see Clark and Walsh, 2016; Li et al., 2018).

Since the sharing of this emotion can benefit relationships, it would be overly simplistic to suggest that individuals always refrain from sharing schadenfreude feeling with others. As Cropanzano and colleagues (2017) explained, the social sharing of positive emotions, such as schadenfreude, can have positive implications for the relationships if the feelings are mutual. For example, many individuals bond together over sharing their schadenfreude when traditionally highly successful football teams lose a game unexpectedly (e.g., Collingwood in Australia or New England Patriots in the USA). The sharing of schadenfreude builds camaraderie in these circumstances – but only if the other person shares the same feeling, or if the schadenfreude is the ambivalent type that is less intensely felt (Li et al., 2018). It is therefore advisable to have some prior understanding of how the other individual will respond prior to sharing feelings of schadenfreude (regardless of the schadenfreude target). Does the other person feel the same way? Do they share the schadenfreude feelings with you? You need to know your audience, or else the schadenfreude shared may have very negative social outcomes.

This advice dovetails with the notions of self-awareness and social astuteness. Key aspects of the broader political skill construct, these constructs describe one's ability to monitor and understand the other members of a social situation (e.g., Ferris et al., 2007). As we are all aware, these skills do not always come naturally. They are, however, vitally important for interpreting situational, verbal, and non-verbal cues as to the appropriateness of sharing schadenfreude in a given situation. Fortunately, it is generally accepted that individuals can work to improve their self- and social awareness, and their overall political skill (e.g., Perrewé et al., 2000).

Similarly, individuals may sharpen their schadenfreude sharing skills by working to develop their emotional intelligence. Salovey, Mayer, and Caruso (2004) explain that emotional intelligence is the ability to accurately perceive emotions, to access and generate emotions so as to assist thought, to understand emotions and emotional knowledge, and to reflectively regulate emotions. Thus, emotional intelligence can help individuals manage their emotional displays. Is now the right time to outwardly express my schadenfreude feelings, or should I try to manage it? It also helps with being able to anticipate the emotions of others (see Antonakis et al., 2009). Will my colleagues also feel the same schadenfreude I do when my boss is fired for financial incompetence? Thus, being emotionally skilled will help with the earlier practical advice about knowing your audience and anticipating their emotional responses.

CONCLUSIONS AND FUTURE STUDY

In this chapter, we have offered a balanced view of the sharing of schadenfreude with others. We have presented the positive outcomes of socially sharing schadenfreude with other individuals, as well as the possible downsides that may arise. Our aim was to stimulate thinking about this rarely discussed emotion, and to ignite research interest in this area.

Future research in organizational contexts could uncover more about this phenomenon by taking a longitudinal approach. For example, diary studies could capture the frequency with which employees observe others expressing schadenfreude over a given time period. Such approaches are required to establish patterns of emotional expression – and their consequences across levels of analysis – over time. Such approaches are required to form more accurate perceptions of personality (see also Fleeson et al., 2014).

We also need to consider measures of schadenfreude. Schadenfreude is often assessed through self-report measures about emotions felt (e.g., Dasborough and Harvey, 2017) or self-reported behaviors, such as watching YouTube videos of people being hurt (Porter et al., 2014). Yet, given that some individuals may wish to hide their schadenfreude for social desirability purposes they may not report feeling any schadenfreude, or perhaps they report lower levels of schadenfreude than they are really feeling. For this reason, we encourage the use of objective measures. For example, after capturing video data to assess schadenfreude, scholars could code the smile intensity of the focal individual (e.g., Porter et al., 2014), using the Facial Action Coding System (FACS; Ekman et al., 2002), or use other psychophysiological measures instead (e.g., facial EMG, EEG; see Vanman, 2015).

Perhaps most importantly, research aimed at understanding the social functional role of schadenfreude is needed. Despite being a wide-spread emotion, schadenfreude's taboo status seems to limit both the "talk" about the emotion and the study of it (Kuipers, 2014). As the brevity of our summary of research-based practical advice above suggests, there is a disconnect between the role schadenfreude plays in organizational life and the attention paid to it by organizational scholars. Again, we hope that this chapter will inspire readers to work towards addressing that disconnect – lest practitioners continue to feel schadenfreude every time our work is criticized for lacking practical relevance!

REFERENCES

Antonakis, J., Ashkanasy, N. M., and Dasborough, M. T. (2009). Does leadership need emotional intelligence? *The Leadership Quarterly, 20*(2), 247–261.

Ames, D. R., Rose, P., and Anderson, C. P. (2006). The NPI-16 as a short measure of narcissism. *Journal of Research in Personality, 40*(4), 440–450.

Baker, A., Black, P. J., and Porter, S. (2016). The truth is written all over your face! Involuntary aspects of emotional facial expressions. In C. Abell and J. Smith (eds), *The Expression of Emotion: Philosophical, Psychological and Legal Perspectives* (Studies in Emotion and Social Interaction, pp. 219–244). Cambridge, UK: Cambridge University Press.

Barsade, S., Brief, A. P., Spataro, S. E., and Greenberg, J. (2003). The affective revolution in organizational behavior: the emergence of a paradigm. *Organizational Behavior: A Management Challenge, 1*, 3–50.

Bénabou, R., and Tirole, J. (2002). Self-confidence and personal motivation. *The Quarterly Journal of Economics, 117*(3), 871–915.

Boecker, L., Likowski, K. U., Pauli, P., and Weyers, P. (2015). The face of schadenfreude: differentiation of joy and schadenfreude by electromyography. *Cognition and Emotion, 29*(6), 1117–1125.

Buckels, E. E. (2012). The pleasures of hurting others: behavioral evidence for everyday sadism. (Unpublished master's thesis).

Buckels, E. E., Jones, D. N., and Paulhus, D. L. (2013). Behavioral confirmation of everyday sadism. *Psychological Science, 24*, 2201–2209.

Buckels, E. E., Trapnell, P. D., and Paulhus, D. L. (2014). Trolls just want to have fun. *Personality and Individual Differences, 67*, 97–102.

Buckley, F. H. (2014). 14 Schadenfreude and laughter. In W.W. van Dijk and J. W. Ouwerkerk (eds), *Schadenfreude: Understanding Pleasure at the Misfortune of Others* (pp. 219–226). Cambridge, UK: Cambridge University Press.

Bushman, B. J., and Baumeister, R. F. (1998). Threatened egotism, narcissism, self-esteem, and direct and displaced aggression: does self-love or self-hate lead to violence? *Journal of Personality and Social Psychology, 75*(1), 219–229.

Chervonsky, E., and Hunt, C. (2017). Suppression and expression of emotion in social and interpersonal outcomes: a meta-analysis. *Emotion, 17*(4), 669–683.

Christie, R., and Geis, F. L. (1970). *Studies in Machiavellianism.* New York, NY, USA: Academic Press.

Cikara, M. (2015). Intergroup schadenfreude: motivating participation in collective violence. *Current Opinion in Behavioral Sciences, 3,* 12–17.

Cikara, M., Bruneau, E., Van Bavel, J. J., and Saxe, R. (2014). Their pain gives us pleasure: how intergroup dynamics shape empathic failures and counterempathic responses. *Journal of Experimental Social Psychology, 55,* 110–125.

Clark, O. L., and Walsh, B. M. (2016). Civility climate mitigates deviant reactions to organizational constraints. *Journal of Managerial Psychology, 31*(1), 186–201.

Cohen, B. (2015, 12 June). Schadenfreude is in the zeitgeist, but is there an opposite term? Retrieved from: https://www.wsj.com/articles/schadenfreude-is-in-the-zeitgeist-but-is-there-an-opposite-term-1434129186.

Combs, D. J., Powell, C. A., Schurtz, D. R., and Smith, R. H. (2009). Politics, schadenfreude, and ingroup identification: the sometimes happy thing about a poor economy and death. *Journal of Experimental Social Psychology, 45*(4), 635–646.

Cropanzano, R., Dasborough, M. T., and Weiss, H. M. (2017). Affective events and the development of leader–member exchange. *Academy of Management Review, 42*(2), 233–258.

Dasborough, M.T. (2018). Tall poppy syndrome. In T. K. Shackelford and V. A. Weekes-Shackelford (eds), *Encyclopedia of Evolutionary Psychological Science.* New York, NY, USA: Springer.

Dasborough, M. T., and Ashkanasy, N. M. (2002). Emotion and attribution of intentionality in leader-member relationships. *The Leadership Quarterly, 13*(5), 615–634.

Dasborough, M., and Harvey, P. (2017). Schadenfreude: the (not so) secret joy of another's misfortune. *Journal of Business Ethics, 141*(4), 693–707.

Dickinson, K. A., and Pincus, A. L. (2003). Interpersonal analysis of grandiose and vulnerable narcissism. *Journal of Personality Disorders, 17*(3), 188–207.

Ekman, P. (1993). Facial expression and emotion. *American Psychologist, 48*(4), 384–392.

Ekman, P., Friesen, W. V., and Hagar, J. C. (1976/2002). *Facial Action Coding System: The Manual on CD-ROM.* Salt Lake City, UT, USA: Network Information Research Corporation.

Feather, N. T. (1989). Attitudes towards the high achiever: the fall of the tall poppy. *Australian Journal of Psychology, 41*(3), 239–267.

Feather, N. T. (2008). Effects of observer's own status on reactions to a high achiever's failure: deservingness, resentment, schadenfreude, and sympathy. *Australian Journal of Psychology*, *60*(1), 31–43.

Feather, N. T., and Nairn, K. (2005). Resentment, envy, schadenfreude, and sympathy: effects of own and other's deserved or undeserved status. *Australian Journal of Psychology*, *57*(2), 87–102.

Feather, N. T., and Sherman, R. (2002). Envy, resentment, schadenfreude, and sympathy: reactions to deserved and undeserved achievement and subsequent failure. *Personality and Social Psychology Bulletin*, *28*(7), 953–961.

Feather, N. T., Wenzel, M., and McKee, I. R. (2013). Integrating multiple perspectives on schadenfreude: the role of deservingness and emotions. *Motivation and Emotion*, *37*(3), 574–585.

Ferris, G. R., Treadway, D. C., Perrewé, P. L., Brouer, R. L., Douglas, C., and Lux, S. (2007). Political skill in organizations. *Journal of Management*, *33*(3), 290–320.

Fischer, A. H. (2014). Schadenfreude, concluding notes. In W. W. van Dijk and J. W. Ouwerkerk (eds), *Schadenfreude: Understanding Pleasure at the Misfortune of Others* (pp. 304–311). Cambridge, UK: Cambridge University Press.

Fleeson, W., Furr, R. M., Jayawickreme, E., Meindl, P., and Helzer, E. G. (2014). Character: the prospects for a personality-based perspective on morality. *Social and Personality Psychology Compass*, *8*(4), 178–191.

Gabbard, G. O. (1998). Transference and countertransference in the treatment of narcissistic patients. In E. F. Ronningstam (ed.), *Disorders of Narcissism: Diagnostic, Clinical, and Empirical Implications* (pp. 125–145). Washington, DC, USA: American Psychiatric Press.

Heider, F. (1958). *The Psychology of Interpersonal Relations*. Hillsdale, NJ, USA: Lawrence Erlbaulm Associates.

Hoogland, C. E., Schurtz, D. R., Cooper, C. M., Combs, D. J., Brown, E. G., and Smith, R. H. (2015). The joy of pain and the pain of joy: in-group identification predicts schadenfreude and gluckschmerz following rival groups' fortunes. *Motivation and Emotion*, *39*(2), 260–281.

James, S., Kavanagh, P. S., Jonason, P. K., Chonody, J. M., and Scrutton, H. E. (2014). The Dark Triad, schadenfreude, and sensational interests: dark personalities, dark emotions, and dark behaviors. *Personality and Individual Differences*, *68*, 211–216.

Jonason, P. K., Wee, S., Li, N. P., and Jackson, C. (2014). Occupational niches and the Dark Triad traits. *Personality and Individual Differences*, *69*, 119–123.

Jones, D. N., and Paulhus, D. L. (2009). Machiavellianism. In M. R. Leary and R. H. (eds), *Handbook of Individual Differences in Social Behavior* (pp. 93–108). New York, NY, USA and London, UK: The Guilford Press.

Jung, K. (2017). Happiness as an additional antecedent of schadenfreude. *The Journal of Positive Psychology*, *12*(2), 186–196.

Keltner, D., and Haidt, J. (1999). Social functions of emotions at four levels of analysis. *Cognition and Emotion*, *13*(5), 505–521.

Kessler, S. R., Bandelli, A. C., Spector, P. E., Borman, W. C., Nelson, C. E., and Penney, L. M. (2010). Re-examining Machiavelli: a three-dimensional model of Machiavellianism in the workplace. *Journal of Applied Social Psychology*, *40*(8), 1868–1896.

Kramer, T., Yucel-Aybat, O., and Lau-Gesk, L. (2011). The effect of schaden-freude on choice of conventional versus unconventional options. *Organizational Behavior and Human Decision Processes*, *116*(1), 140–147.

Krizan, Z., and Johar, O. (2012). Envy divides the two faces of narcissism. *Journal of Personality, 80*(5), 1415–1451.

Kuipers, G. (2014). Schadenfreude and social life: a comparative perspective on the expression and regulation of mirth at the expense of others. In W. W. van Dijk and J. W. Ouwerkerk (eds), *Schadenfreude: Understanding Pleasure at the Misfortune of Others* (pp. 259–294). Cambridge, UK: Cambridge University Press.

Leach, C. W., and Spears, R. (2008). "A vengefulness of the impotent": the pain of in-group inferiority and schadenfreude toward successful out-groups. *Journal of Personality and Social Psychology*, *95*(6), 1383–1396.

Leach, C. W., Spears, R., Branscombe, N. R., and Doosje, B. (2003). Malicious pleasure: schadenfreude at the suffering of another group. *Journal of Personality and Social Psychology*, *84*(5), 932–943.

Li, X., McAllister, D., Ilies, R., and Gloor, J. (2018). Schadenfreude: a counter-normative observer response to workplace mistreatment. *Academy of Management Review*.

Lindebaum, D. (2017). *Emancipation Through Emotion Regulation at Work*. Cheltenham, UK and Northampton, MA, USA: Edward Elgar Publishing.

Lindebaum, D., and Jordan, P. J. (2012). Positive emotions, negative emotions, or utility of discrete emotions? *Journal of Organizational Behavior*, *33*(7), 1027–1030.

Lindebaum, D., and Jordan, P. J. (2014). When it can be good to feel bad and bad to feel good: exploring asymmetries in workplace emotional outcomes. *Human Relations*, *67*(9), 1037–1050.

Lindebaum, D., Geddes, D., and Gabriel, Y. (2017). Moral emotions and ethics in organisations: introduction to the Special Issue. *Journal of Business Ethics*, *141*(4), 645–656.

McNamee, M. J. (2003). Schadenfreude in sport: envy, justice, and self-esteem. *Journal of the Philosophy of Sport*, *30*(1), 1–16.

McNamee, M. J. (2007). Nursing schadenfreude: the culpability of emotional construction. *Medicine, Health Care and Philosophy*, *10*(3), 289–299.

Međedović, J., and Petrović, B. (2015). The Dark Tetrad: structural properties and location in the personality space. *Journal of Individual Differences, 36*, 228–236.

Meier, A. J. (2000). The status of "foreign words" in English: the case of eight German words. *American Speech*, *75*(2), 169–183.

Miller, J. D., Dir, A., Gentile, B., Wilson, L., Pryor, L. R., and Campbell, W. K. (2010). Searching for a vulnerable Dark Triad: comparing factor 2 psychopathy, vulnerable narcissism, and borderline personality disorder. *Journal of Personality, 78*, 1529–1564.

Muris, P., Merckelbach, H., Otgaar, H., and Meijer, E. (2017). The malevolent side of human nature: a meta-analysis and critical review of the literature on the Dark Triad (narcissism, Machiavellianism, and psychopathy). *Perspectives on Psychological Science*, *12*(2), 183–204.

Nietzsche, F. (1954). On truth and lie in an extra-moral sense. In W. Kaoufmann (ed. and Trans.), *The Portable Nietzsche* (pp. 42, 46–47). New York, NY, USA: Viking.

Nietzsche, F. (1967). *The Will to Power* (W. Kaufmann, ed.; R. J. Hollindgale and W. Kaufmann, Trans.) New York, NY, USA: Random House [1901].

Ouwerkerk, J. W., and van Dijk, W. W. (2014). Intergroup rivalry and schadenfreude. In W. W. van Dijk, and J. W. Ouwerkerk (eds), *Schadenfreude: Understanding Pleasure at the Misfortune of Others* (pp. 186–199). Cambridge, UK: Cambridge University Press.

Paulhus, D. L., and Williams, K. M. (2002). The Dark Triad of personality: narcissism, machiavellianism, and psychopathy. *Journal of Research in Personality*, *36*(6), 556–563.

Perrewé, P. L., Ferris, G. R., Frink, D. D., and Anthony, W. P. (2000). Political skill: an antidote for workplace stressors. *The Academy of Management Executive*, *14*(3), 115–123.

Porter, S., and ten Brinke, L. (2008). Reading between the lies: identifying concealed and falsified emotions in universal facial expressions. *Psychological Science*, *19*(5), 508–514.

Porter, S., Bhanwer, A., Woodworth, M., and Black, P. J. (2014). Soldiers of misfortune: an examination of the Dark Triad and the experience of schadenfreude. *Personality and Individual Differences*, *67*, 64–68.

Pozner, J. L. (2010). *Reality Bites Back: The Troubling Truth About Guilty Pleasure TV*. Berkeley, CA, USA: Seal Press.

Salovey, P., Mayer, J., and Caruso, D. (2004). Emotional intelligence: theory, findings, and implications. *Psychological Inquiry*, *15*(3), 197–215.

Santamaría-García, H., Baez, S., Reyes, P., Santamaría-García, J. A., Santacruz-Escudero, J. M., Matallana, D., Sigman, M., García, A. M., and Ibáñez, A. (2017). A lesion model of envy and Schadenfreude: legal, deservingness and moral dimensions as revealed by neurodegeneration. *Brain*, *140*(12), 3357–3377.

Schumpe, B. M., and Lafrenière, M. A. K. (2016). Malicious joy: sadism moderates the relationship between schadenfreude and the severity of others' misfortune. *Personality and Individual Differences*, *94*, 32–37.

Szameitat, D. P., Alter, K., Szameitat, A. J., Wildgruber, D., Sterr, A., and Darwin, C. J. (2009). Acoustic profiles of distinct emotional expressions in laughter. *Journal of the Acoustical Society America*, *126*, 354–366.

Tangney, J. P., Stuewig J., and Mashek D. J. (2007). Moral emotions and moral behavior. *Annual Review of Psychology*, *58*, 345–372.

van Dijk, W. W., Goslinga, S., and Ouwerkerk, J. W. (2008). Impact of responsibility for a misfortune on schadenfreude and sympathy: further evidence. *The Journal of Social Psychology*, *148*(5), 631–636.

van Dijk, W. W., Ouwerkerk, J. W., Goslinga, S., Nieweg, M., and Gallucci, M. (2006). When people fall from grace: reconsidering the role of envy in schadenfreude. *Emotion*, *6*(1), 156–160.

van Dijk, W. W., van Koningsbruggen, G. M., Ouwerkerk, J. W., and Wesseling, Y. M. (2011). Self-esteem, self-affirmation, and schadenfreude. *Emotion*, *11*(6), 1445–1449.

Vanman, E. (2015). Trust, schadenfreude, guilt, and the shapes of rocks on a New Hampshire farm. *Frontiers in Human Neuroscience. Conference Abstract: ASP2015 – 25th Annual Conference of the Australasian Society for Psychophysiology*, doi: 10.3389/conf.fnhum.2015.219.00054.

Veselka, L., Schermer, J. A., Martin, R. A., and Vernon, P. A. (2010). Relations between humor styles and the Dark Triad traits of personality. *Personality and Individual Differences, 48*(6), 772–774.

Wai, M., and Tiliopoulos, N. (2012). The affective and cognitive empathic nature of the Dark Triad of personality. *Personality and Individual Differences*, *52*(7), 794–799.

Walker, B. R., and Jackson, C. J. (2017). Moral emotions and corporate psychopathy: a review. *Journal of Business Ethics*, *141*(4), 797–810.

Watanabe, H. (2016). Effects of self-evaluation threat on schadenfreude toward strangers in a reality TV show. *Psychological Reports*, *118*(3), 778–792.

Zweig, J. (2009, February 12). Financial crisis has an upside: 'The joy of schadenfreude'. [Wall Street Journal Blog]. Retrieved from: http://blogs.wsj.com/wallet/2009/02/12/wall-street-crisis-schadenfreud/tab/article/.

11. Ashamed of your shame? How discrepancy self-talk and social discourse influence individual shame at work

Sandra A. Kiffin-Petersen*

INDIVIDUAL SHAME AT WORK

Shame is a self-conscious, moral emotion that evolved to increase an individual's chances of acceptance in a social group by signalling to them when they have violated the group's moral standards or social norms (e.g., organization, work team) (Weisfeld, 1997). Appeasement is therefore, both a core function and potential outcome of shame (Keltner and Buswell, 1997). Lindebaum (2017) has suggested however, that shame can also be used to manipulate workers into conforming to organizational norms in a way that may be detrimental to them personally. This may be particularly true in Western cultures where shame is often enmeshed in secrecy, such that workers try to conceal their shame from others (Kaufman, 1989) and this can lead to depression (Kim et al., 2011). Indeed, Kaufman (1989, p. 3–4) suggests the "taboo on shame is so strict ... that we behave as if shame does not exist." A chain reaction can then occur where the employee strives to intrinsically regulate the intensity of their shame (i.e., up-regulate through for instance, distraction or cognitive reappraisal), as well as how they express and direct their shame during interpersonal interactions at work (i.e., down-regulate through, for instance, suppression) (Gross et al., 2011; Gross, 2013).

While emotions have biological roots (Frijda, 1988), people also internalize societal expectations and norms about how a particular emotion should be directed and expressed, which then shapes how people respond to that emotion (i.e., its emotionology) (Fineman, 2008). Emotionology is broadly concerned with understanding, "the attitudes or standards that a society maintains towards basic emotions and their appropriate expression; ways that institutions reflect and encourage these attitudes in human conduct" (Stearns and Stearns, 1985, p. 813). Since societal attitudes and standards give meaning to our emotions and inform our judgments, they can also affect the person's appraisal of the significance of a specific emotion (Lazarus, 1991). Individual identities and the organizations where we work are also influenced by how people think and talk about specific emotions (Solomon, 1993). In line with this, Brown (2012) argued that society needs to be more empathetic towards shame, because shame-bound relationships and individual blame are common at work, and this can inhibit employees from speaking up. While shame can occur at individual and collective levels in the workplace, the antecedents, processes, and consequences may differ (Lindebaum and Geddes, 2016; Murphy and Kiffin-Petersen, 2017). The focus of this chapter is on episodic shame at the within-person level, including the influence of cognitions and social discourse on how individuals respond.

Prior research has shown that individuals can respond to shame with an adaptive approach orientation (e.g., apologizing and making reparations; self-improvement), or a more maladaptive avoidant pattern (e.g., displaced aggression; withdrawal) (Leach and Cidam, 2015). While shame does typically cause considerable psychological discomfort, it may still be thought of as adaptive if it ultimately increases inclusivity into a social grouping (Henniger and Harris, 2014). A maladaptive response is more likely among shame-prone individuals who are typically less empathetic, blame others for their feelings, and express their shame as anger and hostility towards those they deem responsible for their feelings (i.e., the so-called shame-rage spiral; Scheff, 1987) (Tangney et al., 1992). Meta-analytic findings have shown that shame is also associated with depression (Kim et al., 2011). For example, a professional employee reportedly experienced major psychological trauma and intense shame after they were publicly vilified and then sacked from their corporate communications job, for an allegedly racist tweet posted while on holiday (Ronson, 2015). The central question examined in this chapter then, is how do shame and the social discourse about shame combine to influence its functionality in the workplace, such that workers respond more constructively to episodic shame, rather than with maladaptive behaviors, such as avoidance or aggression?

To address this question, the chapter is structured into three sections. First, it is important to understand the nature of shame as a self-conscious and moral emotion, including its biological basis and core social function. Shame is typically elicited in situations at work that involve a serious violation of a moral standard or a performance failure (Haidt, 2003; Tangney et al., 2007). In practice however, identifying the cause of shame can be difficult, because the emotion appears to arise from a unique pattern of cognition (Kiffin-Petersen and Murphy, 2016), which over time can become dissociated from the originating event (e.g., see Henderson et al., 2012). Understanding shame at the within-person level including the need for emotional up-regulation and how between-person differences in shame-proneness impact on those feelings, are a key focus in this section.

Exploring possible pathways by which the adaptive function of shame may be subjugated in order to repress and control workers' behavior (Lindebaum, 2017) is the focus of the second section. The prevailing view is that shame more often leads to an avoidance response and this can mean emotional down-regulation during interactions. Leach and Cidam's (2015) recent meta-analysis has shown that shame is much more contextually contingent than previously considered, and hence, interference with the appeasement function of shame may be more likely to occur in situations where the person's transgression or failure appears *less reparable*. A key contextual factor that potentially impacts on an ashamed worker's response may be how other employees react to them, including how they talk about shame.

In the final section, various ways to foster a more adaptive orientation to how shame is managed at work, including lifting the taboo on the talk about shame, encouraging forgiveness, and fostering a belief that restoring the relationship is possible, are explored. The implications for future research into shame at work are then discussed, followed by concluding comments.

SHAME: A SELF-CONSCIOUS MORAL EMOTION

Evolutionary perspectives emphasize emotions as motivational states that are not inherently good or bad, but rather serve to energize the organism to engage in certain types of behaviors (e.g., Frijda, 1988; Haidt, 2003). Each specific emotion carries its own distinctive motivational tendency or action orientation (Frijda, 1988). Frijda refers to the *Law of Concern* in which a negative affective response is elicited because of a concern about a particular situation. While the core relational concern of shame involves failing "to live up to an ego ideal" (Lazarus, 1991, p. 826), the appropriateness of that ego ideal is also fundamentally influenced by social norms and standards (Lindebaum, 2017). Hence, shame is considered a self-conscious emotion because the person believes their personal deficiencies, whether real or perceived, are not only known to themselves (Fischer and Tangney, 1995). Shame has an inherent "innate, functional, biosocial action and expression system" that differentiates it from other discrete negative emotions (Fischer et al., 1990, p. 84). Each of these elements are discussed next, because if individuals understand the cause of shame they can learn to change their thought processes, and thereby, may experience different outcomes.

The physiology of shame is apparent when participants are asked to draw, rather than talk about how they feel – shame is often described as a "hot" emotion because of the magnitude of the accompanying somatosensory changes (Nummenmaa et al., 2014). In Nummenmaa et al.'s study, participants colored in two body silhouettes to show where sensation increased or decreased after they were exposed to words, stories, movies, and/or facial expressions related to shame. The map for shame was statistically separable from thirteen other emotions including fear and anxiety, and was also consistent across West European and East Asian samples. The defining sensations include elevated physiological activity in the head, eyes, central chest and abdominal areas, with decreased activity in all four limbs. Using body maps, Nummenmaa et al. showed that feelings of shame transcend cultural, linguistic, and language differences, consistent with a biological basis to shame. While words help us to explain what is happening to us, we do not require them to actually experience shame (Lazarus, 1991).

Early twentieth-century developmental psychology observed that shame develops to help a child learn what is expected of them to fit into the social group necessary to their long-term survival (Abe and Izard, 1999). Once the child has internalized these societal standards, shame then acts as a type of internal barometer signalling to them when they have transgressed (or have thought about transgressing with anticipatory shame) from what is expected by other members of their social group (Tangney et al., 2007). For example, Grasmick and Bursik (1990) showed the threat of shame significantly inhibited participants' inclination to engage in tax cheating and drunken driving (although the authors did treat shame and guilt as interchangeable). Thus, anticipatory shame appears critically important to adaptive learning since it signals how others may judge our future actions, and hence, provides necessary feedback to avoid future violations. Anticipatory shame can also elicit ongoing self-regulation as a means to avoid transgressing in a way that might rupture valuable social relations (Creed et al., 2014). Hence, shame is also considered a moral emotion (Haidt, 2003).

Lewis (1971) raised the idea of unacknowledged shame with respect to there being another layer of concealment, suggesting a strong link between shame and the ego-defensive mechanism of denial to protect the self from further harm. The fear that disclosing our shame may elicit further shame (i.e., "ashamed of your shame"), can lead to increased regulatory efforts to hide our true feelings from others (Goldberg, 1991). Goldberg notes that while many people consult clinical therapists for help with depression, addictions, and marital breakdowns, few of them realize it is help with their unrecognized shame that is actually needed. Difficulty distinguishing shame from guilt can also make it more challenging for individuals to regulate their within-person cognitions (Tangney et al., 1992). Thinking of the two emotions as differing only in intensity can also make it hard to find accurate language to describe them (Cohen, 2003).

Lewis (1971) and other seminal shame researchers (i.e., Niedenthal et al., 1994; Tangney, 1995) have converged on the view that the attribution that one's *self* is at fault rather than a specific behavior, is what differentiates shame from guilt (for an opposing viewpoint see Solomon, 1993, pp. 301–303). For example, "I *am* a bad person" with shame, versus "I *did* a bad thing" with guilt. Understanding this distinction is important, because adaptive learning is potentially more challenging with shame, since with self-blame it is more difficult for the person to know what (or how) to change (Murphy and Kiffin-Petersen, 2017).

Cooley's (1922) notion of the "looking glass self" links together the idea that imagining others' negative judgments of ourselves elicits the self-conscious feeling of shame. The concept is also central to self-discrepancy theory, whereby shame arises because of the gap between our actual self and what we imagine significant others view as our ideal self (Higgins, 1987). All types of perceived self-discrepancies (i.e., between the actual self and our "ideal self", or the actual self and the "ought self" as suggested by societal standards and norms) can elicit shame (Tangney et al., 1998). For example, "I'm so stupid/an idiot/a fool" are all examples of discrepancy-based thinking that might accompany shame; whereas, the self-talk of guilt is typically behavior-based. One way to disentangle shame from other negative emotions experienced at work, therefore, is for individual employees to become more self-aware of the focal point of their thinking.

Niedenthal and others (1994, p. 593) compared participants' efforts to undo shame and guilt through differing counterfactual thoughts such as, "if only I were (or were not) such and such kind of person" versus, "If only I had (or had not) done such a thing." They found consistent differences in the foci between the self with shame and behavior for guilt. A chain reaction can then occur, where emotional experiences are associated with specific ways of thinking, and this pattern of cognition reinforces and sustains that same feeling state. For example, in Henderson and other's (2012) qualitative study of the obstacles preventing sick doctors from returning to work after an extended absence due to mental (or physical) illness, the doctors internalized the negative reactions of their colleagues, with some also feeling stigmatized. Doctors' feelings of failure ultimately developed into a generalized self-perception that was dissociated from the loss of their work role, and as a result "there was shame, there was fear ... there was low self-esteem" (Henderson et al., 2012, p. 6).

There is a greater likelihood that workers will continuously engage in discrepancy self-talk or ruminate about the event that triggered their shame than is found with guilt (Orth et al., 2006). Gold and Wegner (1995, p. 1246) describe ruminations as ". . . thoughts about events that have occurred in the past. Ruminations contain an irreversible or irrevocable quality, and at times an even pointless quality as well, because they are typically about events that cannot be altered or changed." In Orth and other's study (2006), rumination mediated the shame–depression relationship in both mothers and fathers following marital separation, potentially explaining why depressive symptoms are more severe with shame (Kim et al., 2011). Ruminative thoughts have a driven, unpleasant quality to them such that they form unwelcome intrusions anywhere and at any time (Gold and Wegner, 1995). The intrusive sub-scale of the Impact of Events Scale-Revised (IES-R) illustrates the repetitive mental processes that can occur: "I thought about it when I didn't mean to" and "I had waves of strong feelings about it" (Weiss and Marmar, 1997, pp. 408–409). Efforts to suppress ruminative thoughts to avoid taboo topics is often ineffectual and sometimes only serves to further fuel the emotion or thoughts the person is trying to avoid.

Nonverbal displays of gaze aversion, body collapse, and physical avoidance are unique to shame's expressive system (Keltner, 1995; Keltner and Buswell, 1997). The physical sensations of shame reportedly include increased heart rate, feeling small and weak, and wanting to hide (Keltner and Harker, 1998). Keltner asserted that these nonverbal behaviors serve a critical social function as appeasement gestures that allow the ashamed individual, in a sense, to apologize to others for their transgression (whatever the cause of their failure). By displaying a submissive and conciliatory posture the transgressor may then elicit the sympathy of others including offers of forgiveness, which can mitigate their negative sense of self and help their reintegration back into the social group. Keltner et al. (1997) refer to this process as a reactive type of appeasement that is triggered by shame.

Organizational and societal factors, including how shame is talked about (or not) can interfere with the appeasement process of shame (Keltner et al., 1997; Lindebaum, 2017). For instance, physicians who internalized a medical error as a personal failure suffered in silence when they were prevented from talking about their shame and from making appeasement gestures, such as an apology to the patient (Plews-Ogan et al., 2016). Plews-Ogan et al. suggest that helping physicians to cope with their error requires inter alia a change in the unattainable standards of a wider medical culture that expects physicians to be infallible. Hence, factors such as social discourse are important because they help set standards and social norms that trickle down to affect individuals in the workplace, and from which members' also judge the seriousness of an individual's violation. The influence of social discourse on the functionality of shame therefore, is the focus of the next section.

SOCIAL DISCOURSE: THE TALK (OR NOT) ABOUT SHAME

Emotions themselves are not value-laden; rather, it is society that places a subjective value on emotions and on acceptable ways for people to express those emotions and hence, on specific action tendencies that may be more, or less, acceptable to others (Henniger and Harris, 2014). Kaufman (1989) stressed in an early treatise that the intensity of a person's shame is determined not only by individual differences, but also by the social context. Similarly, Lindebaum (2017) argued that how shame is talked about in society can override its intended function such that it can become a means to increase social control, potentially to the detriment of the individual at work. Lindebaum suggested two possible pathways by which social discourse and attitudes towards shame could interfere with its core function such that it can become a tool for social control in the workplace, shame metaphors and emotionologies.

SHAME METAPHORS

Metaphorical language is often used to convey mental images of our emotional experiences to others, which also then helps to define ourselves and the world in which we live (Solomon, 1993). The importance of shame metaphors to this discussion is the notion that they help create social realities, which in effect can become self-fulfilling prophecies (Lakoff and Johnson, 2006). According to Solomon, the "hydraulic" metaphor, which likens emotions to the steam that can build up inside an engine, infiltrates much of the early conceptual thinking of emotions as essentially biological experiences. The young bride who suddenly experiences "cold feet" at the thought of getting married is another example (Nummenmaa et al., 2014). Solomon argues that these types of metaphors are problematic however, because they convey passivity, rather than recognizing that individuals have a choice and responsibility in how they feel. In line with this, Wood, Lupyan and Niedenthal (2016) suggest the primary function of metaphors is regulatory and not expressive, since the choice of language serves to control and inhibit our own (e.g., see Solomon, 1993), and others' emotional states (e.g., see Lindebaum, 2017).

Kövecses (2000, pp. 32/48) suggested some metaphorical source domains are unique to shame including, "having no clothes on" (e.g., "I felt so *naked*; so *exposed*"), "decrease in size" (e.g., "I felt *this big*"), and "blocking out the world" (e.g., "I wished the *ground would just swallow me up*"). The first domain is unique, because it is both a potential cause and a typical feeling associated with shame. According to Kövecses, people may also use language from other non-specific and overlapping domains when talking about shame, including passivity, lack of control, intensity, difficulty, divided self, and harm (physical damage). For example, passivity is pervasive in this example: "'felled' by shame, as a tree by an ax [*sic*]" (Solomon, 1993, p. xv). Intensity of shame may be conveyed using the "fluid in a container" metaphor, such as: "The memory *filled* him with shame" (Kövecses, 2000, p. 32). Similarly, Creed and others (2014, p. 283, italics added) suggested, "… we all *swim in a sea of shame*, all day, every day." Passivity, lack of control, smallness, physical harm, and remaining hidden, all seemingly underlie Brown's (2012) powerful metaphor that likens the effects of individual shame to the structural damage that millions of tiny termites can inflict on a house over time.

These various shame metaphors share images of passivity, lack of control, smallness of size, and the need to hide from others, which can reinforce discrepancy self-talk and encourage a maladaptive response. Leach and Cidam (2015) concluded that when ashamed workers believe their transgression is reparable they are more likely to respond constructively. Observers' choice of metaphors may signal to the ashamed worker that little can be done to redress their lack of moral character or personal failure, and this can lead them to increase their emotional up-regulation to conceal their shame from others and thereby interfere with the appeasement process (e.g., the sick doctors who felt negatively judged by their colleagues). Next, emotionologies are explored as a second possible pathway that can also influence how workers respond to shame.

EMOTIONOLOGIES OF SHAME

Emotionologies help us to understand how societal-level discourse and attitudes towards shame can impact on individuals in institutions, such as the workplace (Fineman, 2008). This relates back to Cooley's (1922) looking glass self, in which the person imagines others' judgments of themselves – those judgments are shaped by emotionologies (e.g., physicians who are afraid to confess their mistake because of internalized expectations of perfection; Plews-Ogan et al., 2016). The lack of references to shame in recent American literature and in social and political discourse illustrates just how undesirable shame has become in some societies (Cohen, 2003). According to Brown (2012), almost everyone is afraid to talk about shame because the emotion carries with it the fear of disconnection, of being found not worthy to be accepted by people we care about. Emotionologies help to also shape individuals' appraisals of shame-inducing events and hence, how they respond to shame in the workplace.

Stearns and Stearns (1985) suggest that emotionologies are dynamic, in that they develop and change both across space, and over time, in response to various religious, economic, political, and social trends. Geographically, different cultures may lead to some emotions being valued more than others (Kitayama et al., 2006), and this may be reflected in how that emotion is treated in the workplace. Occupation-wise, white-collar workers are often subject to differing emotional standards than blue-collar employees (Stearns and Stearns, 1985). For example, in the United States, the public considers it more likely that street criminals will be caught and severely punished, than white-collar criminals who commit fraud (e.g., bankers), even though both crimes are perceived as on par (Schoepfer et al., 2007). Male and female workers have also been held to differing standards at different times, particularly in relation to female stereotypes and leadership roles (e.g., see Johnson et al., 2008). Next, three areas in which emotionologies may influence the functionality of shame are explored: culture, language, and sensemaking.

Culture. Workers' construction of their experience of shame is at least, in part, culturally determined because particular societies promote specific emotions and responses that help them to achieve their respective cultural goals (Kitayama et al., 2006). Ha (1995) argued that shame tends to be hypercognized in Asian societies, because it provides important information for a harmonious daily life in a collectivistic culture. In contrast, shame is talked about and reported less often in the more individualistic culture of the United States (Boiger et al., 2013a, 2013b;

Cohen, 2003; Kitayama et al., 2006). This may be because employees are less aware of shameful feelings in cultures that emphasize continuous positive self-regard (Creed et al., 2014). Shame appears more conducive to self-improvement in collectivistic cultures (e.g., Japan), where individual goals tend to be subverted for social harmony (Boiger et al., 2013a, 2013b).

In the context of the workplace, cultural differences can directly impact on employees' responses to shame as illustrated in two studies of sales workers. Individualistic Dutch sales workers responded to their shame with avoidance behaviors during customer interactions, negatively impacting on the customer relationship (Verbeke and Bagozzi, 2002). In a second study, the protective behaviors of Dutch salespeople negatively impacted on their performance and lead to poorer customer relations; whereas Filipino salespeople responded constructively and tried to repair the damage that had been done to their customer relationship to the extent that their performance was not affected (Bagozzi et al., 2003). These findings suggest that appeasement behaviors, such as self-improvement aimed at atoning for a performance failure for example, may be more likely in workplaces where social harmony and interdependence are valued.

Language. Lexicographical studies can be helpful in understanding shame because they provide insight into its everyday meaning across time (Hurtado-de-Mendoza et al., 2012). The etymological origins of shame in the Oxford English Dictionary show that features, such as "guilt" that emerged in the seventeenth century, have become more central to shame in contemporaneous lexicographic representations (Hurtado-de-Mendoza et al., 2012). This finding is consistent with recent research into moral emotions, which has shown shame and guilt to be closely related (Haidt, 2003). The two main features of "indignity" and "disgrace" of shame have endured since Old English times, while features such as "modesty" appear later (thirteenth century), and then disappear by the nineteenth century. The concept of honor is also extremely relevant to understanding shame in both Western and non-Western cultures (particularly in the context of saving face). Metaphors that portray shame as a difficult and harmful emotion are consistent with this language use. A shameless person then, can be thought of as someone who lacks qualities of virtuousness, and to "have not internalized community norms" (Cohen, 2003, p. 1084). Since a state of being ashamed is also possible, there is a degree of linguistic complexity in how workers may talk about and express their shame at work.

To fully grasp how shame functions at work it is important to consider its verb form. Shame can encompass actions intended to cause feelings of shame in others (whether that be an individual or a community) (Cohen, 2003). For instance, shaming may be used as a form of social control when supervisors or co-workers deliberately set out to publicly shame an employee for failing to meet performance targets at work (Lindebaum, 2017). Norms that stigmatize shame may challenge a worker's positive self-views and exploit them into conforming in order to avoid experiencing shame. Threatening to name and shame an employee can deter them from engaging in undesirable organizational behaviors or practices.

Sensemaking. Maitlis et al. (2013) theorized that sensemaking processes triggered by shame at work differ significantly to other emotions, because individuals may withdraw from organizational activities and discussions and engage in more solitary sensemaking. The function of sensemaking is to help reduce ambiguity and confusion by creating a sense of shared meaning through conversations and discussions, which allows a decision or solution to be made (Gephart et al., 2010). For instance, when an Israeli public bus company unilaterally changed the color of its fleet to green to improve its environmental image, employees experienced disgust and shame when they interpreted the company's actions as instrumentally driven (Rafaeli and Vilnai-Yavetz, 2004).

The close nexus that exists between shame and fear may further compound solitary sensemaking in organizations. For instance, physicians who attribute a medical error to a personal failure and experience shame as a result, may be afraid to step forward and share their experience and this may prevent system-wide changes being made to help prevent future errors (Plews-Ogan et al., 2016). The Volkswagen emissions scandal has also been attributed in part, to a corporate environment that promoted the public criticism and disciplining of employees, who were therefore reluctant to disclose any negative information or discuss problems with their superiors (Dishman, 2015). These examples suggest that negative attitudes can discourage employees from believing they can appease those affected by their violation and this can lead them to withdraw, as suggested by Leach and Cidam (2015). In the next section, the implications of these research findings for workplace practices are explored, and future research directions suggested.

IMPLICATIONS: WORKPLACE PRACTICE AND FUTURE RESEARCH

The discussion so far has shown that contextual influences in the choice of metaphors and societal discourse about how shame is talked about, as well as how workers' internalize those expectations, combine to influence individual responses to shame. Interventions that foster the belief that a transgression or performance failure is reparable could be directed at two levels: within-person and interpersonal relationships. It should be noted however, that relying solely on within-person approaches such as cognitive reappraisal, may cover up questionable management practices including the need for forgiving and supportive cultural values that prevent stigmatization of shame. In the absence of such structural changes however, Lindebaum (2017) hopes that once workers understand how shame may be used to repress and control their behavior at work they will be motivated to emancipate themselves.

Implications for Workplace Practice

Within-person approaches. Given the moderate relationship between shame and depression (Kim et al., 2011), various clinical approaches used to improve psychological well-being may also help employees at work. Relevant approaches could include compassionate mind training or mindfulness techniques (Gilbert and Procter, 2006; Woods and Proeve, 2014), and acceptance and commitment therapy (Luoma et al., 2012). Compassionate mind training emphasizes practicing self-compassion and mindfulness through techniques, such as breathing awareness, compassion-focused imagery, and compassionate letter writing (Gilbert and Procter, 2006), with the emphasis being on cognitive reappraisal (i.e., up-regulation of emotions) by changing the dialogue of the person's internal critic to that of a compassionate friend in order to inhibit the self-criticism. Indeed, Plews-Ogan et al. (2016) found that physicians reported they often struggle with imperfection and self-forgiveness. As emphasized earlier, if a person is able to become aware of their discrepancy self-talk, they can also alter those thought patterns through reappraisal, and thereby, also potentially be able to respond in a more constructive way.

Woods and Proeve (2014) have shown that regular meditation to improve self-compassion and mindfulness was effective in reducing ruminative thoughts and hence, the intensity of shame in high shame-prone individuals. Shapiro, Wang and Peltason (2015) argue that because mindfulness training cultivates awareness and acceptance even of distressingly painful negative emotions, it can help to reduce the intensity of shame. In mindfulness training, individuals attempt to counteract the effect of their thoughts and feelings by treating them as passing events, rather than buying into the literal nature of the self-talk that accompanies the emotional experience. Replacing ruminative thought patterns with metaphors invoking control, as used in acceptance and commitment therapy, may also assist people in the workplace to better manage their shame. Shifting the focal point of the person's thinking away from the self to images of inanimate objects, such as "leaves floating on the stream" and "passengers on the bus" for example, could help to reduce shame (Hayes et al., 1999).

Findings from a comprehensive, multi-study research project showed that "small shifts in the language people use to refer to the self during introspection consequentially influence their ability to regulate their thoughts, feelings, and behavior under social stress, even for vulnerable individuals" (Kross et al., 2014, p. 304). Kross and others found that if people use their own name and/or other non-first-person pronouns to refer to the self during introspection, they were more able to distance themselves from the experience or decision and hence, reflect on what happened without ruminating. The shift in focal thinking helped to distance the person from ruminative thought patterns. Improved self-awareness and training in this technique could prove helpful to workers experiencing shame.

Zhao and others (2014) suggest that people can use problem-focused and emotion-focused coping (Folkman and Lazarus, 1985) to manage the negative emotions that arise as a result of making an error at work. Problem-focused coping is particularly useful because it can allow the person to learn from their mistake by engaging in a collective sense-making process, rather than a solitary one. Emotion-focused coping is more often related to the desire to protect oneself from experiencing further harm, an action tendency often seen with shame. In contrast, problem-focused coping involves the person directing their attention at analyzing the cause of their distress and specific actions to address the problem. By engaging with others, the transgressor may also display appeasement gestures that may help them to be reintegrated back into their social group. In this way, self-protective emotion-focused coping may reinforce rumination and discrepancy self-talk; while problem-focused coping requires talking to others about what has occurred. Hence, within-person approaches provide some useful ways for individual workers to help regulate their shame through increased self-awareness and control over their internal narratives. The next section considers how the context, including the talk about shame, can encourage a more adaptive response.

Interpersonal relationships. Brown (2012) argues people heal best when their shameful feelings are also addressed interpersonally and that empathy from others is, therefore, critical to an adaptive response. Atkins and Parker (2011) suggested that practicing compassion in organizations is an effective way of healing pain and reducing suffering when strong negative emotions are being experienced by a co-worker or team member. Compassionate responding, which involves four essential processes including noticing, appraising, feeling, and acting towards the person for whom we have feelings of compassion, could be of value here. Such an approach is needed to reduce the taboo surrounding shame.

Expressions of compassion and forgiveness through careful choice of metaphorical language may help to alleviate the suffering of those who feel ashamed, and potentially reduce the stigma. The sick doctors in Henderson and other's (2012) study would have experienced fewer obstacles to returning to work if their colleagues had responded more positively. Similarly, Plews-Ogan and others (2016, p. 238) found that physicians who experience shame after making a serious error often carry "dissociated narratives for years, unrevealed and unresolved" because it is so culturally unacceptable to openly discuss and accept that such events can occur in medicine.

Appeasement behaviors, such as offering a sincere apology, may be helpful in repairing interpersonal relationships in the workplace following episodic shame. Hareli and Eisikovits (2006) found in their study of university students that when others perceived the person's shame had motivated them to apologize, they were more likely to be forgiven. This finding is consistent with the appeasement core function of shame. Individuals who are allowed to apologize are also less likely to engage in subsequent deviant behavior (Keltner et al., 1997). Keltner and others argue however, that in some institutional contexts appeasement may be prevented or strategically avoided, such as negotiations where displays of weakness are to be avoided. Furthermore, Doern and Goss (2014) found that shame can still be directed at the self in situations when appeasement behaviors are not freely chosen (e.g., Russian entrepreneurs who felt forced into colluding in unethical practices by paying bribes to officials). Lessons learned from these studies suggest that the healthy management of shame at work likely involves a workplace context in which appeasement behaviors are supported as a matter of choice, rather than compliance.

Implications for Future Research

Based on the review of the shame literature thus far, there are several implications for future research into how changes in the talk about shame and its emotionologies could influence emotion regulation and shame. Since shame underpins all interpersonal relationships the first line of inquiry could focus on identifying how societal trends may be impacting on the way in which organizations address perceived wrong-doers. Analysis of publicly available data on shameful events, such as the Volkswagen emission scandal, could be insightful here. Lexographic methodologies would be particularly useful in understanding the emotionology of shame through an examination of the linguistic richness of descriptions of shame. Since shame is a social emotion, Stearns (2015) has also argued for the need to conduct more interdisciplinary research including an historical perspective, rather than the current predominance of studies in social psychology. In this regard, digitized books have made possible the quantitative analysis of written references to shame, which Stearns showed had steadily declined from a peak in the 1860s to the 1960s based on data from the New York Times and Google Books, suggesting a lessening desire to publicly talk about shame. Examining newspaper articles, books and company reports may give some indication as to whether this decline has continued.

Second, there is an obvious need to better understand how major societal changes influence how shame is experienced in the workplace. Leaders face a dilemma as to how best to create a culture that promotes an adaptive approach to shame, rather than using it as a means to control others. Clough (2010) argues that to prevent shame from being abused for the purpose of social control, supervisors need to value individual employees and work towards a culture that supports emotional expression. This is potentially more challenging in individualistic cultures such as the United States where shame is considered an undesirable emotion because it emphasizes a person's flaws and not feeling good about oneself (Boiger et al., 2013a). Coupled with a high achievement motive and a focus on individual performance common to Western workplaces, cultural goals may also reinforce workplace norms encouraging avoidance.

Finally, since shame is a multilayered emotion it is important that future research also consider how social discourse affects collective shame in the workplace (i.e., at the group and organizational levels) (Murphy and Kiffin-Petersen, 2017). Gross (2013) suggests that while intrinsic emotion regulation has already received considerable research attention, more studies of how people regulate their emotions in their interpersonal interactions are needed. This observation seems particularly applicable to shame and how it is managed at work.

CONCLUSION

There is a need to address the taboo on shame found in Western individualistic societies, in order to help individuals find ways to acknowledge and express this difficult self-conscious emotion. Pressures for conformity arising from the ubiquitous nature of shame signal to employees the need for them to self-regulate their shame, both intrinsically and interpersonally. Since cognitive appraisal mechanisms underpin emotional experiences, metaphorical language and emotionological changes across space and time can impact on those experiences particularly once individuals internalize expectations (Stearns and Stearns, 1985).

One approach advocated by Scheff (2014) is for researchers to study taboo topics. Future research is needed about stigmatized phenomena in the workplace (e.g., moral transgressions, scapegoating, sexual harassment, bullying, and mistakes/errors), and concomitantly how shame is related to those events. While the use of shaming as a tool of social control may be beneficial for the organization, such approaches are potentially detrimental to the individual and have longer term implications for the types of organizations where employees want to work and the values such practices reinforce. Organizations should play a more prominent role in building corporate cultures that encourage self-forgiveness, and empathy and compassion towards workers who experience shame.

At an interpersonal level, the onus is also on workplaces to create a culture that encourages courageous conversations about shame in a way that builds social relations and restores relationships. The importance of taking a more contextualized approach to studying workplace shame using the lens of social discourse and emotionology has been highlighted because, as Boiger et al. (2013b, p. 12) point out, emotions provide "powerful connections between inner psyches and outer worlds." Such an approach can provide a more nuanced understanding of the complex multilevel layers that influence shame and how it is talked about (or not) in the workplace.

NOTE

* Acknowledgements: the author would like to thank Steven Murphy, Paul Harvey, and Dirk Lindebaum for their helpful comments and suggestions on this chapter.

REFERENCES

Abe, J. A., and Izard, E. C. (1999). The developmental functions of emotions: an analysis in terms of differential emotions theory. *Cognition and Emotion, 13,* 523–549.

Atkins, P., and Parker, S. (2011). Understanding individual compassion in organizations: the role of appraisals and psychological flexibility. *Academy of Management Review, 37,* 524–546.

Bagozzi, R. P., Verbeke, W., and Gavino, J. C. (2003). Culture moderates the self-regulation of shame and its effects on performance: the case of salespersons in the Netherlands and the Philippines. *Journal of Applied Psychology, 88,* 219–233.

Boiger, M., De Deyne, S., and Mesquita, B. (2013a). Emotions in "the world": cultural practices, products, and meanings of anger and shame in two individualist cultures. *Frontiers in Psychology, 4,* 1–14.

Boiger, M., Mesquita, B., Uchida, Y., and Barrett, L. F. (2013b). Condoned or condemned: the situational affordance of anger and shame in the United States and Japan. *Personality and Social Psychology Bulletin, 39,* 540–553.

Brown, B. (2012). *Daring Greatly: How the Courage to be Vulnerable Transforms the Way we Live, Love, Parent, and Lead.* New York, NY, USA: Penguin.

Clough, M. (2010). Shame and organisations. *International Journal of Leadership in Public Services, 6,* 25–33.

Cohen, D. (2003). The American national conversation about (everything but) shame. *Social Research, 70,* 1075–1108.

Cooley, C. (1922). *Human Nature and the Social Order.* New York, NY, USA: Scribners.

Creed, W. D., Hudson, B. A., Okhuysen, G. A., and Smith-Crowe, K. (2014). Swimming in a sea of shame: incorporating emotion into explanations of institutional reproduction and change. *Academy of Management Review, 39,* 275–301.

Dishman, L. (2015). How Volkswagen's company culture could have led employees to cheat. Retrieved from http://www.fastcompany.com/3054692/ the-future-of-work/how-volkswagens-company-culture-could-have-led-employees-to-cheat.

Doern, R., and Goss, D. (2014). The role of negative emotions in the social processes of entrepreneurship: power rituals and shame-related appeasement behaviors. *Entrepreneurship Theory and Practice, 38,* 863–890.

Fineman, S. (ed.) (2008). *The Emotional Organization: Passions and Power.* Oxford, UK: Blackwell Publishing.

Fischer, K. W., and Tangney, J. P. (eds) (1995). *Self-conscious Emotions: The Psychology of Shame, Guilt, Embarrassment, and Pride.* New York, NY, USA: The Guilford Press.

Fischer, K. W., Shaver, P. R., and Carnochan, P. (1990). How emotions develop and how they organise development. *Cognition and Emotion, 4,* 81–127.

Folkman, S., and Lazarus, R. S. (1985). If it changes it must be a process: study of emotion and coping during three stages of a college examination. *Journal of Personality and Social Psychology*, *48*, 150–170.

Frijda, N. H. (1988). The laws of emotion. *American Psychologist*, *43*, 349–358.

Gephart, R. P., Topal, C., and Zhan, Z. (2010). Future-oriented sensemaking: temporalities and institutional legitimation. In T. Hernes and S. Maitlis (eds), *Process, Sensemaking, and Organizing* (pp. 275–312). New York, NY, USA: Oxford University Press.

Gilbert, P., and Procter, S. (2006). Compassionate mind training for people with high shame and self-criticism: overview and pilot study of a group therapy approach. *Clinical Psychology and Psychotherapy*, *13*(6), 353–379.

Gold, D. B., and Wegner, D. M. (1995). Origins of ruminative thought: trauma, incompleteness, nondisclosure, and suppression. *Journal of Applied Social Psychology*, *25*, 1245–1261.

Goldberg, C. (1991). *Understanding Shame*. Northvale, NJ, USA: Jason Aronson.

Grasmick, H. G., and Bursik, R. J. Jr. (1990). Conscience, significant others, and rational choice: extending the deterrence model. *Law and Society Review*, *24*, 837–861.

Gross, J. J. (2013). Emotion regulation: taking stock and moving forward. *Emotion, 13*, 359–365.

Gross, J. J., Scheppes, G., and Urry, H. L. (2011). Emotion generation and emotion regulation: a distinction we should make (carefully). *Cognition and Emotion*, *25*, 765–781.

Ha, F. I. (1995). Shame in Asian and western cultures. *American Behavioral Scientist*, *38*, 1114–1131.

Haidt, J. (2003). The moral emotions. In R. J. Davidson, K. R. Scherer, and H. H. Goldsmith (eds) *Handbook of Affective Sciences* (pp. 852–870). Oxford, UK: Oxford University Press.

Hareli, S., and Eisikovits, Z. (2006). The role of communicating social emotions accompanying apologies in forgiveness. *Motivation and Emotion*, *30*, 189–197.

Hayes, S. C., Strosahl, K. D., and Wilson, K. G. (1999). *Acceptance and Commitment Therapy: An Experiential Approach to Behavior Change*. New York, NY, USA: The Guilford Press.

Henderson, M., Brooks, S. K., del Busso, L., Chalder, T., Harvey, S. B., Hotopf, M., Madan, I., and Hatch, S. (2012). Shame! Self-stigmatisation as an obstacle to sick doctors returning to work: a qualitative study. *BMJ Open*, *2*, e001776.

Henniger, N. E., and Harris, C. R. (2014). Can negative social emotions have positive consequences? An examination of embarrassment, shame, guilt, jealousy, and envy. In W. G. Parrott (ed.), *The Positive Side of Negative Emotions* (pp. 76–97). New York, NY, USA: The Guilford Press.

Higgins, E. T. (1987). Self-discrepancy: a theory relating self and affect. *Psychological Review*, *94*, 319–340.

Hurtado-de-Mendoza, A., Molina, C., and Fernández-Dols, J. M. (2012). The archeology of emotion concepts: a lexicographic analysis of the concepts shame and vergüenza. *Journal of Language and Social Psychology*, *32*, 272–290.

Johnson, S. K., Murphy, S. E., Zewdie, S., and Reichard, R. J. (2008). The strong, sensitive type: effects of gender stereotypes and leadership prototypes on the evaluation of male and female leaders. *Organizational Behavior and Human Decision Processes*, *106*, 39–60.

Kaufman, G. (1989). *The Psychology of Shame: Theory and Treatment of Shame-based Syndromes*. New York, NY, USA: Springer.

Keltner, D. (1995). Signs of appeasement: evidence for the distinct displays of embarrassment, amusement, and shame. *Journal of Personality and Social Psychology*, *68*, 441–454.

Keltner, D., and Buswell, B. N. (1997). Embarrassment: its distinct form and appeasement functions. *Psychological Bulletin*, *122*, 250–270.

Keltner, D., and Harker, L. A. (1998). The forms and functions of the nonverbal signal of shame. In P. Gilbert and B. Andrews (eds), *Series in Affective Science. Shame: Interpersonal Behavior, Psychopathology, and Culture* (pp. 78–98). New York, NY: Oxford University Press.

Keltner, D., Young, R. C., and Buswell, B. N. (1997). Appeasement in human emotion, social practice, and personality. *Aggressive Behavior*, *23*, 359–374.

Kiffin-Petersen, S. A., and Murphy, S. (2016). *Ashamed of being ashamed: talk-inhibiting, soul-stifling feelings of shame*. Paper presented at the 10th EMONET Conference in Rome, 4–5 July.

Kim, S., Thibodeau, R., and Jorgenson, R. S. (2011). Shame, guilt, and depressive symptoms: a meta-analytic review. *Psychological Bulletin*, *137*, 68–96.

Kitayama, S., Mesquita, B., and Karasawa, M. (2006). Cultural affordances and emotional experience: socially engaging and disengaging emotions in Japan and the United States. *Journal of Personality and Social Psychology*, *91*, 890–903.

Kövecses, Z. (2000). *Metaphor and Emotion: Language, Culture, and Body in Human Feeling*. Cambridge, UK: Cambridge University Press.

Kross, E., Bruehlman-Senecal, E., Park, J., Burson, A., Dougherty, A., Shablack, H., Bremner, R., Moser, J., and Ayduk, O. (2014). Self-talk as a regulatory mechanism: how you do it matters. *Journal of Personality and Social Psychology*, *106*, 304–324.

Lakoff, G., and Johnson, M. (2006). Metaphors we live by. In J. O'Brien (ed.), *The Production of Reality: Essays and Readings on Social Interaction* (4th ed., pp. 103–114). Thousand Oaks, CA, USA: Pine Forge Press.

Lazarus, R. S. (1991). Progress on a cognitive-motivational-relational theory of emotion. *American Psychologist*, *46*, 819–834.

Leach, C. W., and Cidam, A. (2015). When is shame linked to constructive approach orientation? A meta-analysis. *Journal of Personality and Social Psychology*, *109*, 983–1002.

Lewis, H. B. (1971). *Shame and Guilt in Neurosis*. New York, NY, USA: International Universities Press.

Lindebaum, D. (2017). *Emancipation Through Emotion Regulation at Work*. Cheltenham, UK and Northampton, MA, USA: Edward Elgar Publishing.

Lindebaum, D., and Geddes, D. (2016). *The emotion, and the talk about the emotion at work*. Symposium presented at the 10th EMONET Conference in Rome, 4–5 July.

Luoma, J. B., Kohlenberg, B. S., Hayes, S. C., and Fletcher, L. (2012). Slow and steady wins the race: a randomized clinical trial of acceptance and commitment therapy targeting shame in substance use disorders. *Journal of Consulting and Clinical Psychology, 80*, 43–53.

Maitlis, S., Vogus, T. J., and Lawrence, T. B. (2013). Sensemaking and emotion in organizations. *Organizational Psychology Review, 3*, 222–247.

Murphy, S. A., and Kiffin-Petersen, S. (2017). The exposed self: a multilevel model of shame and ethical behavior. *Journal of Business Ethics, 141*, 657–675.

Niedenthal, P. M., Tangney, J. P., and Gavanski, I. (1994). "If only I weren't" versus "If only I hadn't": distinguishing shame and guilt in counterfactual thinking. *Journal of Personality and Social Psychology, 67*, 585–595.

Nummenmaa, L., Glerean, E., Hari, R., and Hietanen, J. K. (2014). Bodily maps of emotions. *Proceedings of the National Academy of Sciences, 111*, 646–651.

Orth, U., Berking, M., and Burkhardt, S. (2006). Self-conscious emotions and depression: rumination explains why shame but not guilt is maladaptive. *Personality and Social Psychology Bulletin, 32*, 1608–1619.

Plews-Ogan, M., May, N., Owens, J., Ardelt, M., Shapiro, J., and Bell, S. K. (2016). Wisdom in medicine: what helps physicians after a medical error? *Academic Medicine, 91*, 233–241.

Rafaeli, A., and Vilnai-Yavetz, I. (2004). Emotion as a connection of physical artifacts and organizations. *Organization Science, 15*, 671–686.

Ronson, J. (2015, February 12). How one stupid tweet blew up Justine Sacco's life. *The New York Times*. Retrieved from http://www.nytimes.com/2015/02/15/magazine/how-one-stupid-tweet-ruined-justine-saccos-life.html.

Scheff, T. J. (1987). The shame-rage spiral: a case study of an interminable quarrel. In H. B. Lewis (ed), *The Role of Shame in Symptom Formation* (pp. 109–149). Hillsdale, NJ, USA: Erlbaum.

Scheff, T. J. (2014). Toward a concept of stigma. *International Journal of Social Psychiatry, 60*, 724–725.

Schoepfer, A., Carmichael, S., and Piquero, N. L. (2007). Do perceptions of punishment vary between white-collar and street crimes? *Journal of Criminal Justice, 35*, 151–163.

Shapiro, S. L., Wang, M. C., and Peltason, E. H. (2015). What is mindfulness, and why should organizations care about it? In J. Reb and P. W. B. Atkins (eds), *Mindfulness in Organizations: Foundations, Research, and Applications* (pp. 17–41). St Ives, UK: Cambridge University Press.

Solomon, R. C. (1993). *The Passions: Emotions and the Meaning of Life.* Indianapolis, IN, USA: Hackett Publishing Company.

Stearns, P. N. (2015). Shame, and a challenge for emotions history. *Emotion Review*, 1–10, doi: 10.1177/1754073915588981.

Stearns, P. N., and Stearns, C. Z. (1985). Emotionology: clarifying the history of emotions and emotional standards. *The American Historical Review, 90*, 813–836.

Tangney, J. P. (1995). Recent advances in the empirical study of shame and guilt. *American Behavioral Scientist, 38*, 1132–1145.

Tangney, J. P., Niedenthal, P. M., Covert, M. V., and Barlow, D. H. (1998). Are shame and guilt related to distinct self-discrepancies? A test of Higgins's (1987) hypotheses. *Journal of Personality and Social Psychology*, *75*, 256–268.

Tangney, J. P., Stuewig, J., and Mashek, D. J. (2007). Moral emotions and moral behavior. *Annual Review of Psychology*, *58*, 345–372.

Tangney, J. P., Wagner, P., Fletcher, C., and Gramzow, R. (1992). Shamed into anger? The relation of shame and guilt to anger and self-reported aggression. *Journal of Personality and Social Psychology*, *62*, 669–675.

Verbeke, W., and Bagozzi, R. P. (2002). A situational analysis on how salespeople experience and cope with shame and embarrassment. *Psychology and Marketing*, *19*, 713–741.

Weisfeld, G. E. (1997). Discrete emotions theory with specific reference to pride and shame. In N. L. Segal, G. E. Weisfeld, and C. C. Weisfeld (eds), *Uniting Psychology and Biology: Integrative Perspectives on Human Development* (pp. 419–443). Washington, DC, USA: American Psychological Association.

Weiss, D. S., and Marmar, C. R. (1997). The impact of event scale – revised. In J. P. Wilson and T. M. Keane (eds), *Assessing Psychological Trauma and PTSD* (pp. 399–411). New York, NY, USA: The Guilford Press.

Wood, A., Lupyan, G., and Niedenthal, P. (2016). Why do we need emotion words in the first place? Commentary on Lakoff (2015). *Emotion Review*, *8*, 274–275.

Woods, H., and Proeve, M. (2014). Relationships of mindfulness, self-compassion, and meditation experience with shame-proneness. *Journal of Cognitive Psychotherapy: An International Quarterly*, *28*, 20–33.

Zhao, B., Olivera, F., and Edmondson, A. (2014). Learning from errors in organizations: the effects of negative emotions on motivation and cognition. In J. A. Miles (ed), *New Directions in Management and Organization Theory* (pp. 23–61). Newcastle upon Tyne, UK: Cambridge Scholars Publishing.

Index